Anton Francesco Doni

The Earliest English Version of the Fables of Bidpai

Anton Francesco Doni

The Earliest English Version of the Fables of Bidpai

ISBN/EAN: 9783744797764

Printed in Europe, USA, Canada, Australia, Japan

Cover: Foto ©ninafisch / pixelio.de

More available books at **www.hansebooks.com**

Five hundred and fifty copies of this Edition have been printed, five hundred of which are for sale.

The Fables of Bidpai.

Ballantyne Press
DALLANTYNE, HANSON AND CO.
EDINBURGH AND LONDON

The earliest English version of the Fables of Bidpai,

"*The Morall Philosophie of Doni*"
by Sir Thomas North, whilom
of Peterhouse, Cambridge
Now again edited and induced
by Joseph Jacobs, late of
St. John's College,
Cambridge.

LONDON. M.D.CCCLXXXVIII. PUBLISHED BY DAVID NUTT, IN THE STRAND.

TO

MY DEAR WIFE.

PREFACE.

OF late years nearly all the Western versions of the "Fables of Bidpai" have been printed, either again or for the first time. The Greek, the Hebrew, the Old Spanish, the German, the Latin, the Croatian, and the Old Slavonic have been given afresh to the world, and it seemed fitting that the earliest English version, made by Sir Thomas North of Plutarch fame, should also be made to see the light of day again. On my suggesting this to Mr. Nutt, he readily consented to add a reprint of the book to his "Bibliothèque de Carabas," and the present volume is the result.

The need of a reprint of North's version became evident during the search for a copy of the original. Mr. Quaritch has been on the look-out for me for the last five years in vain. Of the first edition the British Museum, Cambridge

University, Trinity College, Cambridge, and the Lambeth Libraries do not possess a copy, nor are the noble collections of the Duke of Devonshire, Mr. Huth, or the late Mr. Dyce richer in this respect than the public libraries. The only complete copy of the first edition that I have been able to trace is in the Bodleian, and the present volume has been printed from a transcript of this, though I have collated with an imperfect copy possessed by Dr. Williams' Library. There was a second edition in 1601, but this is even rarer, only the British Museum copy being known to me.

The first edition received the license of the Stationers' Company sometime towards the end of 1569 or the beginning of 1570, as we learn from the entry in their books (Arber *Transcript* i. fol. 184), " Recevyd of henry Denham for his lycense for pryntinge of a boke intituled phelophye (*sic*) of the Aumcyant ffaythers xijd." It is a small quarto of 116 leaves, divided into four parts, of which the last two have separate title-pages, as in the Italian original : the last is dated 1570. We have exactly reproduced its typographical peculiarities for the first forty pages, after which the whole book was in gothic, for which

PREFACE. ix

we have substituted ordinary type, as less trying to the eyes. The book is illustrated with woodcuts imitated from the Italian. We have reproduced nine of the quaintest and most characteristic.

I believe I have opened a new chapter in the already voluminous Bidpai literature by showing that the illustrations of the Fables were regarded as an integral part of the text, and were "translated," so to speak, along with it. We have therefore given an example of these traditional illustrations from the *editio princeps* of the Latin version of John of Capua (p. lxiii.). From the other end of the world we give as a frontispiece to the volume one of the Indian designs which adorn the fine Persian MS. of the Fables preserved at the British Museum (Add. MS., 18,579). This was executed in 1610 for Tana Sahib, the last Rajah of Golconda (See Rieu, *Cat. Pers. MSS.* p. 756). The plate represents the first meeting of Dimna and Senesba, the two chief actors in the main story, and may be contrasted with the representation of the same personages given in the English text on p. 100.

It remains to perform the pleasant task of

PREFACE.

thanking those to whom this volume owes its external attractions or internal correctness. My best thanks are due to Mr. E. Burne-Jones for the beautiful design which forms the frontispiece to the book itself, and embodies the ideal of Oriental Tradition. The Duke of Devonshire was good enough to send his copy of the Italian original to the British Museum for comparison, and the Trustees of Dr. Williams' Library gave me facilities for collating with their precious copy of the first edition.

INTRODUCTION.

———◆◆———

> "*Pilpay, sage indien. Sa livre a été traduit dans toutes les langues. Les gens du pays le croient fort ancien et originel à l'égard d'Ésope si ce n'est Ésope lui-même.*"
> —LA FONTAINE, *Avertissement au second recuiel*, 1678.

THE work I am to introduce to the reader is the earliest English representative of a cycle of stories which has passed into every civilised tongue, and into many not civilised. The bare description of the "Morall Philosophie of Doni" will suffice to indicate how wide a traveller it had been before it reached these shores. It is the English version of an Italian adaptation of a Spanish translation of a Latin version of a Hebrew translation of an Arabic adaptation of the Pehlevi version of the Indian original. And this enumeration only indicates one of many paths which these fables took to reach Europe. To trace these paths is a fascinating pursuit for the bibliographer

—and for him alone. Luckily, bibliographical work, which is so necessary but so dry, needs only to be done once if done well, and the work in this case has been done admirably by the late Mr. Keith-Falconer in the introduction to his translation of the later Syriac version of "Bidpai's Fables" (Cambridge, Pitt Press, 1885).[*] I have endeavoured to summarise the seventy erudite pages which he has taken to enumerate the various translations and editions in the accompanying genealogical table. From this I calculate that the tales have been translated into thirty-eight languages, in 112 different versions, which have passed into about 180 editions.

We must not, however, dismiss the earlier stages of the history of the Fables so summarily. In these days, research after paternity in such matters is encouraged rather than forbidden in the code of scholarship. In the present instance,

---

[*] A less complete enumeration is given in Table II., attached to Mr. T. Rhys Davids' translation of the *Jataka Tales* (Trübner, 1880). Table I. deals with the Indian variants with greater fulness than in Mr. Keith-Falconer's work. I have included some of these, as well as a few unconsidered trifles that had escaped the notice of these two scholars in Schultens, Graesse, the British Museum Catalogue, and Landau, *Quellen des Decamerone*.

the search is rendered peculiarly difficult, and therefore fascinating, by the fact that the Indian original has disappeared, and its features can only be guessed at by the family likeness shown in its earliest descendants. By combining the common features of the nearest of kin to the Sanskrit original—the Old Syriac, the Arabic and the Tibetan versions—Professor Benfey has produced a "composite portrait" of the original (Introduction to *Kalilag,* pp. vi.-x.) From this it appears that the source of this multifarious literature was a "Mirror for Princes," in thirteen books of tales and fables connected together by an ingenious framework, which brought the stories to bear upon the problems of conduct. An Indian sage named variously in the versions Vishnuçarman, Bidpai, Pilpay, or Sendebar, tells them to his king to incite him to virtue. It is in this device of a framework to connect the stories that the literary significance of the book consists, and it is owing to this that it has managed to keep the component tales together through so many vicissitudes.

Many of the tales occur in another connection, and enclosed in another "frame," in the Jātaka Tales, or Buddhist Birth Stories, which may detain us a moment, as they serve to establish the date of the original Bidpai, and throw some light on the framework device. These *Jatakas* are tales supposed to have been told by the Buddha, and to be in each case experiences undergone by him or witnessed by him during one or other of his former manifestations on earth. This is obviously a very convenient form by which to connect a number of stories even about birds, beasts, and fishes, since the Bodisat (or Buddha) is thought to have appeared in animal shape. Thus the eleventh, or *Lakkhana Jataka* (Rhys-Davids, p. 194), begins: "At that time the Bodisat came to life as a deer," and it has been calculated that, of the 550 Birth Stories, 108 relate to the appearances of the Buddha as a monkey, deer, lion, wild duck, snipe, elephant, cock, eagle, horse, bull, serpent, iguana, rat, jackal, &c. (*l.c.* Table VII. p. ci.) It is therefore probable that most of these Fables were first brought into connection with one another as Birth Stories of the Buddha, and some of them may actually have been composed by him, as it was clearly his custom to inculcate moral truths by some such apologues. Benfey had already seen the Buddhistic tone of the whole collection (*Pant.* i. p. xi), and Mr.

Rhys-Davids has clinched the matter in his interesting translation of a number of the Jatakas (*Buddhist Birth Stories*, vol. i., Trübner, 1880). These include two which have passed into North's version, and are reprinted at the end of the present Introduction.

The latest date at which the stories were thus connected is fixed by the curious fact that some of them have been sculptured round the sacred Buddhist shrines of Sanchi, Amaravati,* and Bharhut, in the last case with the titles of the Jatakas inscribed above them (Rhys-Davids, p. lix., and Table VIII.) These have been dated by Indian archæologists as before 200 B.C., and Mr. Rhys-Davids produces evidence which would place the stories as early as 400 B.C. Between 400 B.C. and 200 B.C., many of our tales were put together in a frame formed of the life and experience of the Buddha.

We have them now in quite a different order and connection, and the question arises, When were they taken out of the one frame and placed in the present one? This could only have been when the influence of Buddhism was declining in India, and I am therefore inclined to date

* Now on the grand staircase of the British Museum.

them in their present connection about 200–400 A.D., and to attribute them to the new Brahmanism of that period, possibly as rivals to the Jatakas. Of their later history in Buddhist countries little is known definitely. They passed into Thibet and China, and in the Indian peninsula parts of the original work appear in the *Pantschatantra* or Pentateuch, which contains five of the original thirteen books, in the *Hitopadesa*, which includes four of these, in the *Mahabharata*, which contains another three books, and the *Katha-sarit-sagara*, (Ocean of Stories), of Somadeva, which has many of the stories in a detached form; these are late, and often give us less information about the original than the more faithful Western versions.

The moment we start on the Western travels of the Fables we are on firmer ground. They were translated into Pehlevi (or Old Persian) by Barzoye, by the orders of Khosru Nushirvan (fl. 550 A.D.), under circumstances which are related to us in the book itself (pp. 34–40). Firdausi thought the event of such importance that he devoted a section to it in his *Shahnameh*, or poetical chronicle of Persia (Mohl's translation, vi., 356–65). This Pehlevi version was almost immediately translated into Syriac by a Priest named Būd or Bōd, about 570 A.D. The history of the rediscovery of this Old Syriac version forms one of the romances of modern scholarship, which must, however, here remain untold. (See Benfey's letter, translated in Professor M. Müller's *Selected Essays*, i., pp. 549-55.)

When Islam turned to science and literature, one of the earliest works translated into Arabic was the Pehlevi translation of our Fables by 'Abdullah Ibn al-Mokaffa', a Persian convert from Zoroastrianism to Islam, who was therefore a most appropriate intermediary. There is, however, another account how the book got into Arabic, which may be given here for its intrinsic interest as well as from the fact that it is one of the few things overlooked by Mr. Keith-Falconer. Abraham Ibn Ezra, a wandering Jew who visited many lands, England among them in 1158, and wrote on many subjects—grammar, arithmetic, exegesis, poetry, and astronomy—gave the following account of the Arabic translation in one of his astronomical tracts.*

* See Steinschneider, *Zur Geschichte der Uebersetzungen aus dem Indischen in's Arabische*, ZDMG. xxiv. 325-392.

INTRODUCTION.

"In olden times there was neither science nor religion among the sons of Ishmael that dwell in tents till the [author of the] Koran arose and gave them a new code of religion after his desire . . . till the great king in Ishmael, by name Es-'Saffa'h [fl. 750 A.D.], arose, who heard that there were many sciences to be found in India . . . and there came men saying that there was in India a very mighty book on the secrets of government, in the form of a Fable placed in the mouths of dumb beasts, and in it many illustrations, for the book was greatly honoured in the eyes of the reader, and the name of the book was Kalila and Dimna, that is, the Lion and the Ox, because the story in the first chapter of the book is about them. The aforesaid king fasted therefore forty days, so that he might perchance see the Angel of dreams, who might allow him to have the book translated in the Ishmaelitish tongue. And he saw in his dream according to his wish. Thereupon he sent for a Jew who knew both languages, and ordered him to translate this book, for he feared that if an Ishmaelite versed in both tongues were to translate it he might die. And when he saw that the contents of the book were extraordinary —as indeed they are—he desired to know the science [of the Indians] [and he accordingly sends the Jew to Arin, whence he brings back the *Indian numerals* and several important astronomical works]."

There are two ways of explaining this account, supposing it to be substantially true. Either Al-Mokaffa employed the Jew as a "ghost" or "devil," or there were two Arabic versions, one made from the Pehlevi, the other from the Sanskrit. In the former case it would not be surprising to receive different accounts from the "devil" and the advocate. But it would be difficult to account for the biography of the Persian Barzoye in a translation from the Sanskrit, and I am therefore inclined to think that Ibn Ezra's account points to an independent translation by a Jew from the Sanskrit direct into Arabic. I am confirmed in this belief by the remarkable variations in the Arabic MSS., which clearly indicate two prototypes (Guidi, *Studij sul testo arabo del libro di Calila e Dimna*, Rome, 1873), but must reserve details for another place. And in this connection it is interesting to observe the reference to *illustrations* in the Indian book in Ibn Ezra's account. We have seen that some of the Jatakas, or Buddhist Birth Stories, were sculptured round sacred shrines as early as the third century B.C., and the temptation is strong to connect these Indian illustrations of the same stories with the sculptures. When we come to the Arabic version, we need no longer rely on mere references to illustrations. They are still extant: three of De Sacy's MSS. (*Anciens fonds* 1483, 1492; *St. Germain de Près*, 139) have illustrations, and two others (*Anc. fonds* 1489, 1502) have places where the figures are not, but were clearly intended to be. The latter fate has unfortunately attended the only MS. of the Hebrew version of R. Joel which remains to us. But that there were illustrations in other MSS. of this Hebrew version is testified by a curious fact. A certain Rabbi Isaac Ibn Sahula wrote in 1281 a goody goody collection of tales termed "Tales of the Olden Time" (*Mashal Hakadmoni*) in order to wean the Jewish public from such books as *Kalilah wa Dimnah*, which he expressly mentions. He tells us that he has added illustrations so that his book might be equally acceptable, and these illustrations were given in the first edition of his book* (Brescia, 1491 ?). Thus it is clear that illustrations formed one of the attractions of the Hebrew version of the Fables of Bidpai, and, though we have them no longer, we have a list of them inserted in their proper places in the unique MS., and in M. Derenbourg's excellent edition of it. Now, on comparing the list with those actually given in the *editio princeps* of the Latin version, which was made from the Hebrew, a remarkable result appears. I cannot display this better than by giving for a few of the chapters in parallel columns a translation of the list of illustrations *referred to* in the Hebrew text, and an account of the plates which are actually *given* in the first edition of the *Directorium*, as well as in the first German and Spanish versions, which have the same plates.†

* The British Museum possesses a unique copy of this, with seventy-one illustrations, thirty-four of which are of animals. On fol. 18*b* is one of two jackals, which might easily pass for Kalila and Dimna.

† Benfey has shown (*Orient and Occident*, i. 165) that the plates were originally made for the German, as it has seven more than the Latin, which issued from the same press.

Chap. VI.

Referred to in Hebrew.	*Given in Lat., Germ., Span.*
Ape in tree and reptile in water.	Ape on tree, reptile in water.
Animals in water.	Ape and reptile in water.
Ape on tree and reptile in water.	
Lion and ass running away.	Lion, ass, man, ape.
Lion seizing ass and fox looking on.	Lion seizing ass, ape above.

Chap. VII.

	Ascetic striking pot of honey [= La Perrette].
Child and dog killing serpent.	Child, dog killing serpent [= Gellert].

Chap. VIII.

Cat in net, bird on tree, dog and mouse.	Cat in net, bird on tree, dog and man.
Mouse gnawing net.	Mouse gnawing net.*
Mouse, net, cat in tree, and hunter going away.	Mouse, net, cat in tree, and hunter going away.

Chap. IX.

Child killing little bird.	Child killing little bird.
Pinza taking child's eyes out.	Bird like a gryphon [= Pinza] taking child's eyes out.
King calling Pinza on a mountain.	King calling Pinza on a mountain.

---

* In German, not in Latin, for want of room. It passed into the Spanish, showing that the latter used the German (Benfey, *l.c.*).

There is only one conclusion to be drawn from the identity of the two lists. John of Capua must have taken into his version the illustrations in the Hebrew or copies of them. And combining this with our other evidence about the Indian and Arabic versions, there seems every reason to believe that the illustrations were regarded as an integral part of the text and were translated, if one may say so, along with it. No notice has been hitherto taken of this migration of illustrations, yet it may one day afford as interesting a chapter in the history of art as the Fables themselves have given to the history of literature.*

This traditional illustration of the Fables ceases after the first editions of the Latin, German, and Spanish appeared in print. Henceforth the work of the illustrator was done "out of his own head." Thus, the plates accompanying the Italian and English, some of which are here reproduced, cannot be brought into connection with India. We give, however, a sample of the traditional illustrations on p. lxiii., to accompany the text of the *Baka Jataka*, and it is surprising how exactly a design by a German artist of the fifteenth

* I have already collected materials for the Gellert story, as illustrated in the MSS. and early editions.

century can be made to illustrate a tale told probably by the Buddha nearly two thousand years before.

These traditional illustrations may also be made to play an important part in the criticism of the Bidpai literature. They would serve as the readiest means of testing the affiliation of texts. In particular, they may bring order into the confusion which now reigns as to the Arabic version. I trust that henceforth no description of an Arabic MS. of the Fables will be considered complete without a list of its illustrations. We may thus determine the question whether there are not two distinct families of Arabic MSS. of the *Kalilah wa Dimnah*, one of which was derived directly from the Sanskrit by a Jewish dragoman, according to the tradition given by Abraham Ibn Ezra, which formed the starting point of this long, but, I hope, not uninteresting or unimportant digression.

Whether any Jew was concerned in bringing the Fables from India or no, there is no doubt that Jewish intermediation brought them into mediæval Europe. The Arabic version appeared under the name of "Kalilah wa Dimnah," a softened form of the Pehlevi Kalilag and Dimnag, which represent the two jackals, Karaṭaka and Damanaka, of the first chapter of the Indian original. From Arabic it was translated into the languages of all the countries of Islam. Besides the late Oriental versions, like the Persian and the Turkish, *Kalilah wa Dimnah* reached the West mainly through three offshoots. The first of these was a Greek version, done by Symeon Seth, a Jewish physician at the Byzantine court in the eleventh century: from this were derived the Old Slavonic and the Croat versions. Then there was an Old Spanish version which I have elsewhere (*Jewish Chronicle*, 3d July 1885), shown to have been translated in the College of Jewish translators of Arabic works of science, established by Alphonso the Good at Toledo, about 1250; this gave rise to a Latin version. And finally, there was a Hebrew version made by by one Rabbi Joel, from which a Latin version was made by John of Capua, a converted Jew, under the title of *Directorium humane vite*, and this gave rise to German, Spanish, Czech, Italian, Dutch, Danish, and English versions.

It will thus be seen that the work before us enjoys the unique distinction of having appealed to all the great religions of the world. Originated in Buddhism, it was adopted by Brahmanism, passed on by Zoroastrianism to Islam, which transmitted it to Christendom by the mediation of Jews.

Besides the wide spread of the tales as a whole by translation, several of them passed into popular literature in more or less modified form. The chase after these scattered references is a very alluring one, but almost all the game has been already bagged by that mighty hunter, Benfey. In that eminent scholar's introduction to his translation of the *Pantschatantra* (Leipzig, 1859) he has traced each of the tales in its wanderings with an amount of erudition which is phenomenal, even in the land of erudition. Some idea of this may be given by Professor Max Müller's charming essay "On the Migration of Fables" (*Chips from a German Workshop*, vol. iv. pp. 145–209; *Selected Essays*, i. pp. 500–576). Professor Müller has forgotten to mention that this is a chip from another German's workshop,* yet as a matter of fact, every reference to the tale of the milk-maid who counts her chickens before they

---

* I have felt obliged to say this, first, because Professor Müller has not done so, and secondly, because in consequence he has been credited with original work on the subject.

are hatched, is given in § 209 of Benfey's *Einleitung*, and nearly every one of its 239 sections affords material for a similar monograph. In the analytical table of contents which I have appended to this introduction, I have given Benfey's references to each tale, so that the reader may judge of their relative popularity.

Besides this spontaneous spread through Europe of the Fables of Bidpai, there has been, during the past two centuries, what may be termed a learned diffusion of the various Oriental versions of the Fables. As Orientalists became aware of the interest and value of the Fables, they edited or translated the Eastern versions, and thus a mass of materials was collected which required wide linguistic knowledge to master. The investigation of the Bidpai literature began with Bishop Huet in 1670, and was then carried on by Stark, by Schultens, by Sylvestre de Sacy, and by Loiseleur Deslongchamps, till, at the present day, there is scarcely an Orientalist of note who has not had his say and said something worth saying about the Fables of Bidpai. Two names, however, in the present generation, stand out most prominently as the masters of all that is to be known on this subject—Theodor Benfey and

Joseph Derenbourg. Thus, by a curious coincidence, as the Jews were the chief agents in the spontaneous spread of the Fables, so Jewish scholars have done most for the scientific study of that spread.

Owing to this learned diffusion of the Fables, it has come about that, within the last hundred years, no less than twenty English translations of various versions of Bidpai's Fables have been published. Of these, fourteen are from various Indian offshoots (for which see Mr. Rhys-Davids' Table I.),* of which the most important are the *Hitopadesa*, of which there are five English versions,† and Somadeva's *Katha-sarit-sagara*, or Ocean of the River of Tales. Besides these we have Knatchbull's translation of the Arabic, Eastwick's and Wollaston's versions of the Persian *Anvari Suhaili*, besides J. Taylor's translation of the French version of its first four chapters, which is interesting as being the first work with

---

* Adding M. Müller's (interlineary) translation of the *Hitopadesa*, Tawney's *Katha-sarit-sagara*, Winford's version of the Tamil *Panchatantra*, Manuel's translation of the Urdu, and Fausböll's, Mr. Rhys-Davids', and Dr. Morris' versions of the Jatakas.

† The earliest of these by Wilkins (Bath, 1787) has been reprinted by Professor Morley in his Universal Library (No. 30).

the title "Fables of Pilpay" (1699).* And finally, we have Mr. Keith-Falconer's version of the Later Syriac, and Mr. Ralston's reproduction of Schiefner's curious "find" of the Tibetan version. All this may serve to justify the reprint of the earliest of the twenty English translations, and to indicate that to the many stories contained in the book itself, must be added one more wonderful still—the story of its wanderings.

North's version, here republished, bears traces of these peregrinations almost in every section. Notwithstanding the warning to the reader of the necessity of reading the book in connected order, it is really an *omnium gatherum* from almost every country and tongue through which the original fables had passed on their way to England. Thus, the appeal "to the Reader" is from the Italian. The Prologue appears first in Arabic, though the tales in it can be traced to Indian sources. The Argument of the book goes a step farther back, and must have been in the Pehlevi. An interesting trait is omitted in the English version, for Barzoye in the original asks as his only reward that his life and exploits should be added to the Fables of Bidpai, as indeed they

* Reprinted recently in the Chandos Library.

have been. The First Part is really a continuation of the "Argument" and, though it is not so stated, is an abstract of Barzoye's account of his religious views, a kind of *Religio Medici*, in which the Buddhistic influence is strong. This again can only go back as far as Persia, though the celebrated tale with which it concludes occurs also in "Barlaam and Josaphat," or the Life of St. Buddha.* It is only with the Second and Third Parts that we come upon the earliest stratum of the Fables. These correspond to the first book of the original Fables represented in the first book of the *Pantschatantra* and in the second of the *Hitopadesa*. The Fourth Part again is originally an addition of Al-Mokaffa's in the Arabic version. The only things quite English in the book are, if we may be excused the Hibernicism, the Italian sonnet to North, and the other two poems (pp. 7–10). The remaining three quarters of the Indian original are not represented in North's version, which is confined more strictly than any of the others to the story of Kalila and Dimna. These appear in the anonymous form of the ass and the mule. Thus the illustration on p. 100 gives us

* In the illustration, the gentleman who is running away from the four lions (four elements) is the same as he that has fallen into the well.

the original jackal, Damanaka, of the Indian tale under the form of "his Moyleship."

The proper names of the books also bear traces of the phonetic detrition they have undergone, owing to the wear and tear of ages. A German scholar could easily fill this whole Introduction with a dissertation on these proper names.* I must content myself with one or two examples. Though I have called the stories throughout "the Fables of Bidpai,"—the name by which they are best known—in the book itself they are attributed to the sage Sendebar. The reader might not think it, but this can be traced back to the same original as the name Bidpai. As thus: Bidpai was originally Baidaba,† and in the Arabic MS. used by the holy‡ Rabbi Joel, the diacritical points

* Most of Benfey's Introduction to the Old Syriac version is devoted to this subject, and most properly so, since it affords the crucial test of literary origin.

† It is doubtful whether the original was the Pehlevi *Wedawaka* (Nöldeke) or the Sanskrit *Vidyapati*, "lord of knowledge" (Benfey). Other variants are Nadrab, Sendebar, Sanbader, Bundabet, Bendabel, Barduben, for which see Keith-Falconer, p. 271.

‡ I use this epithet on the same principle as a youthful friend of mine who, on being told by his nurse that she must not read stories on Sunday, replied, "But surely you may read holy Grimm." At the same time our only authority for attributing the Hebrew Version to Joel is the poor one of Doni.

which distinguish between *b, t,* and *th* had been omitted, and the Rabbi who had also translated the far-famed book of *Sindibad*, jumped to the conclusion that these fables were also due to that sage, and thought the reading to be *Thindiba*, which he took the liberty of changing into *Sindibad*. But revenge soon overtook him, for in Hebrew there is a similar resemblance between the letters *d* and *r*, and his translator, John of Capua, read Sindibad as Sendebar, Q.E.D. A similar misunderstanding of the Hebrew, according to Derenbourg, has changed the Shah Nurshirvan into Anestres Castri (p. 34).

So much at present for the external history of the work before us, which lends it so much of its interest. But its contents claim our attention in equal degree, for it has been claimed for them that in them, or rather in their Indian original, is to be found the *fons et origo* of all folk-tales, or at any rate of all tales about beasts. No one now-a-days would perhaps go so far as to hold that we can trace every folk-tale back to India, and to this particular collection, but the temptation is often very strong to do so, with M. Cosquin, for example (*Contes populaires* *de Lorraine*, Paris, 1882), or with Mr. Clouston (*Popular Tales and Fictions*, 1887). As regards the origin of folk-tales, the view is too extreme to need much discussion.* Those who hold it overlook the fact that the "tell me a story" instinct is as universal as any craving of mankind. Indeed I wonder that some one has not defined Man as a tale-telling animal (with the corollary of Woman as a tale-bearing one). The only plausibility which is given to the derivation of all folk-tales from the East is given by the amazing erudition of Benfey. At first sight it might seem that all European folk-tales, and more also, had been swept into the net of his *Einleitung*. But if we take any particular collection and investigate what proportion of it is to be found referred to by Benfey, we get a more sober estimate of the influence of the Orient on folk-tales.

* I have not thought it worth while to refer to the further refinement of those who, like Professor de Gubernatis (*Storia delle Novellini populari*, Milan, 1883), besides tracing all folk-tales back to India (he does this for ten selected examples in the accompanying *Florilegio*) traces them when there to degradations of meteorological myths about sun, moon, and stars. Even Professor Müller, who applies his "sparrow-grass" theory of things to most things in heaven and earth, would not go this length (*Sel. Ess.* i. 510).

Thus, out of the two hundred *märchen* collected by the Brothers Grimm, only eighteen are quoted as parallels by Benfey,* and in many of these cases the parallelism is only so far justified that there seems to be no point of contact between the two tales except that afforded by the common human nature underlying them. Or working from the other end we may attempt to calculate the proportion of any country's tales which can be traced to the East. Professor Crane has selected from the voluminous folk-literature of Italy 107 of the most characteristic tales in his *Italian Folk-Tales*, and of these he only traces a dozen (xxxvii.-xlviii.) to Oriental sources, a somewhat higher percentage than in the German collection, as is but natural, considering the closer proximity and connection of Italy, and especially Sicily, with the East. Altogether we shall not be far out if we restrict the proportion of Oriental tales among the folk-tales of Western Europe to one in ten.

Another consideration will modify the somewhat exaggerated claims that have been made for the influence of our collection upon European

* §§ 36, 92, 106, 120, 150, 155, 159, 165-8, 181, 186, 195, 208, 209, 212, 227.

folk-tales. It is true that these tales passed into all the languages of Europe in translations, but a large part of them never emerged from within the covers of the translations, as may be seen by referring to our analytical list of the stories. At first sight it seems to argue a wide spread for a story to see it quoted from "Anvari-Suhaili," "Hitopadesa," "Directorium vite humane," "Panchatantra," "Exemplario," "Stephanite i Ichnelate," "Del governo degli animali," and so on. Mr. Clouston especially is fond of ringing these changes (*Popular Tales, pass.*) But after all this is much the same as if one were to state that a saying appeared in "the Torah" and "ἡ παλαία διαθήκη" and "Das erste Buch Mose" and "the Vulgate" and "the Peshitto" and "Les saintes écritures" and "Genesis" and "the Douay Version," and all the other names under which the Bible is known in translation. All these are but one book, and though the various translations may very properly be quoted as testimonies to the popularity of the book, they cannot be counted over and over again as proving the popularity of each story. Or rather, if a story occurs only in these translations, this tells dead against its popularity *per se.** For what does this imply? Surely that in the struggle for existence among popular tales many of those which found a footing in written or printed literature failed to find any vogue in oral literature. That there was an exosmose of ideas and tales between the literate and illiterate is undoubtedly the fact, but we know little of the laws of intercommunication, and are likely, from our ignorance of the exact processes of oral tradition,† to exaggerate its amount. Whenever clear cases of the interfusion occur, as when we can clearly trace the Grimms' story *Simeliberg* (No. 142) to the *Forty Thieves* of the Arabian Nights, the literary *form* of the original has left its traces in some significant word or phrase, (in that case the pass-word "Sesame"). Altogether

---

* Of the forty stories or so contained in this volume only about ten (C1, C4, D7c, D9, D9a, E4a, E6, E9, E10, and F4) can be said to be really popular. At the same time, it should be added, that stories that are so popular may be almost counted on the fingers.

† The only kind of oral tradition extant among us consists in the stories—more broad than long—that circulate among young men in smoking rooms. In my sallet days I have heard stories of this nature told me by a Canadian, which I had previously heard with exactly the ame turns of expression in Australia.

we may say that the *onus probandi* falls upon those who assert the Oriental origin of folk-tales, and in their proof we cannot be content with the assertion of a common "formula," which can only show that some rural wit in Germany had observed the fickleness of woman or the vanity of man in somewhat the same form as a brother sage in India had done some hundreds of years before. We have an exact analogy in the case of novels: one of these days we may obtain a scientific scheme of "formulæ" for the huge mass of novels, yet it would be hasty to assume that every novel which might come under the formula of "the lost heir" or "the innocent accused," had been derived from the same original.

There is still another reason why it is improbable that the Bidpai literature should have had such influence on European folk-tales as has been attributed to it. Incredible as it may seem, the Fables were translated in the first period of their spontaneous spread, not for the story-interest of them, but on account of their moral interest—their "moral philosophy" as the title of the Italian and English versions testifies. They were regarded as homilies, and the tales were only tolerated as so much jam to give a relish to the "morality." It was therefore appropriate that these Asiatic tales with their Buddhistic tendencies should be introduced just at the period when Europe was Asiaticising. For if we may generalise about such big things as continents, may we not say that the ideal of Asia has been *to be,* that of Europe *to do ?* * And was it not the striving of mediæval Europe *to be,* and not primarily *to do,* that makes it seem so alien to us moderns who have recovered the old European tradition of Greeks and Romans and Teutons? With touching simplicity, the mediævals, like the Asiatics, thought it only necessary to know, in order to do, the right, and hence their appeal to Oriental wisdom: alas, we moderns know better! It is important to notice this aspect of the book, as it makes it still more remarkable that it should have been accepted as a sort of secular Bible, if we may so term it, by men of so many different religions. There must have been something essentially human in this Buddhistic book that it should have been welcomed as a moral encheiridion by Zoroastrians, Moslems,

* Lindley Murray would perhaps have added that the ideal of Africa has been *to suffer.*

Jews, and Christians. Perhaps we may account for this universal acceptance of its doctrines because they seemed to come from the mouths of those who could not be suspected of heresy —from our dumb brethren, the beasts.

And this leads me to discuss the claim of our book, or its original, to be the source of all beast-fables—a claim for which a somewhat better case has been made out. For India is the home of metempsychosis, and there, if anywhere, the idea of animals talking and willing like men might seem most natural. Accordingly, Benfey would trace all stories in which animals act in this way back to India, though, curiously enough, he claims a Western (Greek) origin for beast-tales in which animals act "as sich." Against this a claim has recently been set up for South Africa by Professor Sayce, who points to the existence of such fables quite independent of Indian influence (Bleek, *Reynard the Fox in South Africa*, 1872). He connects with beast-fables, by some link of association which is not too evident, the existence in the South African languages of special "clicks" which accompany each animal in the narration* (*Science of Language*, ii. 280–3).

* Thus we might tell the rhyme of *the House that Jack*

INTRODUCTION.

From the Bushmen or their ancient representatives, it seems to be suggested, it may have passed on to Egypt, and thence have percolated to Phœnicia, Assyria, Greece (may not Æsop be connected with Aἰθίοψ, it is asked), and India. Benfey himself gives some support to this contention by suggesting that in the first instance metempsychosis was derived from Egypt.

But against all this inquiry about the place from which beast-fables first came may be urged the probability that they came from nowhere, because they have always been everywhere where nomad man was. The doctrine of metempsychosis itself we now know, thanks to Mr. Tylor, to be merely an extension of the general tendency of early races towards an "animistic" theory of things, by which the savage observer of Nature projects his personality into all surrounding objects, whether animate or inanimate. The

---

built with appropriate "clicks" as follows : "This is the cock that crowed in the morn (*Cock-a-doodle-doo*) to wake the priest all shaven and shorn (*Pax vobiscum*), who married the man all tattered and torn (*Haha-ha-ha*), unto the maiden all forlorn (*Hehe-he-he*), that milked the cow with the crumpled horn (*Mooooo*), that tossed the dog (*bow-wow*), that worried the cat (*mieaou*), that killed the rat (*week*)," &c.

prevalence of totemism is another proof of the intense interest of men in the hunting stage in the ways of animals. And if we may apply the inverse method and argue back from the infancy of the individual to the infancy of the race, we may notice that the "gee-gee" and the "bow-wow" are the first objects of interest to the little ones.* Sir Richard Burton would even go further, and sees the essence of the beast-fable in "a reminiscence of *Homo primigenius* with erected ears and hairy hide, and its expression is to make the brother brute to hear, think, and talk like him with the superadded experience of ages."† One hesitates to dissent from so great an authority as Sir R. Burton on all that relates to the bestial element in man.

* George Eliot's infantile imagination was first touched by Æsop's Fables (*Life*, i. 20), and M. Bert sensibly begins his *First Year of Scientific Knowledge* with Animals.

† I owe this quotation and my knowledge of Sir R. Burton's views generally on this subject to an article by Mr. T. Davidson on "Beast-Fables," in the new edition of Chambers's Cyclopædia, which sums up admirably the present state of opinion on this subject, and a very confused state it is. Mr. Davidson quotes section 3 of the notorious Terminal Essay of the *Thousand Nights and A Night*.

But it may be pointed out what an unconscionably long memory the originators of beast-fables must have had if it could bridge over the long lapse of years required to turn the Darwinian *Homo* into Man the Speaker. And as all men *ex hypothesi* would have the same reminiscence of their original identity with the beasts, it seems rather inconsistent in Sir R. Burton to stand out, as I understand he does, for an exclusively African origin of beast-fables.

But we need not depend on imaginative hypotheses of pre-historic psychogony in opposing the contention for any single centre of dispersion for beast-fables. Their exclusively Indian origin at any rate, with which we are more particularly concerned, is at once disproved by traces which we can find of them in Egypt, Assyria, and Judæa (Jotham's fable, *Judges* ix.), before any connection with India can be established. Indeed on the strength of Jotham's fable and the many fables given or mentioned in the Talmud,* Dr. Landsberger some years ago argued that Judæa was the original home of the Fable

---

* On these see Hamburger's *Realencyclopädie des Talmuds* s.v. Fabel, and a series of papers by Dr. Back in Graetz's *Monatschrift* for 1881.

(*Fabeln des Sophos*, 1859). But the Talmud is late (150–450 A.D.), and the Rabbis to whom the fables are attributed may easily have learned their beast-fables from the Romans, just as they took the chief elements of their culture from Rome. M. Halévy has even suggested that the Fables of Bidpai were known to the Talmudic Doctors (*Revue des études juives*, xi., 195-200). He finds a pair of words which with a little coaxing can be made to resemble *Karirak* and *Damonak*. The words seem to mean in the text a set of fire-irons, whence the connection with fire-worshippers and with Persians, and so, with the Pehlevi text of our fables is made out to the satisfaction of M. Halévy, who is on this occasion even more ingenious than usual, which is saying a great deal, but even less convincing than usual, which is saying more. But apart from all this, priority of time is against our deriving Indian fables from the Talmudic ones or even asserting the independence of the latter.

Remoteness of locality might seem to be equally effective in proving independence or priority of time. For this reason the African collections of Fables are especially interesting, and have been adduced by Professor Sayce and

Sir R. Burton, as we have seen, to establish Africa as the origin of the Fable. Yet Benfey promises (*Pant.* i., pp. 102, 183) to show traces of Indian influence on the fables of the Senegal negroes (Roger, *Fables sénégalaises*, 1828), and on those of the Bechuanas (Grimm-Hunt, ii. pp. 544-554), through the medium of Arab slave-traders. He nowhere carried out this promise, so far as I can ascertain, but I think I can confirm his conclusion by evidence from a most unexpected quarter. Most of my readers will remember the amusing collection of beast-fables from the slave-states of America known by the name of *Uncle Remus*. Nothing could seem more autochthonous or more remote from Indian influences, and they have already been adduced as convincing evidence of the ubiquity of beast-fables. Yet I am much mistaken if I cannot connect the celebrated incident of the "Tar-Baby," which forms the nucleus of the collection as motivating the enmity of Brer Rabbit and Brer Fox, with one of the Jatakas or Buddhist Birth-stories. Every one will remember how Brer Rabbit, annoyed at the incivility of the Tar-Baby, chastises it with his right paw and left paw, with right leg and left leg, all of which stick to the "Baby," till at last he butts at the obnoxious infant with his head, and is then at the mercy of Brer Fox, who all the time has "lain low." Now compare with this the following passage from the Jataka of the Demon with the Matted Hair (Fausböll, i. pt. ii. p. 272) as translated by Professor J. Estlin Carpenter* (*Three Ways of Salvation*, 1884, p. 27). The Bodisat in one of his former births as "Prince Five-Weapons" assails the Demon of the Matted Hair in the midst of a gloomy forest, "And with a resolute air he [the future Buddha] hit him with his right hand, *but his right hand and his left hand, his right foot and his left foot, were all caught in turn in the Demon's hair, and when at last he butted at him with his head that was caught too.*" The situation is so unique and the parallelism so close that we cannot avoid assuming a causal connection between the two versions. Yet if that be so, the Jataka of the Demon of the Matted Hair must have passed from India to Africa with Hindoo merchants or Arab slave-traders, must then have crossed Equatorial Africa before

* I was put on the track of this by Mr. F. H. Jones, Dr. Williams' Librarian, who heard Professor Carpenter's address and was struck with the resemblance.

Livingstone or Stanley, then took ship in the hold of a slaver across the Atlantic and found a home in the log-cabins of South Carolina. No wonder Brer Rabbit was so 'cute, since he is thus shown to be an incarnation of the Buddha himself.

This remarkable instance of the insidious spread of Buddhistic fables is at anyrate sufficient to give us pause before assuming that distance from India proves independence from Indian influences. We can only prove this by examples of beast-fables known to have been in existence before any contact with India can be shown. Besides the instances of Egyptian, Assyrian, and Bible fables, before referred to, we have the case of Greece, which, as the home of Æsop, deserves more particular attention. We find a fable in Hesiod (*Op. et Dies*, 202), two fables of Archilochus are known, and almost the only poetical thing in Byron's *English Bards*:

> "So the struck eagle, stretch'd upon the plain,
> No more through rolling clouds to soar again,
> View'd his own feather on the fatal dart,
> And wing'd the shaft that quiver'd in his heart," *

is from a fable contained in a fragment of

---

* Byron got the idea from Waller, *To a Lady singing a Song of his composing.*

Æschylus' *Myrmidons*, which by the way does something to confirm the African origin, since the poet adds ὡς δ'ἐστὶ μύθων τῶν Λιβυστικῶν λόγος (Schol. in Arist. *Aves*, 808). Aristophanes again has several references to Æsopean fables, and as we all know, Socrates in his last days occupied his leisure with "tagging" Æsop. All this was before any Indian influence could come in, and Benfey accordingly goes so far as to trace the Indian fables of an Æsopic type (*i.e.*, where the animals do not act as men, but *in propriâ personâ*) to Greek or Western influence. But the reasoning on which he bases this somewhat startling result (I. p. xxi. §§ 58, 130, 162) does not give one as much respect for his judgment as for his erudition. And at anyrate it is now generally recognised that *our* Æsop, the mediæval collection passing under that name, is strongly impregnated with Indian elements from the Bidpai literature.

Whether Phædrus, and Babrius from whom he borrows, can be traced back to the influence of the *Jatakas*, and so to the original of our present work, has not been thoroughly threshed out.* But

* "The History of the Greek Fable" forms the second introductory Essay to Mr. W. G. Rutherford's *Babrius*.

I would point to a feature common to the *Jatakas*, the Fables of Bidpai, and those of Babrius and Phædrus. And that is the "moral-pidgin," as Mr. Leland's Chinaman would say, that is inseparably connected with all these forms of the fable, though, if one thinks of it, the very *raison d'être* of the Fable is to imply its moral without mentioning it. The whole book before us seems to be written in the spirit of the Duchess in *Alice's Adventures* who, it will be remembered, concludes every statement of hers with the remark "And the moral of that is —." This moralising tendency is so distinctive a feature that one is tempted to trace it to a definite and single source, which can only be the *gatha* or "moral" verse, of the Buddhistic *Jatakas* (see Appendix). That there was time for them to reach the Hellenic world is shown by the fact that as early as the time of Augustus a *sramanakarja* (teacher of the Ascetics) created a great impression by burning himself alive at Athens, where his tomb was long afterwards to be seen with the inscription Ζαρμανοχηγὰς Ἰνδὸς ἀπὸ Βαργόσης [Barygaza, then

---

He decides against any Indian influence in a very trenchant manner, but more trenchant than convincing, as it seems to me.

a Buddhist centre] κατὰ τὰ πάτρια Ἰνδῶν ἔθη ἑαυτὸν ἀπαθανατίσας κεῖται.*

Thus, although we cannot trace all beast-fables to India, we may, I think, give Buddhism, as represented by the book before us, the credit of those that have a moral attached, which is the case with most forms of the Æsopic fable. And arrived at the end of our inquiry into the influence of the book, we may trace it all to the Buddhism latent in it. For we have seen its wide acceptance due to the moral interest in it, and its influence on the so-called Fables of Æsop also due to the "morals" attached to them, and these moralities are the special things in the book which are due to Buddhism. And still more curiously the peculiar literary form of the book, which, as we shall see, has been even wider in its influence, can be traced back directly to the person of the founder of the religion.†

---

* See Lightfoot, *Colossians*, p. 390–6, who, however, for polemical purposes, dates Indian influence on the West as late as possible. The learned Bishop, however, considers that St. Paul derived from this incident his striking remark, "Though I give my body to be burned and have not charity, it availeth nothing" (1 *Cor.* xiii. 3).

† Against this Mr. Rhys-Davids points to the fact that several of the Jatakas are already "frames;" the

INTRODUCTION.

The idea of stringing a number of stories together by putting them in a frame as in Boccaccio's *Decamerone*, Chaucer's *Canterbury Tales*, Basile's *Pentamerone*, and so on down to Mr. Pickwick and Mr. Stevenson, is one that is distinctly to be traced to the East in the Fables of Bidpai, the book of Sindibad, and the *Arabian Nights*. The last is late, and was influenced by the others,* but the other two books which went through much the same history are offshoots of Buddhism, and in the case of Bidpai's Fables we have seen how the idea of a frame arose in the *Jatakas* or Birth Stories of Buddha. It is in the tendency to collect all the "good things" of India about the great exemplar of good in India that we must see the origin of the literary device of "the frame," which has done so much to keep intact the book we have been discussing during its long travels across the ages. Considering all these

---

Ummaga-Jataka contains 150 stories. But the vogue of the "frame" was due to Buddhism.

   * Professor de Goeje has made out a plausible case for tracing the frame story of *the Thousand and One Nights* to the story of Esther (*Ency. Brit.*, sub voce), as Shahzará is mentioned by Firdausi as a Jewish wife of Artaxerxes I. But the idea of a "frame" must have been suggested by the Indian books.

things, and remembering that Bidpai is only a lay figure who takes the place of Buddha in "moralising" the stories, may we not sum up our conclusions as to their origin and influence by roundly stating that the Fables of Bidpai are the Fables of Buddha ?*

As the experienced reader might suspect from all this insistence on the extrinsic interest of the book before us that intrinsically it is as dull as most books of Oriental apologues are, I hasten to reassure him on the point. And in order to do so, I must remind the reader of the man to whom we owe it, and of his position in our literature. Of the external events of Sir Thomas North's life little definite is known, and that little has been put together with his customary diligence and accuracy by the late Mr. Cooper in his *Athenæ Cantabrigienses* (ii. p. 350–1). That Thomas,

* All this on the assumption that the remaining nineteen-twentieths of the Jataka tales are as full of the Fables as the hundred or so that have been translated by Fausböll, Mr. Rhys-Davids, Dr. Morris, and the Bishop of Colombo. I suspect, however, that the Pali scholars have already played their strongest trumps. Benfey held almost as good a hand thirty years ago: at anyrate *our* two Jatakas are duly noted by him in their proper places (§§ 60, 84; see also §§ 61, 82, here D10, E4).

second son of Edward, Lord North of Kirtling, was educated at Peterhouse, Cambridge, entered Lincoln's Inn in 1557, was presented with the honorary freedom of Cambridge in 1568,* was appointed captain of three hundred men raised at Ely in the Armada times, had something to do with the gaugers of ale and beer in 1591, was reduced to accept a relief of £20 from the town-council of Cambridge in 1598, and that he and his son received further help from his brother's will in 1600—these are the facts that form the exoskeleton of his life. We are at present more concerned with his literary productions. These are three; all of them translations. The first was a version of Antonio de Guevara's *Libro aureo*, a Spanish adaptation of Marcus Aurelius's *Meditations*, which had an extraordinary vogue throughout Western Europe at this time: North translated mainly from the French version, but did the last part into English from the original.

* From his familiarity with French and Italian, we might surmise a grand tour about this time. The "G. B." who wrote one of the introductory sonnets of our book was probably an Italian friend thus acquired. Could he have been Giordano Bruno, who came over to England thirteen years later, and had therefore relations with this country?

This was published in 1568, and two years later appeared "The Morall Philosophie of Doni,"* and in 1579 came his most important work, the translation of Plutarch, after the vigorous French of Amyot. This was one of the most popular books of the period, running through eight editions within the century after its first appearance. Most of us know it, or know of it, as the source of Shakespeare's picture of the Roman world.

Yet, if recent research is to be trusted, North's first book, the translation of Guevara, which he called *The Dial of Princes*, had almost as much influence as his Plutarch. For Dr. Landmann in an ingenious essay (*Der Euphuismus*, Giessen, 1881) has attempted to trace Euphuism to the influence of Guevara. It is true Mr. S. L. Lee interprets this to mean that Euphuism had for

* As we are on biographies, a word or two may be spared to the Doni, who forms part of the title of our book. He was a real person—Antonio Francesco Doni—flourishing in Italy in the middle of the sixteenth century (*b*. 1513, *d*. 1574) as a kind of journalist at Florence, his birthplace; Venice, where he wrote the *Moral Philosophia* in 1552; Ancona, whither he retired from fear of the Inquisition; and at Montselice, where he died. He was a novelist as well as a fabulist, and in the former capacity appears in Roscoe's *Italian Novelists*, where eight of his novels are translated.

its literary parent Lord Berners, the translator of Froissart, who also Englished Guevara's book before North in 1539 (see his edition of Berners' *Huon of Burdeux*, E.E.T.S. iv. pp. 785–6). But Berners' version was made from the French, and it is difficult to see how the Spaniard's style could be caught except in a version made from the Spanish, as was in large measure that of North, who must therefore be regarded as the father of Euphuism, if that style is to be traced to Guevara alone. But as a matter of fact such a tendency to over-ornamentation as is shown in Euphuism came to all the literatures of West Europe as a natural development after they had passed the apprenticeship of translation, and became conscious of the delights of literary artifice.

North came just mid-way between the exaggerated Ciceronianism of Berners, Elliot, and Ascham, his chief predecessors, and the exaggerated Guevarism (if it must be so) of Lyly and his school; and because he did so, we see in him Tudor prose at its best. In the Elizabethan period our language attained both ease and dignity, but the ease of Greene and the pamphleteers was never dignified, and the dignity of such men as Hooker was rarely easeful. North alone, so far as I know, had ease with dignity, and so ranks rightly as the first great master of English prose. He alone of his era had the art of saying great things simply, as he does so often in his Plutarch.

If I mistake not, the book here brought again to light displays these qualities in no less a degree. It comes as a happy medium between the stateliness of his Guevara and the grandeur of his Plutarch, with its Italian vivacity tempered with far off echoes of Oriental gravity. It argues a master of language to have been equal to so many styles.* Let us hear a couple of his sentences: "To be alone it griueth vs: to be accompanied it troubleth vs: to live long it werieth vs: and sufficient contenteth vs not." That might have come from one of the finest of the Homilies: notice the subtle turn of the last clause just when the parallelism is beginning to cloy. Again: "His Moyleship brauely yerked out with both legges and liuely shook his eares and head. He brayed and flong as he had bene madde." There is vigour and crispness.

---

* North's French prototype, Amyot, showed the same versatility of style, being equally successful with Plutarch and with *Daphnis and Chloe*. (Saintsbury, *French Lit.*, 232.)

North is at his best in the dialogues and soliloquies which are scattered so frequently through the book, and it is there too that he departs most freely from the Italian version, which as a rule he follows closely. The flexibility of his style comes out in these speeches: contrast, for example, the vigour of the exulting speech of "the Moyle" (Dimna) when he has entrapped the Bull (p. 177) with the courtier-like gravity with which he has just approached King Lion (p. 129), and the friendly persuasion with which he has won over the Bull (p. 147).

Another mark of the fine instinct which North displays as a literary artist is the fact that so few of his words have become obsolete. There are scarcely a dozen passages in the book which fail to yield their meaning on a first reading owing to this cause.* And yet with all this the book is full of those racy quaintnesses which give to Elizabethan English something of the charm of the pretty prattlings of early childhood: the

---

* Some readers may be glad to have the following equivalents:—flight (p. 55) = fled; draffe (82) = dregs; bucke (95) = lye (?); girned (103) = mocked; dole (127) = share. Few will care to know that 'cockle' (113) = *Angrostemna githago*, Linn., and I should like to know what 'coccomber' (178) means.

interjections in particular, "Tut a figge," "What a goodyere," and the like, resemble the inarticulate cries of childhood, and come most appropriate in a literature after a New Birth.

And the book which North has clothed in this style has greater claims to artistic unity than most collections of Oriental tales. With happy tact, he did not translate the second part of Doni (*Trattati diversi*), which contains a farrago of Oriental tales culled from all quarters, which produce the same bewildering effect as most of the Oriental collections. North, by confining himself to the first part of the *Moral Philosophia*, corresponding to the first chapter of the original Sanskrit,* has given a certain amount of consistency to his version of Bidpai which is lacking in all the others. Three-quarters of the book represent the intrigues of the wily Dimna against the simple-minded Senesba.

Here I must stop. One who edits a "find" cannot hope to be trusted about its artistic merits.

---

* It must not be supposed that our book contains only one-thirteenth of the original. The first chapter is exceptionally long, so that our version represents about one-fourth of the original Sanskrit, and rather more than a third of the Arabic version, from which most of the European representatives come.

If I go on further, I foresee the sort of mental dialogue which will pass between my reader and myself. "What," the reader will exclaim, "the first literary link between India and England, between Buddhism and Christendom, written in racy Elizabethan with vivacious dialogue, and something distinctly resembling a plot. Why, you will be trying to make us believe that you have restored to us an English Classic!" "Exactly so," I should be constrained to reply, and lest I be tempted into this temerity, I will even make a stop here.

APPENDIX.

BUDDHIST BIRTH-STORIES OCCURRING IN THE *MORALL PHILOSOPHIE*.

I. BAKA JĀTAKA.

The Cruel Crane Outwitted.

[Fausböll, No. 38 ; Rhys Davids, pp. 315-321 ; North, *infra*, pp. 118-122].

𝕿𝖍𝖊 𝖛𝖎𝖑𝖑𝖆𝖎𝖓, 𝖙𝖍𝖔𝖚𝖌𝖍 𝖊𝖝𝖈𝖊𝖊𝖉𝖎𝖓𝖌 𝖈𝖑𝖊𝖛𝖊𝖗. *This the master told when at Jetavana about a monk who was a tailor [and used to cheat his customers by changing old clothes patched up, for new cloth. He is however outwitted by a tailor from the country, who cheats him by taking the cloth in exchange for old clothes dyed to look like new]. And one day the monks sat talking about this in the Lecture Hall, when the Teacher came up and asked them what they were talking about, and they told him the whole matter.*

Then the Teacher said, "Not now only has the Jetavana robe-maker taken other people in in this way, in a former birth he did the same. And not now only has he been outwitted by the countryman, in a former birth he was outwitted too." And he told a tale.

Long ago the Bodisat was born to a forest life as the Genius of a tree standing near a certain lotus pond.

Now at that time the water used to run short at the dry season in a certain pond, not over large, in which there were a good many fish. And a crane thought, on seeing the fish—

"I must outwit these fish somehow or other and make a prey of them."

And he went and sat down at the edge of the water, thinking how he should do it.

When the fish saw him, they asked him, "What are you sitting there for, lost in thought?"

"I am sitting thinking about you," said he.

"Oh, sir! what are you thinking about us?" said they.

"Why," he replied; "there is very little water in this pond, and but little for you to eat; and the heat is so great! So I was thinking, 'What in the world will these fish do now?'"

"Yes, indeed, sir! what *are* we to do?"

"If you will only do as I bid you, I will take you in my beak to a fine large pond, covered with all the kinds of lotuses, and put you into it," answered the crane.

"That a crane should take thought for the fishes is a thing unheard of, sir, since the world began. It's eating us, one after the other, that you're aiming at!"

"Not I. So long as you trust me, I won't eat you.

But if you don't believe me that there is such a pond, send one of you with me to go and see it."

Then they trusted him, and handed over to him one of their number—a big fellow, blind of one eye, whom they thought sharp enough in any emergency, afloat or ashore.

Him the crane took with him, let him go in the pond, showed him the whole of it, brought him back, and let him go again close to the other fish. And he told them all the glories of the pond.

And when they heard what he said, they exclaimed, "All right, sir! You may take us with you."

Then the crane took the old purblind fish first to the bank of the other pond, and alighted in a Varaṇa-tree growing on the bank there. But he threw it into a fork of the tree, struck it with his beak, and killed it; and then ate its flesh, and threw its bones away at the foot of the tree. Then he went back and called out—

"I've thrown that fish in; let another come!"

And in that manner he took all the fish, one by one, and ate them, till he came back and found no more!

But there was still a crab left behind there; and the crane thought he would eat him too, and called out—

"I say, good crab, I've taken all the fish away, and put them into a fine large pond. Come along. I'll take you too!"

"But how will you take hold of me to carry me along?"

"I'll bite hold of you with my beak."

"You'll let me fall if you carry me like that. I won't go with you!"

"Don't be afraid! I'll hold you quite tight all the way."

Then said the crab to himself, "If this fellow once

got hold of fish, he would never let them go in a pond! Now if he should really put me into the pond, it would be capital; but if he doesn't—then I'll cut his throat and kill him!" So he said to him—

"Look here, friend, you won't be able to hold me tight enough; but we crabs have a famous grip. If you let me catch hold of you round the neck with my claws, I shall be glad to go with you."

And the other did not see that he was trying to outwit him, and agreed. So the crab caught hold of his neck with his claws as securely as with a pair of blacksmith's pincers, and called out, "Off with you, now!"

And the crane took him and showed him the pond, and then turned off towards the Varaṇa-tree.

"Uncle!" cried the crab, "the pond lies that way, but you are taking me this way!"

"Oh, that's it, is it!" answered the crane. "Your dear little uncle, your very sweet nephew, you call me! You mean me to understand, I suppose, that I am your slave, who has to lift you up and carry you about with him! Now cast your eye upon the heap of fish-bones lying at the root of yonder Varaṇa-tree. Just as I have eaten those fish, every one of them, just so I will devour you as well!"

"Ah! those fishes got eaten through their own stupidity," answered the crab, "but I'm not going to let you eat *me*. On the contrary, it is *you* that I am going to destroy. For you in your folly have not seen that I was outwitting you. If we die, we die both together; for I will cut off this head of yours, and cast it to the ground!" And so saying, he gave the crane's neck a grip with his claws, as with a vice.

Then gasping, and with tears trickling from his eyes, and trembling with the fear of death, the crane

BAKA JATAKA.   lxiii

beseeched him, saying, "O my Lord! Indeed I did not intend to eat you. Grant me my life!"

"Well, well! step down into the pond, and put me in there."

And he turned round and stepped down into the pond, and placed the crab on the mud at its edge. But the crab cut through its neck as clean as one

would cut a lotus-stalk with a hunting-knife, and then only entered the water!

When the Genius who lived in the Varaṇa-tree saw this strange affair, he made the wood resound with his plaudits, uttering in a pleasant voice the verse—

> "The villain, though exceeding clever,
> Shall prosper not by his villany.
> He may win indeed, sharp-witted in deceit,
> But only as the Crane here from the Crab!"

APPENDIX.

When the Teacher had finished this discourse, showing that " Not now only, O mendicants, has this man been outwitted by the country robe-maker, long ago he was outwitted in the same way," he established the connexion, and summed up the Jātaka, by saying, "At that time he [the crane] *was the Jetavana robe-maker, the crab was the country robe-maker, but the Genius of the Tree was I myself."*

The part in italics is called "The Story of the Present," and that in ordinary type is "The Story of the Past," of which the verses (*gatha*) in old Pali probably formed the literary nucleus, and were handed on as a peg on which the stories hung. Both the stories were ultimately written down as a commentary on the verses with the first line of which the Jataka begins.

On the wide extension this story has found when divorced from its connection with the Buddha, see note in Analytical Table of Contents, *infra*, p. lxxiv. It is to be found in the *Morall Philosophie*, pp. 118–22, and considering that it has passed through more than a thousand years, and no less than seven languages on its way from Pali to English, it has preserved its identity with remarkable success.

The illustration is from the *editio princeps* of the Latin (reduced), and, as I have shown, has a traditional connection with the story in its Indian form, and may one day, I hope, be traced to a rock carving representing this very Jataka, on one of the Buddhist stupas.

APPENDIX.

II. KACCHAPA JĀTAKA.

The Talkative Tortoise.

[Fausböll, No. 215, also *Five Jatakas*, 1871, pp. 16, 41; Rhys-Davids, pp. viii-x; North, *infra*, pp. 170-175].

Once upon a time, when Brahma-datta was reigning in Benāres, the future Buddha was born in a minister's family; and when he grew up, he became the king's adviser in things temporal and spiritual.

Now this king was very talkative: while he was speaking, others had no opportunity for a word. And the future Buddha, wanting to cure this talkativeness of his, was constantly seeking for some means of doing so.

At that time there was living, in a pond in the Himālaya mountains, a tortoise. Two young haṁsas (*i.e.*, wild ducks) who came to feed there, made friends with him. And one day, when they had become very intimate with him, they said to the tortoise—

"Friend tortoise! the place where we live, at the Golden Cave on Mount Beautiful in the Himālaya country, is a delightful spot. Will you come there with us?"

"But how can I get there?"

"We can take you, if you can only hold your tongue, and will say nothing to anybody."

"Oh! that I can do. Take me with you."

"That's right," said they. And making the tortoise bite hold of a stick, they themselves took the two ends in their teeth, and flew up into the air.

Seeing him thus carried by the haṁsas, some villagers called out, "Two wild ducks are carrying a tortoise along on a stick!" Whereupon the tortoise wanted to say, "If my friends choose to carry me, what is that to you, you wretched slaves!" So just as the swift flight of the wild ducks had brought him over the king's palace in the city of Benāres, he let go of the stick he was biting, and falling in the open courtyard, split in two! And there arose a universal cry, "A tortoise has fallen in the open courtyard, and has split in two!"

The king, taking the future Buddha, went to the place, surrounded by his courtiers; and looking at the tortoise, he asked the Bodisat, "Teacher! how comes he to be fallen here?"

The futute Buddha thought to himself, "Long expecting, wishing to admonish the king, have I sought for some means of doing so. This tortoise must have made friends with the wild ducks; and they must have made him bite hold of the stick, and have flown up into the air to take him to the hills. But he, being unable to hold his tongue when he hears any one else talk, must have wanted to say something, and let go the stick; and so must have fallen down from the sky, and thus lost his life." And saying, "Truly, O king! those who are called chatter-boxes—people whose words have no end— come to grief like this," he uttered these Verses—

> "Verily the tortoise killed himself
> Whilst uttering his voice;
> Though he was holding tight the stick,
> By a word himself he slew.

> "Behold him then, O excellent by strength!
> And speak wise words not out of season.
> You see how, by his talking overmuch,
> The tortoise fell into this wretched plight!"

KACCHAPA JATAKA.

The king saw that he was himself referred to, and said, "O Teacher! are you speaking of us?"

And the Bodisat spake openly, and said, "O great king! be it thou, or be it any other, whoever talks beyond measure meets with some mishap like this."

And the king henceforth refrained, himself, and became a man of few words.

This again is a very widely extended tale, (see Table of Contents, E4a), and has lost little of its effectiveness in North's version. The quaint illustration, p. 174, would serve for the Pali original equally well as for its English great-great-great-great-great-great-grand-child.

ANALYTICAL TABLE OF CONTENTS.

With Parallels to the Tales mainly from Benfey and Derenbourg.

Tr. = Translations. *Ad.* = Adaptations. *Plls.* = Parallels.

	PAGE
To the Reader	5
[*Italian* at back of Title-page.]	
Al Lettore, G. B., T. N. to the Reader; E. C. to the Reader	7–10
[Only in *English*, second by North.]	
A. THE PROLOGUE	13–33

[Originally in *Arabic* of Abdallah ibn Almokaffa De Sacy, 45-59 (Knatchbull, 47-64), as 3rd chapt. *Tr.* Persian I., Greek, 22-33, Latin, 4-13, Hebrew II., 313-18, Spanish, II., ii.-v*a*, German, A. ii. a-A., vi. b, Italian, 2; Benfey, § 14.]

(1) Of a husbandman who lost the treasure he found . . . 17–20
    [*Tr.* as above; *Ad.* Baldo and Raymond in Edeléstand du Méril *Poesies inedites*, 218.]

(2) Of a simple man desirous to seem learned 20–22
    [*Tr.* as above; *Ad.* Méril, 219.]

CONTENTS. lxix

	PAGE
(3) Too slothful to catch thieves	22–24

[*Tr.* as above; *Ad.* Méril, 220.]

(4) One trying to obtain the greater of two heaps of corn gets the less by his own cunning 25–27

[*Tr.* as above; two stories of original Arabic being omitted.]

(5) A robber surprised leaves his money behind 28–31

[*Tr.* as above; the gold and silver in the cape added by *Germ.*, and hence into Spanish II., Italian, and North.]

B. THE ARGUMENT OF THE BOOK . . 34–41

[Must have been in *Pehlevi* (now lost), hence into Arabic, as Chapter II. (Knatchbull, 32 seq.); Persian I. *Not.* 103-112; Greek, 7, &c.; Latin, 14-16; Hebrew II., 319-320; Spanish I., 13 *b.* {The same account in Firdausi, *Shahnameh* (Mohl, vi. 354-365). On the Indian tree of life, Renaud, *Memoire sur l'Inde,* 130; Burnouf, *Lotus,* 83.]

C. THE FIRST PART. 43–46

[Properly a spiritual biography of "Berozias," and therefore in *Pehlevi,* thence into Arabic, 61, and other translation following above (Argument); also in Syriac II., 375 (Keith-Falconer, 248-267). Cf. Malcolm, *Sketches in Persia,* I., 143-148, B § 17.]

(1) A thief caught riding the moonbeams 47–52

[*Tr.* as above; *Plls. Discip. Cler.,* xxv., *Gest. Rom.,* cxxxvi.; Cf. Dunlop-Liebrecht, 195-196, Note 262ª, Oesterley, *ad loc.,* p. 734.]

	PAGE
(2) The lover enticed by a husband into a jakes . . . . [*Tr.* as before.]	54–55
(3) A jeweller has to pay for letting his workman play to him . . [*Tr.* as before.]	56–58
(4) A parable of this world: a man in the midst of all manner of dangers falls to eating honey . . . [*Tr.* as before (but skipping three stories in Arabic and offshoots, among them the Dog and Shadow fable). *Plls.*, Dubois, *Mœurs de l'Inde*, II., 127; Somadeva, v. 38–97; Sinhâsana, pp. 23 *seq.*; Julien, *Avadanas*, i. 132, 191; Barlaam, c. 12; Dunlop-Liebrecht, Note 72ᵃ; *Gesta Rom.*, 168 (Oesterley, 739ᵇ); Dchelaleddin *Diwan* (Hammer, 183); Grimm, Deut. Myth., I., 758; Rückert, *Ges. Schr.*, I., 51; Homayun Namah, iv.; Liebrecht, *Zur Volkskunde*, 457.]	60–63
D. THE SECOND PART . . . . [This and the next part correspond to the first chapter of the *Sanskrit* original, now lost, and of the *Panchatantra*, = *Hitopadesa*, Bk. II., = *Katha-sarit-sagara*, Tar. 49, = Syr. I. ch. i., = Arab. I. ch. v., = Greek I. ch. i., = Latin I. ch. ii. (D 36–100), = Pers. I. ch. iii., = Pers. II. ch. i. (Eastwick, p. 71 *seq.*). On the variations in the main story see B. §§ 6, 21–23, 29, 34, 43, 46–48, 54, 64, 66–69, 74, 75, 81, 88, 90, 98, 102, 107. It also appears in shortened form in a Siamese Buddhistic tale *Asiatic Res.* xx. 348, and in the Tibetan	64–127

CONTENTS.   lxxi

PAGE

Sidikur, Tale 19 (*Sagas from the Far East*, p. 192-197). The names of the two oxen were originally *Sanjivaka* (Arab. *Shanzabeh*, Lat. *Senesba*) and *Nandaka* (Arab. *Banzabeh*, Lat. *Chenedba*), which Firenzuola, and after him Doni and North, altered to Chiarino and Incoronata. The anonymous ass and mule of the English version were in the original two jackals, *Karataka* ("crow," Syr. I. *Kalilag*, Arab. I. *Kalilah*, Lat. I. *Celila*, Span. II. *Belile*), and *Damanaka* ("tamer," Syr. I. *Damnag*, Arab. I. *Dimnah*, Lat. I. *Dimna*). For the *translations* of the various stories it will only be necessary to refer to Benfey's sections giving the Sansk., Arab., Pers., Ger., Span., and Ital. versions, and to Derenbourg's edition of the *Directorium*, which gives the Lat., Heb. I. & II., Syr. I. & II.]

Introduction 64–66

[Only in *Italian*, including the stories of (a) the belly and members, from Livy, and (b) horse and stag, from Æsop, Halm, 175.]

(1) An ape being curious about a woodman splitting a tree with a wedge is caught in the cleft . . . 73–74

[*Tr.* B § 30, D 40 n. 1 (not in Syr. I.). *Plls.* Luther *Fabul Hans*, p. 530. *Cf.* Æsop, Fur. 162, Halm, 362; Syntipas, 46; Vartan, 31.]

(2) Wolf is released from a trap on promising to amend: breaking his promise is restored to the trap and killed 77–78

[This form original to Italian of Doni, B § 36 *ad fin.* Cf. *Disc. Cler.* vii.]

(3) Buriaso fattens a sow and then kills her 82
[Only in *Italian* of Doni.]

(4) A quail is saved from a sparrow-hawk by noticing its acts more than its words 84
[Only in *Italian* of Doni.]

(5) A captured Turkey pretends to be on a visit to his captors till his pride is humbled and he submits to be ransomed 89–91
[Only in *Italian* of Doni.]

(6) A fox, hearing the sound of mule-bells, is afraid; which seeing, he fears no longer 93–94
[B § 41, D 50 n. Originally a drum hanging on tree, but "tympanum" of Latin, translated "schell" by *Germ.* causes change in Span., Ital., and Eng.]

(7) A devout man, entertaining a thief unawares, is robbed by him, and sees three things in pursuing after him 104–111
[B § 50, D 53. *Plls.* This and the three following have passed into the 1001 Nights (Prenzlau, iv. 261–273)].

(7a) Two goats fight; a fox watching them too curiously gets butted and dies 105–106
[B § 50, D 53 n. 8. *Plls.* Reineke Fuchs (ed. Grimm, cclxxvii.); Robert, *Fables,* cxxvi.]

CONTENTS.   lxxiii

(7b) A bawd trying to blow poison into a young man's ear, swallows it herself and dies 106–107
[B § 51, D 53 n. 9; only in *Arabic* and offshoots. *Plls.* Cent. nouv. nouv., ii.; Malespina, No. 37.]

(7c) A husband ties his wife to a pillar at night; a bawd takes her place and has her nose cut off for refusing to speak: the wife returning pretends to call upon heaven to restore her nose as a proof of her innocence 108–111
[B § 50, D 54 n. 3. *Plls.* Vetalapançavincati (in 5 variants); Tutinameh (Kadiri, xvii.; Rosen II. 92); Bahar Danush, II. 83; Barbazan-Méon, iv. 393; Vierzig Viziere (Behrnauer, 173); Aristænetus, *Epist.*, ii. 22; Morlini, *Nov.* 27; Cent. nouv. nouv. xxxv. lxi.; Gesammtabenteuer, xliii.; W. Grimm in *Zt. deut Alt.*, xi. 2, 213, No. 13. *Cf.* Von der Hagen, II., xv.-xviii., xlii.-xlix.; III., xci.; Dunlop (Germ.), 242; Deslongchamps, 33.]

(8) An eagle finding a leveret devoured it notwithstanding the remonstrance of a beetle, which nevertheless avenges the leveret by destroying the eagle's eggs . . 114–116
[Seemingly only in Doni; ? from Lat. Æsop. *cf.* L'Estrange, ccclxxviii.]

(9) A raven whose young are killed by a snake, revenges herself by carry-

CONTENTS.

ing off a jewel to the snake's hole in the presence of men, who pursue it and thereby kill the snake in seeking the jewel . . . 116–122

[B § 58, D 58 n. 2. *Plls.* 1001 Nights (Weil. III., 916); Mahavanso, 128; Gest. Rom., cv. (Oest., 728); Gesammtabenteuer, II., 635; III., clxiii. *Cf.* Æsop, Fur. 1, Halm, 5; Phæd., I., 28; Syntipas, 24; Ugobard, 14; Vartan, 3; Méril, 194; Arist., *Aves,* 652; *Pax.*, 126. B. thinks derived from "Æsop." *Cf.* § 86.]

(9a) A "Paragon," pretending that the lake is to be drained, persuades some fishes to allow him to carry them off, whereupon he devours them; on trying to do the same with a crab, he has his head bitten off 118–122

[B § 60, D 58. *Plls.* Lafontaine, x. 4. A Jataka, says B. *Cf.* Upham, *Sacred Books of Ceylon*, III., 292, and Dhammapada (ed. Fausböll, 155), but compares Æsop, Fur. 231, Halm, 346, where also a crab victorious. The Jataka is given in Rhys-Davids, v. *supra*, pp. lx-lxiii.]

(10) The animals agree to provide a lion with one of themselves daily by drawing lots. The lot falling on the fox, he rouses the lion's jealousy against another lion whom he pretends to be down a well.

CONTENTS.

The lion seeing his own image, jumps down and is killed . . 123–126

[B § 61, D 61 n. 1. *Plls.* Reineke Fuchs (Grimm, cclxxviii.); Disc. Cler., xxiv. (*cf.* Schmidt, 155); Hodgson in *Journ. Asiat. Soc.*, 1836, p. 83 (a Jataka). B. suggests that idea of animals casting lots is derived from the beautiful Jataka of the Banyan Deer (Hiouen Thsang, ed. Julien, I., 361). *Cf.* Rhys-Davids, pp. 205-10.*]

E. THIRD PART 128–215

[Contains continuation of first chapter of Indian original and offshoots; see analytical note to Part Second. The lion who was originally terrified at the roaring of the bull *Chiarino* (=Senesba), has made friends with him through the intermediation of the "Moyle" (=the jackal, Dimna), who finding himself neglected, plots against the bull and sets the lion against him, so that a fight ensues in which the bull is killed.]

(1) Three great fishes are in a lake which is being drained: one escapes by hiding, another by cunning, but the third is destroyed by his own laziness . . . 132–135.

[B §§ 65, 85, D 65 n. 1. *Plls.* Mahabharata, xii., 4889 *seq.*]

(2) A flea revenges itself on a louse by enticing it into the bed of a prin-

---

* This is *figured* in Gen. Cunningham's "Stupa of Bharhut," Pl. xxv. No. 1.

cess whence the flea escapes but the louse is caught and killed . 137–141
[B § 72, D 67 n. 7 ; not in Hitopadesa or Anwari-Suhaili.]

(3) The lion is ill ; the wolf, the fox, and the raven persuade the camel to offer himself for dinner by pretending the same themselves . 153–167
[B § 78, D 76 n. 2. *Plls.* Pantschatantra, I., 16 ; IV., 2 ; Bahar Danush, II., c. 19 ; Æsop Fur. 356, Halm, 243 ; Babr., 95. *Cf.* B § 181 ; Deslongchamps, 37 n. 1 ; Lancereau's Hitopadesa, 253. Alterations in *Germ.* I. have influenced Ital. and North.]

(4) A cock-linnet persists in building his nest by the sea against the advice of his spouse ; the sea rises and destroys the nest 169–176
[B § 82, D 81 n. 5. *Plls.* Æsop Fur. 240, Halm, 29 (from Planudes, who took it from Greek I.) With ending B. compares two Jatakas—Hardy, *Buddhism*, 106 ; Hiouen Thsang, ed. Julien, I., 335. This end has disappeared in Italian and English.]

(4a) A tortoise biting a stick carried by waterfowls through the air opens its mouth to answer birds that mock it and thereby falls . 170–175
[B § 84, D 82 n. 3. *Plls.* Robert, II., 252. A Jataka. *Cf.* Hardy, 309, and Julien *Avadanas*, I., 71–73 ;

cf. 122–126. See now Rhys-Davids, *supra*, pp. lxv.-vii. Derived, according to B., from Æsop Fur. 193, Halm, 419; Phæd., II., 7; VII., 14; Abst., 108.]

(5) Apes trying to light sticks with a glowworm are advised by a popinjay who receives little thanks for her advice 181–184

[B § 93, D 86 n. 8. *Plls.* Luther, *Fabel Hans,* 530. The glowworm appears first in Arabic, the original having guncha berries.]

(6) A magpie tells her master all his wife's misdemeanours; the wife causes the pye to believe there is a storm when it is clear: he is henceforth not credited, and finally killed 185–190

[B § 95, D 89 n. 6. Not in Arabic I., but in Latin I., in same position as in Panchatantra. *Plls.* In the Sindibad cycle in all its offshoots. Gest. Rom. (ed. Graesse, II., 185); 1001 Nights (Weil., I., 70). *Cf.* Keller, cxxxiv.; Deslongchamps, 99 n. 1; Boccacio, vii. 9. Other *plls.* by Crane, *Ital. Folk Tales,* 167-183, and notes 358-360; Clouston, *Pop. Tales,* II. 196-211.]

(7) Two find a treasure and hide it in a tree. One steals it, and, on a trial ensuing, induces his father to get inside the tree and accuse the other. The judge orders fire

CONTENTS.

  to be set to the tree and the fraud
  is discovered 190–202
   [B § 96, D 90 n. 4. *Plls. Delices
   de Verboquet* (1623), p. 41.]

(7a) A bird having its young destroyed
  by a snake that has its hole near,
  entices thither an enemy of the
  snake, which is destroyed and
  the bird too. 198–199
   [§ 97, D 92 n. 1. *Pll.* Here D9. *Cf.*
   Deslongchamps, 42 n. 1. In original
   the enemy is an ichneumon.]

(8) A merchant returning after a long
  absence finds a lad in his house,
  whom his wife avers the snow
  has begotten, witness his name
  "White." The merchant takes the
  boy for a walk and declares the
  sun has melted him . . . 203–206
   [Not in the Bidpai cycle but from
   Italian novels. *Cf.* Dunlop-Liebrecht,
   296, B § 99, *ad fin.*]

(9) A merchant leaves iron with a friend
  who afterwards alleges that the
  rats have eaten it; the merchant,
  pretending to believe, shortly
  after hides away his friend's son
  and alleges a chicken has carried
  it off. The friend confesses, makes
  restoration, and receives his boy
  again 207–212
   [B § 101, D 97 n. 1. *Plls.* Çukasaptati, 38=Tutinameh (Rosen, I., 67;

CONTENTS. lxxix

Iken, III., 25); Cardonne, *Mél. de lit. orient*, II., 63; 1001 Nights (Prenzlau, xi. 259-262). *Cf.* Deslongchamps, 43 n. 2; Crane, *l. c.*, 353 n. 4.]

(10) A woman sent to the apothecary by her husband whiles away her time with him while the assistant changes the drugs for dust. On her return the wife declares she dropped her money in the dust and brought it home in the hope of recovering some of the coins . 213–214

[B § 99, D 95. *Cf.* 94 n. 4. *Plls.* From the Sindibad cycle (and offshoots); introduced first in Latin I. (or Hebrew). Çukasaptati, 32; 1001 Nights, xv. 177; Tutinameh, xxv. *Cf.* Keller, *Romans*, cxliv.]

F. FOURTH PART 216–257

[The "Moyle" (Dimna) being suspected by the lion, is imprisoned, and having made an elaborate defence contained in this part, is executed. This was inserted in *Arabic* of Abdullah ibn Almokaffa, and only appears in its offshoots. B § 109-112. The stories differ much in Pers. II.]

(1) A painter loved a joiner's wife and visited her in a certain mantle, a servant borrows the mantle and visits her in his stead . . . 229–232

[B § 111, D 108 n. 2. *Plls.* Bahar Danush, II., 293; Le Grand d'Aussy, IV., 121; Boccaccio, III., 2. *Cf.* Deslongchamps, 44 n. 1.]

CONTENTS.

                                                  PAGE

(2) An ignorant physician gives arsenic to a princess and is killed . . 242-245
      [B § III, D 119. *Plls.* Probably from Phæd., I., 16.]

(3) A man and his two daughters being captured and stripped, in trying to hide their nakedness, he uncovers himself 248-249
      [B § III, D 122 n. 4. In Heb. I. the two women are the man's wives.]

(4) A servant tries to slander his mistress by teaching a parrot to tell lies of her in a strange tongue, but a sparrow-hawk miraculously exposes him 252-255
      [B § III, D 130. *Plls.* Here E 6. The *three* birds are a misunderstanding by the *Germ.* of the Latin, "cepit duos pullos psittaci et papagilli,"= "und fieng zwen sittikus und ein papagai." *Cf.* D, *l. c.*]

LXXX1

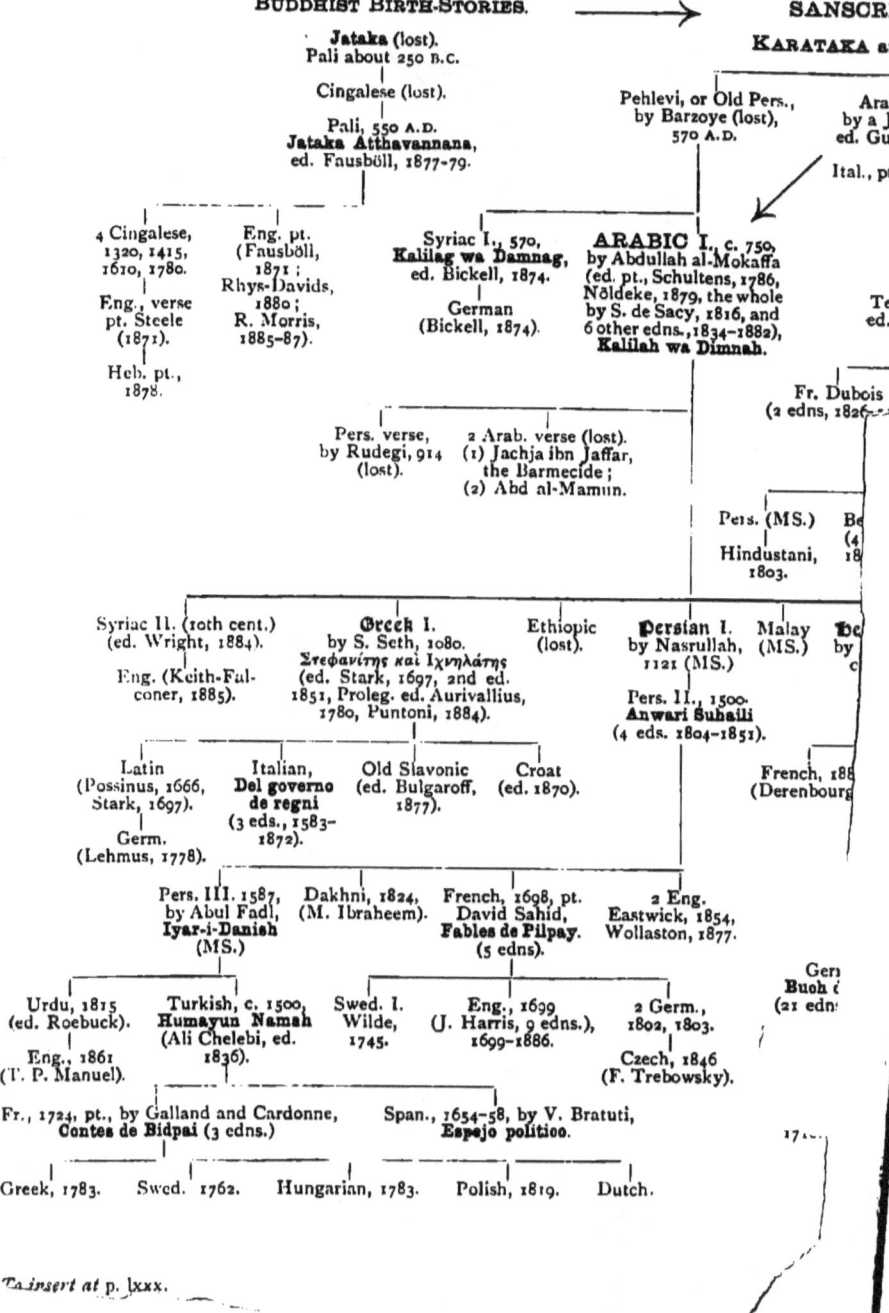

To insert at p. lxxx.

IDPAI LITERATURE.

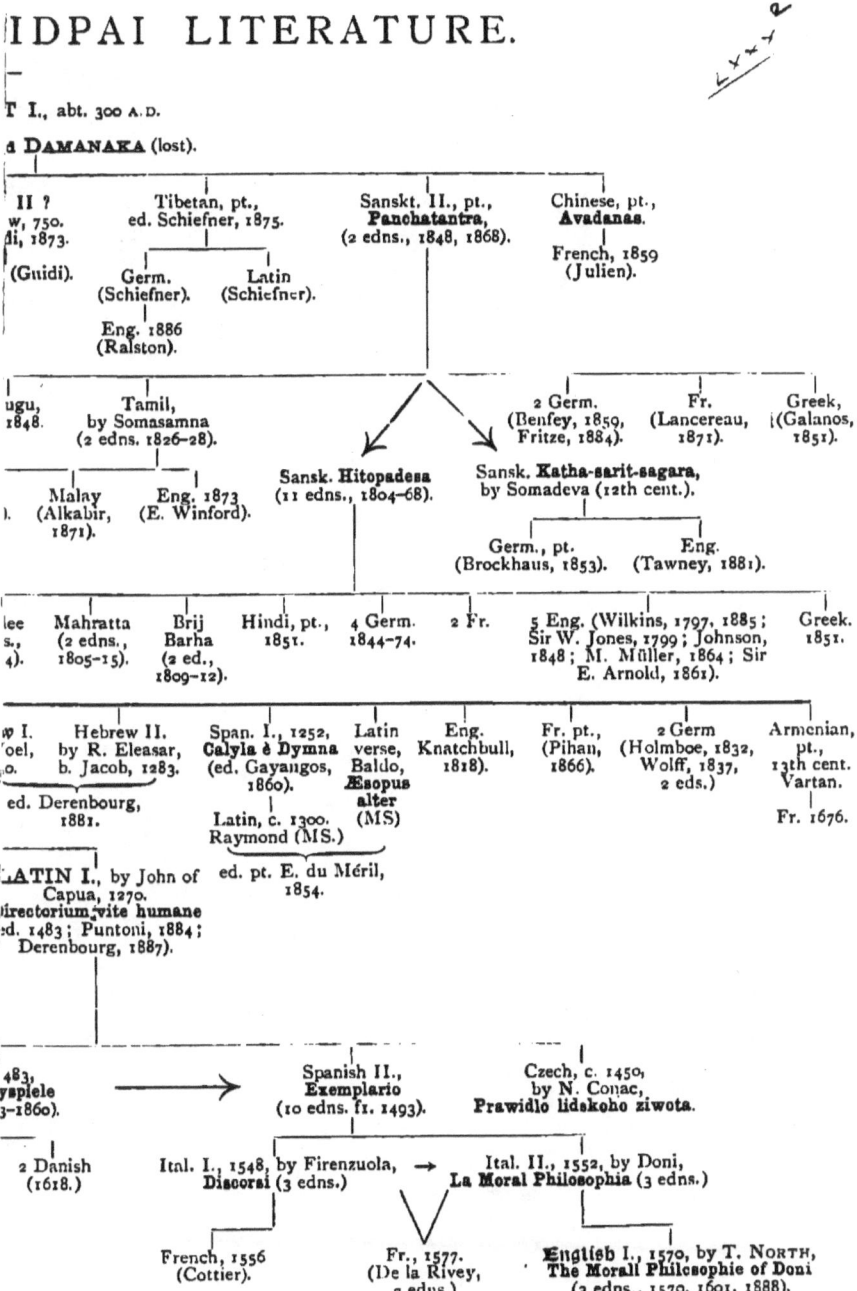

The
Morall Philosophie of Doni.

A

The Morall Philosophie of Doni:

Drawne out of the auncient writers.

A worke first compiled in the Indian tongue,
and afterwardes reduced into divers other
languages: and now lastly Englished
out of Italian by Thomas North,
Brother to the Right Honorable
Sir Roger North Knight,
Lorde North of
Kyrtheling.

THE WISDOME OF THIS WORLDE
IS FOLLY BEFORE GOD.

¶ *Imprinted at London
by Henry Denham.*
1570.

TO THE READER.

HE that beginneth not to reade thys Booke frõ the beginning to the ende and that aduiſedly followeth not the order he findeth written, ſhall neuer profite anything thereby. But reading it through, and oft, aduiſing what he readeth, hee ſhall finde a marveylous benefite thereof. The ſtories, fables, and tales, are very pleaſaunt and compendious. Moreover the ſimilitudes and compariſons doe (as they ſaye) holde hands one with the other, they are ſo linked togithers,

togithers, one ſtill depending of another: which if you feuer, defirous to reade any tale or ſtorie by it felfe, not comparing the Antecedent with the Sequele: befides that, you ſhall be fare from the vnderſtandinge of the matter, you ſhall thinke them ryding tales ſpoken to no purpofe, but to occupie your cares, and confume time. Therefore follow I fay this order giuen you and receyue to you the fruites of my poore traueyle and of your painefull reading.

FAREWELL.

AL LETTORE. G. B.

Il Doni, *che col suo leggiadro stile*
   Augelli, e muti pesci. Armenti, e
   fiere.
Fà ragionar d'Impresa alta, & humile.
   E sotto il falso asconde cose vere.

Non pensò mai, che la ricca Anglia, *e*
   Thyle
   Sapessero di luj, ne che in tal schiere
Venissero le Nimfe a mezzo Aprile
   In freddo Clima a fiori, e frutti
   hauere.

Il Northoé, *che col suo sublime Ingegno*
Fà questo, et alla bella Italia *dona*
Nel suo paese, con sua lingua, stanza.
                                  E

E Perciò, il Doni. *Dona a luj per pegno
Se ifteffo, et dice. Se gia mai perfona
M' Interpretò,* Northoé *quelche hor m' auanza.*

T. N. TO THE READER.

Of wordes and of examples is a fundrie fort
 of fpeache
One felfe fame thing to mindes of men in fun-
 drie wife they teache.
Wordes teache but thofe that vnderftande the
 language that they heare:
But things, to men of fundrie fpeache, examples
 make appeare.
So larger is the fpeache of beafts, though mens
 more certaine bee:
But yet fo larger as conceyte is able them to fee.
Such largeneffe yet at length to bring to cer-
 taine vfe and plane,
God gaue fuch grace to beafts, that they fhould
 Indian fpeach attaine.
And then they learnde Italian tongue, and now
 at length they can,
By help of NORTH, fpeake Englifh well to euery
 Englifh man.
In Englifh now they teache vs wit. In Englifh
 now they faye,

Ye

Ye men, come learne of beaſts to liue, to rule,
    and to obaye,
To guide you wiſely in the worlde, to know to
    ſhunne deceite,
To flie the crooked paths of guile, to keepe
    your doings ſtreight.
As earſt therefore you vſed beaſts, but for your
    bodies neede,
Sometime to clothe, ſometime to beare, ſome-
    time your ſelues to feede.
Now vſe them for behoofe of minde, and for
    your ſoules delite,
And wiſhe him well that taught them ſo to
    ſpeake and ſo to write.

E. C. TO THE READER.

If care to ſhowe, good will to natiue ſoyle,
In ſetting forth, a worke of great auayle:
If how to ſhunne, the vaine & reſtleſſe toyle,
Wherein we wade, for things that ſoone doe fayle.
If graue aduice, bewraydde in ſimple ſhowe,
Forwarning ſtill, the trayne of guilefull waye:
If Wiſedomes lore, the good from yll to knowe,
And by the ſame, our brittle liues to ſtaye.
If this and more, yea more an hundred folde,
Lies open nowe, vnto thy happie gaine:
If theſe I ſaye, worth more than maſſe of golde
Doe well deſerue, by him that tooke this paine
Good Reader than, graunt this my iuſt deſire,
In thankfull ſort, receyue this learned Booke:
For his rewarde, he ſeekes no further hire,
But good report, when thou herein ſhalt looke.
His paines were great, thy gift thus waye but ſmall
Yet be content, and thinkes he reapeth all.

The Philosophie of the wise auncient Fathers.

A Worke first compiled in the Indian tongue, and aftervvardes transferred into divers and sundrie other languages: as the Persian, Arabian, *Hebrue, Latine, Spanish, and* Italian: and now reduced into our vulgar speeche.

THE PROLOGUE.

This precious Jewell (beloued Reader) was first founde written in the Indian tongue, entituled Morall Wisdome: and was thence conueyed into Persia, and was coated with their language, naming it with them The example of good lyfe: and from the Persian speech a long time after by the auncient Fathers (they knowing the wonderfull doctrine thereof) brought into the naigue Arabian and from that translated into Hebrue

Hebrue by Ioel gran Rabi a Iewe; at length reduced into Latine: and passing through many languages became a Spaniarde, with the title of Exemplario: and so in time brought to Venice, and there put into Italian by a company of Gentlemen associated togithers, entituling their Felowship Academia Peregrina: and now lastly out of Italian made vulgar to us. What high doctrine is conteyned in thys Booke, the diligent and curious searche for the same of so many wise and famous men and of so sundrye nations doth witnesse. If therefore you desire the vnderstanding of Royall wisdome, spirituall doctrine, and infinite instructions and examples for man to liue well: reade I say this golden Volume. Surely reader, this booke shall be a looking glasse for thee, wherin thou shalt most liuely beholde the daylie and present daungers and deceytes of mans most miserable lyfe, and the eyes of thy vnderstanding shall be made open to descerne the flatteries of disceytfull men, and the wisdome of this most guileful worlde: by meanes whereof yee may easilye blotte out many malignant effects of this (alas) our crooked age. The style is familier and pleasaunt, and wyll much delight thee. For the first and olde Authors hereof

hereof wrote it doubtlesse with great iudgement, trayned thereto with a feruent desire that their doctrine shoulde not onely remayne in perpetuitie for euer, but that it shoulde also be imprinted in the Readers minde, assuring themselues it shoulde profite all, and dislyke none. For it maye in maner be called an artificiall memorie, to benefite themselues at all times and seasons, and in all argumentes, with euerye perticular thing these wise and graue men haue inuented, shadowed with tales and parables, and wyth the examples of brute and dumme beastes.

The Sages of auncient nations (expert in all the Sciences) difrous to publifhe to thofe that came after them their great knowledge and wifedome, euen with a determinate minde and counfell premeditate decreed to fet foorth a peece of woorke, adapted with diuers fimilitudes and fundrie comparifons of vnreafonable beafts and birds, by which they might greatly beautifie their doctrine, and this they did for diuers refpectes. Firft, to give occafion that their wifedome and learning fhould be knowne to the worlde. Secondly, that men of iudgement and difcretion reading the fame might reape the benefite of their rules to direct this fraile lyfe. Thirdlye, that hee that vnderftandeth vnderſtandeth theſe examples, knowing little, ſhoulde by them knowe much. And fourthly, and laſt of all, if he were yong, and had ſmall delight to reade much: yet he may with a ſhort and pleaſant waye be inſtructed with theſe delightful fayninges, and with thoſe ſimilitudes and examples taſte the ſweetneſſe of the wordes, the pleaſure of the ſentences, accompanied with proper tales: and ſo (Gentle Reader) profite himſelfe, and teache others. In this their treatiſe ſuch wiſe Fathers have hidden from vs woonderfull ſignifications. For a treaſure vndoubtedly of ſo high a myſterye and doctrine as this is to be more eſteemed than all the Jewelles in the worlde. This precious Iemme of knowledge, who ſo ſhall lodge it in the ſecreſie of his memorie, ſhall neuer loſe it, but ſhall rather augment and increaſe it with age in ſuch ſort, that hee ſhall winne a marueylous commodotie to him: and of that plant ſhall taſte the ſauorie, pleaſant, and profitable fruites, no leſſe wonderfull than delectable. To reade ſuch a Booke (worthy Reader) thou muſt call thy wittes togither vniting them and thy vnderſtanding with the due order of the woorke, to knowe why, and to what purpoſe the olde prudent Fathers framed it: leaſt thou be

lyke

lyke to the blinde man, that wanting his fight, taketh vpon him to go ouer Mountaynes, Hilles, and Dales, through moſt daungerous and perillous wayes. He therefore that doth reade muſt vnderſtand what he readeth, and why he readeth it: and not to be ſo deſirous to come to the ende, that he marke not the beginning, and forget the ſenſe (full of knowledge) lincked with the middeſt and end. For he that readeth ſo, readeth without fruite, and rather troubleth the minde, and wearieth his body than otherwiſe, not forcing the benefite and knowledge of the truth. Folow therefore theſe graue precepts and ruled order, and let no vaine thoughts poſſeſſe your mindes to withdraw you from reading it. For to finde ſo riche a treaſure, and not to know how to take and laye it vp: is rightly to folow him, that finding a Maſſe of Golde and Siluer, had not the wyt to take it, and cary it away.

Of a Huſbandeman, and of the treaſure he founde.

A Husbandeman of Perſia going one daye to plough his lande, by chaunce stumbled of a marueylous treasure, fyndinge store of pottes of Coyne

Coyne, of Golde, and Siluer: and woondering at hys great fortune, began to think to lode himselfe, and to beare it home. But seeing the summes so great that scant twentie men coulde carie it awaye, it greeued him much that hee

alone coulde not conuey it, and thus hee sayde to himselfe. If I leaue it here, it is in daunger to be taken from mee, and to watch it daylie, it would to much trouble mee: besides, that that I coulde take with me, would doe mee but small pleasure. Well, hap what hap will, I will

will go fetch company to helpe me home withall, and they shall beare the burden, I will onely pay them, and take mine ease, tush I haue at will to content them: and thus in one day I shal come home and finde my Cofers filled. With this minde resolued forth he goeth and calleth men togithers, bringing them with him to this Golden masse of coyne, where he giueth eche man his burden, and byddeth them hye them to his house. These bearers now departing with their burdens, ouercome with desire of the money, and greedy of this praie, in strade of going to the house of this foolishe and vnluckie man, they went euery one to his owne house. The husband-man after their departure commeth leysurely home without any burden, lyke a man of welth, as one that thought himselfe a Lorde at home, weening to haue founde his richesse there. But when he was entered his house, and hearde no-thing of the goodes nor bearers: then all to late he knew his lack and folly, commending their iudgements that with the burden of theire shoulders had made themselues riche. So that for trea-sure he enioyed sorowe. For hee that might haue beene Lorde of all, discreetly gouerning that which good hap had layde on him, deseruedly
bought

bought the price of hys folly, abyding the bitter smart of pouertie and miserie.

The discrete Reader that shall looke in this Booke must giue attentiue eare, and note eche thing perticulerly he readeth, diligently marking the secret lessons. For alwayes the worke of these sage Fathers carieth two senses withall. The first, knowne and manifest. The second, hidden and secret. Of the first we swetely enioy the taste: but of the second we receyue small knowledge, if we deeply ponder not the wordes. And hereof we may take ensample of the Nut, which giueth no maner of taste to man if he doe not first breake and open the shell, and then comen to the wyshed kernell, he beginneth to taste the sauor thereof, and to reape the fruit of so excellent a doctrine. Let us not doe therefore as the vndiscrete and simple man that had a desire to seeme learned, and to bee counted aloquent in speach as you shall heare.

Of the simple ignorant man desirous to seeme learned.

On a time one earnestly besought a Poet and an excellent Rhetorician (his very friende) to giue him

him something written that might be learned and eloquent, which konning without booke he might recite at pleasure in the companye of wise men, that he might at least seeme no lesse learned than they. His friende consented, and performed his desire, and gaue him in a written booke (faire bounde and lymned with golden letters) many goodly sentences, so that he began to learn by rote his written authorities, and laboring night and daye to commit them to memorie, he determined to show that he was also learned. And being one daye in argument, not vnderstanding the signification of the words he had learned, for that they were not in his owne tongue, hee began to alleadge them quite from the purpose: & being taken with the maner they lawghed him to scorne. Hee being angrye at the matter, lyke an obstinate and ignorant foole, aunswered. What? thinke you I am deceyued, that haue learned that I alleadge out of the booke of a woorthie learned man, yea, and the letters lymned with golde to? at which wordes they laughed him more to scorne than before to see his ignorance.

Every man therefore muſt endeuor himſelfe to vnderſtand that he readeth, and vnderſtanding it well, he muſt diligently obſerue that doctrine, marking

marking to what end and purpose that was written that he hath red, to profit thereby at any time. I knowe there will be wife men that will beleue they can faye and doe more wonders than this commeth to : yet for all that, the more we reade, the more we knowe, and the quicker is our vnderftanding, befides, there is obteined euen profounde knowledge. Learning bringeth with it a great priuiledge ; forby that men are exalted, and to a man of knowledge and vnderftanding it giueth life. But to him that hath iudgement and vnderftanding, and that gouerneth not himfelfe and his actions according to the prefcribed rule of reafon : His knowledge I fay dyeth within him without fruit. As by reading this example folowing you may eafilye perceiue.

A comparifon of the flouthfull man for the Reader.

An honest man lying in his bedde hearde a Theefe going vp and downe in his house : and thinking to page him home (to take the more aduantage of him) suffered him to take his pleasure and loding, that hauing in deede his packe at his backe, he might euen then as he thought

thought take him with the maner, and iustly reward him with the swordes point as he listed. Thus debating with himselfe, imagining to execute his purpose, (the Theefe occupying all this while him selfe taking what he woulde) this sielye good man fell a sleepe againe, and the Theefe with his fardell of the best things without any let at all quietly departeth his waye. This man when he awaked and sawe his house naked, hys chestes emptye and broken open, bitterly sighed and lamented, cursing himselfe and blaming his folly: considering hee might easily haue saued all that he was robbed of (since he knew it and heard the noyse) and for very sloth woulde not once rise and defend it, hauing as it were the theefe in his handes. Knowledge therefore is aptly compared to a tree, whose fruite are the works; and this knowledge is that we al ought to desire, and to exercise ourselues in. Were it not a mad part to leaue the brode beaten hie way, and to take the unknowne and daungerous pathe? Euen so it may be sayde of him which followeth his owne appetite and liking, gouerning himselfe thereby, (and not as he ought with reason and good order,) leauing to these worldlye experiences,

which

which euer desireth that that is profitable, but follow alwayes in deede things that are hurtfull. A man of such life and gouernement we may compare to him that knoweth good meates light of digestion, and the grosse ill and heauie: yet ouercome with desire taketh that that is most hurtfull, and so being hurt, him selfe alone is the cause of all his yll.

Even ſuch a man is he whome affection ſubdueth. He vnderſtandeth and is learned, and able to diſcerne troth from falſehoode, and yet will not put in proofe the true profit, nor once fellow and difire knowledge and wiſedome. We might bring this man in the example of him that hauing his ſight good and perfite, ſhutting his eyes would needes be ledde by a blinde man, ſo that both they falling into a diche were drowned, and miſerably died. Every man will condeme him for a foole, and worſe than mad, that hauing his ſight good and without blemiſhe, that might haue ſeene the daunger and ſcaped it, and of mere fooliſhneſſe would not. Therefore euerie wiſe and diſcrete perſon muſt continually labour to reade, and to vnderſtande that he readeth, and muſt then teache it to as many as defire to knowe it, and to doe the good workes of the knowledge he teacheth, that
every

euery way he may ſhowe the wonderful profit of his doctrine: for in this caſe he may not be like vnto a Well or Spring, which without any profit to it ſelfe quencheth the thirſte of all beaſts. The wiſe man is afterwardes bounde (when he is growne to the perfection of learning) to teech and inſtruct thoſe that knowe not. Provided euer that he can maſter himſelfe, and ſubdue his affections. For to a wiſe man three things are pertinent: to wit, Knowledge, Richeſſe, and Mercie. And of all thinges a man muſt chiefly beware of reprouing his neighbour of that fault he himſelfe is guiltie off. That he be not likened to him which hauing a Perle in his eie found fault with the element that it was alway cloudie, not conſidering the blemiſh of his eie. Yet greater doubtleſſe is our offence when with our neighbours hurt or detriment we winne commodotie to ourſelues. As falleth out many times, which this example following ſheweth vs.

The deceyt lighteth on the
deceyuers necke.

Two friends hauing a great mount of corne in a Garner vndeuided, they fel to parting it, leauing to eche his portion apart (howbeit both in one Garner

Garner still) so that they could not erre to choose eyther heape. But bicause in deede the one heape was greater than the other, hee which had the lesser thought to steale the bigger, and so by deceit to be reuenged of Fortune that had allotted him the least part. Upon this he went to the Garner determining to steale it that night, and bicause he would not misse of his purpose in taking the one for the other, he cast his cloke ouer his fellowes heape being the greater, that he might the easilier knowe his owne in the darke being vncouered. Not long after came to the Garner also the other honest partener to looke to his heape, & to see his deuided part: and when he sawe the loue of his partener to him (supposing simply he had couered his heape of corne for good will he bare him, that it shoulde receiue no dust) as one that would not be thought vnthankfull, nor come behinde his fellow in curtesie, thus he sayde to him selfe. Oh this man is to kinde to mee, that to couer mine leaueth his owne heap bare. And so taking the Cloke off his heape cast it on the others, and couered it as his was, requiting his curtesie with like good will, little suspecting the intended deceyte, but rather reputed his friende ciuile and full of humanitie. At night his false
friende

friende counselled with a theefe and tolde him his intente, saying: if thou wilt goe with me this night I will bring thee to a place where we shall haue a good bootie of Corne as much as we can both carie away with vs. And thus they agreed togithers thereupon, they went both to the Garner where those two heaps of Corne laye, and this partener the theefe groping in the darke to finde the heape his Cloke laye on, laying handes of his Cloke (suposing he had met with his fellowes heape) hee gaue it in praye to the theefe he had brought with him, labouringe both to loade themselues, and so betweene them they conueyed the whole heape: and weening they had stollen from the other honest man, founde at length he was theefe to himselfe. The next morning very earely the two companions (according to appointment) went togithers to the Garner to carie away eche other his portion as it was deuided betweene them. And he that had done this feate, seeing his partener's part whole and vntouched, and his owne gone; like a man halfe deade for sorrow he heauily departed thence to his house, and not a worde he spake, bewayling and lamenting his wretched pretenced craft, not daring once to open the theft to his friende, who so much did trust him.

No man therefore ſhould deale ſo fooliſhly in thinges that haue no certaine ende, and that are hard to bring to paſſe : leaſt that wearied with ſuperfluous labor, he cannot afterwardes exerciſe him ſelfe in thinges certaine and needfull. All our workes and deedes ought rather to tende to profit vs in time to come, then to ſerue the time preſent. For if we abandon and forſake the inſatiable and infinite deſire we haue of this wretched worlde, doubtleſſe in the other worlde to come we ſhall feele no paine. For who that ſerueth God deuoutly and with pure conſcience, and that deſireth riches only to ſupplie neceſſitie, and to doe good workes : him God doth proſper and guide in all his wayes. And let no man diſpaire though he be viſited with ill hap ſome time, doing well notwithſtanding. For God manye times ſendeth his bleſſing and increaſe vnwares to man, and in an houre vnlooked for, which he neuer thought would happen. And heare in what manner.

The good and uertuous ſhould neuer diſpaire in aduerſitie.

There dwelled in a certaine Citie a man of godly life and diſpoſition, who fallen into extreeme pouertie

pouertie, being ashamed to aske for Gods sake, detirmined to prooue his friends, and so he did. And bewraying his miserie, looking for reliefe and pittie,
founde nothing but hardnesse, neither was there any
that once woulde looke vpon the necessitie of that
honest conditioned man. And thus repleate with
griefe, vexed in his minde, he sorrowfullye repaireth
to his poore mansion. And being layde at night
in his bedde to take his rest, the anguishe of his
minde, togither with famine, woulde not suffer
him to rest but kept him waking. And by chaunce
hearing a noyse about the house, lystening diligently what it shoulde be: hee knewe straight it
was some Theefe (hoping of a great bootie) that
went thus ransacking vp and downe. So this
poore man sayde vnto himselfe. Thou hadst
neede looke narrowlye, if thou weene to haue that
thou seekest for: Surely I will see yet what
feates these theefes doe worke when they come into
such places where they finde naught. The Theefe
roming here and there, busily searching and groping in euery corner, founde nothing but a little
pot with Meale: and bicause he would not lose
hys labour, hee determined to drawe his string to
ketch that little morsell, and began to poure it out
into the lappe of his cloke, hauing in the cape
thereof

thereof great store of Iewelles and ready money which he had stolen in an other house where he had beene. The goode poore man which till nowe was whisht and quiet to see the ende of the Theefe, perceyuing hys little discretion, his hart rose against him, considering the billange of thys wretch that woulde not leaue him that sielye quantitie of Meale to sustaine him aliue withall: and thought with him selfe it were better defend it in time to keepe him from famine, than to tarye looking for the late reliefe of his harde friends. So in a great furie he leapt out of his bed and tooke him to his sword, and hauing the same drawne in hys hande with a terrible noyse hee runneth to the Theefe. Which bicause hee would not both lose his honesty and life togither at one instant, (leauing for hast to saue himselfe) hys cloke in paune with the Meale, hauing no ley=sure to caste it on his backe, he was forced to flye for life and let all alone. This honest poore man then at his pleasure poured out the Meale out of his cloke, and put it againe into hys earthen potte where it was before: and thus sayd to him=selfe, a ha, by Saint Marie this geare goeth well, I haue gotten a cloke to boote by the meanes, to defende mee from the colde at least, and putting

his

his hande into the cape, hee met with great riches and Jewels, and happily lighted on those goods which he neuer hoped of: winning that frō his enemie by force which his friends would neuer haue giuen him for loue.

I doe not like in ſuch a caſe to ſay as the common people doe, that God provideth liuing for euery bodie, and that he will not ſee me lacke that that ſhall be neceſſarie for me, ſo as I neede not labor for my liuiug, for ſure it is but a fooliſh phraſe and vaine ſpeach. But rather I will conclude, that euery man is bound to labor to procure his liuing, & he may not make any ſuch caſes preſidents, in which it pleaſed God to ſende great riches without labor as in this. For theſe are only the ſecrets of God, & we ought not to aſke the cauſe of his diuine goodneſſe. The wiſe man therefore muſt endeuour himſelfe to gaine that he may, honeſtly and vp-rightly, truſting always in almightie God: that he will proſper his doings and giue him encreaſe, ſeeking euer to keepe him ſelfe out of trouble and ſorowe: and not to do as the Doue, which breed-ing hir Pigions about the Houſe (making them familiar with the ſame) albeit they are monthly taken from hir and killed, yet ſhe leaueth not for that to returne to hir olde neſt and breede yong againe

againe, though she know they shalbe taken from hir. We finde it written, that God hath odeined the end and terme of all things, and that they can not passe. Therefore saye these wise men, that he that worketh respecting the worlde to come lightneth the burthens and trouble of this frayle life. But he that reposeth his trust in these worldlye thinges and is wrapped in the same, doth waste and consume his yeares. A man ought to labour in these three things, bicause he hath neede of them, to wit. To knowe to keepe the law, and the good statutes thereof. The seconde, to procure things necessarie for mans life. And the thirde, that his workes be pure and cleane with himselfe and among others. Then he must beware and withdrawe himselfe from foure other mortall and damnable. The first, is to be negligent in his art or science, The second, to contemne that the law commandeth, The third, to credit all things lightly. The fourth, to denie knowledge. For he that will be reputed wise in his doings, must first consider well what he taketh vpon him : and if he neede counsell let him aske it of a faithfull friende. When he happeneth to haue great matters in hande, let him not goe about them rashly, but first way the importance thereof. That he be not likened

to

to one which being out of his waye, and going on
ſtill, is the farther of the place he would go to.
And alſo compared to another, which hath but a
little hurt in his eye, and by continuall rubbing of
it he maketh it incurable. A man muſt feare the
diuine iuſtice, inclining him ſelfe to that that is
good, and doing that to his neighbour he woulde
haue done to him ſelfe, helping him in all daungers
as he woulde be holpen himſelfe. And to conclude
this our worke, he that meaneth to vnderſtande
it, muſt order his life according to the lawes
and inſtitutions of Vertue: as ſhoweth
theſe wonderfull and learned examples, and ſententious
authorities.

THE ARGUMENT OF THE BOOKE.

WHAT tyme there reigned in Edon ſo manye Royall crouned Kings, amongſt the reſt there was a King called Aneſtres Caſtri: *who choſe for chiefe of all his Courte one* Berozias, *whome hee made high treaſorer of all his Realme, a man right noble in his deedes, and rich of poſſeſſions; and him he loued and truſted ſo much, that hee put his princelye perſon and whole affaires of his Realme into his handes. It happened one daye there was preſented to the King a Booke, in which was*

was written many goodly dedes and secrets, and amongst the heape this was one. Howe that in India were marueylous hie mountaines, in which there grewe certaine sortes of herbes and trees, which if they were knowen and confected afterwardes in a certaine kinde: they should drawe out of that precious composition such a remedie, as therewith they might raise to life again the dead. The King no sooner read this wonder, but he burned straight to knowe the troth thereof: wherefore in haste (as soone might bee) he dispatched Berozias, *and bade him hie him thither, commaunding him to see if he coulde finde it true. And bicause it was a hard and painefull enterprise, he furnished him with golde and siluer, not onely sufficient, but more than*

than needed, that he ſhoulde not lacke. Then he deliuered him his letters of recommendation to all thoſe Kings of India, praying them to further this worthie man in his noble attempt, purpoſed to good ende. Berozias *licenſed nowe of the King to depart (furniſhed with money and letters) went into that countrie, and arriued in India preſented ſtraight to the King his maiſters letters: by meanes whereof he was receyued of the Magiſtrates as was pertinent to the Jmbaſie of ſo highe a Prince. And his meſſage deliuered, they vnderſtanding the cauſe of his comming, offered themſelues with all the wiſe men they had to fauour his enterpriſe, and to further it all they could. And thus honorably accompaunied of all the ſage and wiſe men, conducting*

conducting him through all the Mountaynes and Countries there abouts, they had and gathered all they found written for the conditing of so precious an electuarie. And all they ioyning togithers to make this confection, prouing it a great while, wuld neuer finde it to worke such effect as to raise any one from death to life againe. So that they saw by proofe that all that was written in the booke concerning the electuarie was meere false and vntrue. This thing grieued much Berozias, *that he should retourne to the King* Anastres *his maister and bring no better newes with him: howbeit consulting with these graue and wise men before his departure, how he might doe, not to retourne home in vaine, there was giuen him by a famous Philosopher of* of that Region, a goodly treatiſe, who ſerched himſelf alſo to finde that ſecrete, and in the ende he vnderſtoode that it was the Booke which was ſo called. And ſo O graue Berozias thou ſhalt ſay vnto the King, and returne to him with ioye.

The hilles which we ought to ſeeke, are the wiſe and learned men. The trees and herbes growing vpon thoſe hilles, doe betoken wiſdome and learning: which ſprings of the vnderſtanding and iudgements of the learned. The medicine or electuarie condited of thoſe herbes, are the bookes full of moſt learned writings, compoſed by the high and deepe wittes, and with this oyle or Baulme they reuive the deade. For with ſuch knowledge the ignorant and vnlearned are inſtructed:
whom

whom wee maye iuſtly recken deade and buried.

Therefore taſting the ſweetneſſe (continually reading) of the doctrine of the ſages, they receiue health and reſurrection. This interpretation greatly reioyced Berozias, in ſo much as hee beſought the Princes and ſage men that they would giue him but the copie of that booke to carie to the King his Maiſter, which (although the booke were alwayes in the handes of thoſe Kings, for that it was ful of Morall Philoſophy) was graunted him, licenſing him to tranſlate it out of the Indian into the Perſian tongue, with the helpe and knoledge of all thoſe learned Philoſophers, which was ſo ſingularlye done that it bare the vaunt of all Morall Philoſophie. The Booke
receiued

receiued with due and infinite thankes rendered to thofe noble Kings and Sages for the great honor and courtefie they had done him: Berozias departeth home, and being come to his maifter, prefented him the booke with relation of his whole entertainement.

The King hearing fo noble an expofition, fo wife and difcreete an interpretation thankefully receyued the Booke efteeming it aboue any other prefent. And thencefoorth he procured with great deligence to haue alwayes bookes, and thofe he ftudied, difirous of knowledge, feeking to entertaine in his Court wife and learned men: iudging (as is true) that bookes and wifdome are the greateft treafure and delight to man. Appointing in his Palaice a great librarie, wherein aboue the reft
he

he placed this booke for cheife, being full of examples and inſtructions for man's life, and alſo of Iuſtice and the feare of God: in praiſe and honour of whom we begin this worke, ſhewing therein the continuall daungers and deceits of this miſerable worlde.

*The firſt Part of the Morall Philoſo-
phie of the auncient Sages, compiled*
by the great and learned Philoſopher *Sendebar,*
In the Indian tongue, who by ſundrie and wonderfull examples bewrayeth the deceyts
and daungers of this pre-
ſent worlde.

WHEN I was come to yeares of diſ-
cretion, borne of a noble houſe,
and of my Genitours put to the
ſtudie of Philoſophye, to learne
Phiſycke, whereof I proceded
Doctor: I knewe that thys worlde was a courſe
of a moſt vehement running ſtreame, but yet
appearing no perill of drowning to him that
paſſed it, bicauſe that harde by the banckes
ſydes it was verie ſhalow, and aboue it ranne
quietly, carying aboue water riches and wares
of great value to the iudgement of thoſe that
beheld

beheld them, by means whereof men drawne with great couetousnesse to have abundance, they ranne towardes them and entred into the riuer, partly wetting themselues, but onely their foote, they tooke a fewe of them. And he that would have mo, going further in, must of necessitie wet his legge and knee, bicause it increased. And he that with furie, (passing the rest) with an insatiable desire would needes go further, plunged his whole bodie in the water. And the others trusting in their force of swimming stucke in the middest, and founde the streame exceeding bigge: for in the bottome it was most swift and raging, and they could not get out of the middest, but euen as much as they coulde doe in swimming to kepe them selues aboue water. And brought to this passe, not finding any waye to get out, they cast of these rich merchandises to this man and to that man, which hauinge no skill to swimme followed them alongest the banckes sides of the riuer. In the ende weried with swimming, not able to labor any more for life, forsaking this merchandise floting aboue the water, downe they sinke, and carying nothing with them, remayne drowned.

Who could in better maner describe our worldly labour? Truly our insatiable desire is
so

so greedie to haue that it liketh and seeth, that to be owner of that we would, we put our selues to all manner of daungers, and intollerable paynes of this world. To be briefe: euery man (little or much) wetteth himselfe in this raging riuer of man's life. He that wetting his foote runneth alongest the bancks side of this terrible Brooke, is a man that is oppressed with bondage, that enioyeth naught else in this world but miserable lyfe. The other that washeth his legge, liueth by his labor, and commeth to take more of the world, and to taste the delights thereof bearing many afflictions. He that thrustes in his whole bodie in this water, hath possessed the seignorie and gouernment of the most wicked and haplesse state of this world. O vnspeakable cruelty, that once passed forwards he entreth perforce into the middest, and reacheth to this man and to that man that he hath, keeping himself alwaies in this daungerous state. But in the ende overtaken by some accident, as warre, treason, poyson, or mans force, he falleth into deathes lappe: and he that hath followed his troublesome life remayneth depriued of all his goodes, bicause wanting the heade, the rest of the members remain vile, filthie, and stincking. Sure this worldly life representeth no more but the little worlde of our bodie, which carrieth a
wonderfull

wonderfull prefence: and that little breath of ours once fpent, it is then but a fhadowe, duft and fmoke. Thefe worldly fauours and temporall goodes in the iudgement of the wife feeme but as fnowe, which with the firft beames of the Sunne diffolveth and commeth to nothing. Lord, what coft do we beftow vpon our heares and face, which when the Barber clippeth of, are defpifed and throwne away? A man fhould neuer truft this foolifhe life. It is but a fire kindled on the coles, which confuming it felfe giueth heate to others. The Phifition truly that cureth the difeafe of the bodie is a worthie fpirite of man: but he that healeth us of our finnes is a celeftiall God. Hee that can fhunne the water of this riuer, which carrieth in his courfe, Pride, vaine glorie, lafciuioufneffe, couetoufneffe, prefumption, infirmities, and loffe: may be called diuine and not humaine. Let no man put his foote into the water of carnall loue, neyther his legge into the falfe waues of thefe goodes, nor wafhe his bodie in the glorie of this malignant time, neyther feeke continually to fwimme in the middeft of thefe felicities: for all paffeth awaye to oure loffe and vndoing. The rich Indian merchaunt *Softrates* richly furnifhed his houfe with fundrie forts of merchaundife with his

great

great trauell, expence of time, and money:
and hauing his houſe full ſtored anew to the
toppe, he could find none that had ſo much
readie money as to paye him for it all at one
time and to carie it away. Then he ſaide to
him ſelfe: If by little and little I ſhould
ſpende it, when ſhall I euer make an ende?
Life will not always laſt, neyther can I liue
ſo long as I woulde: I knowe there can be
no ende of our miſeries: and thus diſpiſing all
pompe and riches he forſooke the deceytfull
life with trouble, and withdrewe him to a
better, taking vpon him another courſe. A
man ought to beleeue the true and diuine
careƈte, and not mans writing: not to truſt
the falſe ſayings of wicked men (which continuallye liue of the ſpoyle of their neighbour
beguiling them) but to his owne experience.
For who ſo eaſily beleeueth the words of light
perſons, falleth into a grieuous errour, to his
owne loſſe and hurt, as ye ſhall heare reading
that that followeth.

Here you may ſee how light
beliefe bringeth damage.

Two theeues very ſkilfull in picking and opening lockes with ginnes (but nothing aduiſed nor
foreſeeing

foreſeeing the daunger) entered one nyght into a knightes houſe, no leſſe wyſe than worſhipfull, and verie riche: where theſe theeues thought to have ſped themſelues for euer, that they ſhould neuer more haue needed to haue exerciſed that arte. This valiant knight awaketh, and hearing the noiſe of their feete in the houſe, imagined (as it was) that there were theeues: and they were euen vpon the point of opening his chamber doore where he laye, when he iogging his wyfe awaked hir, and ſoftly ſaid to hir, Have ye not heard the noyſe of the theeues in the houſe that are come to robbe us? I would haue ye therefore aſke mee ſtreight with great inſtance, after what ſort, whence and howe I came by all that we haue togither in the houſe. And ye ſhall aſke mee ſo lowde that if there were any at the chamber dore he might eaſily heare you: and I will ſeeme to be verie ſcrupulous to tell you, then ſhall you bee more earneſt with mee than before to vnderſtande it: at length you ſhall preſſe mee ſo with importunacie that I will tell it you. The Ladie his wife being verie wiſe and ſubtill, began in this maner to aſke hir huſbande, and thus ſhe ſaide vnto him: O deare ſir, graunt mee I beſeech you one thing this night that I ſo long haue deſired to knowe: to tell me how you haue done to come

by

by all thefe goodes you haue gotten togither. So he gaue hir an anfwere at random, nothing aunfwering hir defire. She contending with him, and he aunfwering, in the ende as he had bene angry he faid to hir: I can but mufe what reafon mooues you (in God's name) to defire to knowe my fecretes, being a thing that little profites you to know them, or not to know them. Be ye contented Madame, and fet your heart at reft: let it fuffice you to fare well, to be richly apparelled, and to be worfhipfully wayted vpon and ferued, although ye do not importune me to tell you fuch a fecret. Thefe are not thinges to be tolde, for I haue hearde it fpoken many a time and oft, that euery thinge hath eares: therefore many times thinges are fpoken which are repented of the partie afterwardes. Wherefore hold your peace, for I cannot tell you. To this anfwere his Ladie replied, and louingly befought him to tell hir, fweetly entifing him with wifely traynes in fuch fort, that the knight wearied with hir importunate fpeach yelded, and faid to hir: All that we haue, and as much as is in the houfe (but fweete hart I charge you let it neuer come from you) is ftollen, and in deede to be playne with you, in the nightes feafon I ftole it from this and that mans houfe, fo that I neuer gate anything trulye. His Ladie amazed to heare that aunſwere, would not yet beleeue it at the firſt, but ſaide: What for ſhame, how can you euer ſpeake this with truth! being reputed here the beſt Gentleman in this citie: and there is none in all this realme I dare well ſaye that would once dare to ſuſpect you for a theefe. Out a theefe, one of your worſhip and credit? nay nay, I will neuer beleeue it. Therefore I pray you without ceremonie, tell mee truly that I have aſked you, or elſe I cannot be in quiet. The knight anſwered hir and ſayd: You think it perauenture a wonder that I haue tolde you: but liſten yet and you ſhall heare more. Euen from my cradell in maner I alwaies had delight to ſteale and filch, and it liked me a life to be amongſt theues that my fingers might euer be walking, ſo ſweete was the craft vnto me. And a Mate amongſt them there was that loued me ſo well, that he taught mee only a ſingular tricke, and ſo rare a ſecret as neuer yet was hearde. And wote ye what it was? a fewe wordes coniurations which I made to the Beames of the Moone, and I ranne ſodenly to embrace them, going vpon them qucklye into euery part where they ſhone. Sometime I came downe vpon them from a high windowe, another time

I

I ſerued my ſelfe with thē to get vp againe to the top of the houſe: ſo I ſtaid and went on them as I liſt, and did what I would. The Moone hearing my coniuration ſeauen times ſhewes me all the money and treaſure that was hidden in that houſe, where I flew thus vp and downe vpon hir beames, by meanes where-of I tooke my choice, and had what I would, carying it quite away with me. And thus good wife (as I haue tolde thee) I made me riche, and now I care for no more.

One of the two theeues (who gaue a liſten-ing eare, ſtanding at the knights chamber dore) heard all that he ſaide, and bare it away with him in memorie, beleuing it was true that he ſpake, knowing this riche knight to be a man of credit and to be beleeued, ſince he was re-puted of all men to be a worthy and courteous knight: ſo that they thought themſelues happie to haue learned ſuch a wonderfull ſecrete in maner (upon his wordes) aſſuring themſelues in ſhort time to be made verie rich. The chiefe theefe apparelled like a woman got vp to the toppe of the houſe, deſirous to prove that in deedes which he had heard in words: ſo he made his exorciſme and enchauntment, repet-ing it ſeuen times, and then embracing the beames of the Moone, his armes throwne abrode,

he

he caſt himſelf on them, thinking to haue gone from windowe to windowe, and ſo hedlong he fell to the grounde in ieopardie to breake his necke. But the Moone for the firſt time fauored him ſo that he killed not himſelfe, but brake his legges and one of his armes as God would haue it: ſo that oppreſſed with paine he cryed out alowde, lamenting his miſſehap chaunced to him, giuing to much credit to an others wordes. And thus not able to creepe nor goe, he pitifully lieth expecting death. The knight leaping out of his bed ran to the crie, and come to the place, he found this vnfortunate and wretched theefe lying on the grounde in womans apparell, and hee gaue him many a faire wounde to lighten the paine of his broken legges and arme, and forced him to tel what cauſe moued him to come to robbe his houſe. Thys miſerable theefe aunſwered him (fearing leaſt hee would kill him) and tolde him the whole cauſe of his comming. But yet that that grieued him worſt of all was ſaide hee, that he was ſuch a fool and beaſt to beleeue his words: and he beſought him though he had at leaſt hurt him to much with his wordes, (which he had dearly bought and repented both), yet that he would vouchſafe not to hurt him in his deedes alſo.

It

It is moſt true that lightly beleuing theſe worldly thinges hath made many a man fall into ſundrie daungers, and hedlong to plunge himſelfe into the deepe miſeries of this worlde. Sometimes men detirmine to obey the lawe. At another time they contemme it and ſet it at naught, following ſenſuall appetite. Oft times they beleeue the counſell of their good friend, but very often they follow the counſell of the flatterer. To-day we are pleaſed with true doctrine: to-morrow we folow the falſe. In euery wit and arte there is abuſe; and who runneth not to this riuer? and the more they weene to gaine, the more they runne in daunger and loſſe of life and ſoule. Behold here is one man pricked in his conſcience, there is another oppreſſed with paſſion and ſorow, and there neuer wanteth ſome that follow the continuall ſeruitude of this deceitfull life, either for goodes, fauor, and eſtimation, or elſe of their owne free willes: and there is neuer none (or fewe at the leaſt) that in ſo ſhort time of life can forget this knowne and manifeſt daunger. For death aſſaulting us, we knowe not whither to retire, and then with all our might we flie the force of his moſt piercing dart: and thus weening to hide our ſelues in ſure place, we hedlong runne to our ſhame and vndoing. As is manifeſtly
ſeene

ſeene by ſundrie examples happened like to this following.

A tale of a Louer and a Gentilwoman.

There was in the citie where I dwelled, harde by my houſe, a fayre yong Gentilwoman nobly borne, the which was but euen in maner newly maried (at leaſt not long before) when this chaunce happened. This younge ſpouſe fell in loue with a proper Gentleman, fayre condicioned, well ſpoken, and of good entertainement: and fortune ſo fauoured hir, that ſhee ſweetly reaped the fruits of hir deſire at all times when ſhe liked to enioye it without let or annoy at all. But to preuent hir huſbandes ſodein comming home at times vnlooked for, this liuely yong wife deuiſed to worke a waye for her louers ſafetie, and the continuance of this ſecond (yea moſt bleſſed) ioye. She cauſed to be conueyed in a well ſhe had a proper vawte, which ſhould ſafely receyue hir yong louer leaping into the ſame, if he were by miſhap at any time diſtreſt with hir huſbandes ſoden comming vpon them. The huſband alſo much about that time called workemen to him, and in a corner of the houſe made

a

a great darke hole and vent (very deepe) for the fincke of the houfe. It happened fo by chaunce one daye that hir yong Louer was no fooner entered into the houfe, and the gate but newly put too, but ftraight the hufband of this wanton wife knocked alfo at the doore. She knowing his knocke, with heauie hart beckened to him to hide himfelfe in the vawte that fhe had made in the well, and this while fhee ftoode ftill, poynting him the place and woulde not open to hir hufbande. This yong man flight with feare (which is euer at hand to amaze the offender) ranne round about like a headleffe flie, and miffing the well (as one ftricken blinde for fodeine feare) leapt into the deepe darke vawte feruing the fincke of the houfe. At which inftant fhe had opened the dore to hir hufband, fo as he faw the yong man when he went into it: and then he knew his wife had born a man more than fhee fhoulde, and that fhee had beguiled him, vnderftanding the late opening of the doore. And ouercome with rage and hir faulte, he fierflye laid hands on hir, and cruellye flue both hir and hir Louer.

To be vnaduifed, and to doe thinges rafhly which we ought not, bringeth many times death,

hurt

hurt and fhame. For no man fhould fo entangle himfelfe in thefe worldly toyles, as he might not euer leaue them at his will. For fo ftraunge and fodein chaunces fall vpon him, as a man would neuer haue imagined, and therefore he cannot vpon fuch a fodeine withftande it, but is forced to yeelde. Wherefore I would wifh no man to be fo caried awaye with thefe fhort pleafures and fweete found of man's life, that they fhould caft behinde them the remembraunce of the right way to doe well: as happened vnto him that would mende and fet his Jewelles.

Of a Jeweller that forgot his profit, and gaue himfelfe to pleafure.

There was a rich Merchant of *Surria* that brought from the *Cair* a great fumme of precious ftones, and bicaufe they wanted fetting in Golde with curious worke to pullifh them, hee agreed with an excellent artificer (moft fkilfull in fuch workes) to giue him daily a certaine fumme of money, bicaufe that during the time he wrought in his Jewelles he fhoulde worke with no other but only attende his bufyneffe. This cunning workeman went euerye morning to thys merchants houfe to worke, carying his tooles wyth him: and working all the daye at his defire, at
night

night he receyued his dayes wages agreed vpon. It happened there was brought to this merchant a goodly inftrument, and excellent to playe vpon (muche like to a Harpe), to fee if he would buye it. The next morning betimes came this workemaifter to follow his worke, and the firft thing that the merchant did was to fhewe him the Harpe. The workeman taking it in his hande (being an excellent mufition, and playing well of this inftrument), he fayd: Sir, is it your pleafure I fhall playe? yea, fayd the merchant. This cunning man paffingly handling this inftrument, playde fo fweetely, and fhewed fuch muficke in fuch ftraunge and rare ftoppes, with fuch voluntarye wythall, that the merchaunt delighted with his heauenly harmonie made him play all daye long. At night this cunning workeman demaunded his dayes hire, as if he had wrought the whole daye in his Jewels. The merchaunt denied it, and would not paye him. The other alledged that he had bene in his houfe all that day (at his requeft) as he was the other dayes before. This matter called before the Judges and brought in tryall, the Judge gaue fentence againft the merchaunt, and forced him to paye the workemaifter for the daye (fuch fumme of money as they were agreed vppon) as if hee had wrought all daye. The merchaunt

yll

yll digefted the Judge's fentence, but much worfe the paiment, greuing him to the heart to paye fo deare for fo fhort a pleafure, where he might haue gotten much by the others worke, if like a foole he had not let him.

Let men that giue themfelues to the pleafures of this vnhappie life be warned by the example of this merchaunt, to leaue afide the fweete deceits of the bodie, and to attende onely to the precious ftone of our foull, pullifhing and keeping that cleane. Lorde howe many are there that leauing profit follow loffe, and all for a fayned fhowe, or worldlye fhadowe. The Greyhounde that hath pinched the Hare, and taken hir in hys mouth, cannot runne after another he feeth go before him and take hir alfo: for fo the one may fcape from him quite, and the other eafily vanifh out of his fight. O miferable worlde, naye rather moft miferable and wretched our mindes and willes: that plainly feeing our hurt and miferie, we ftill hedlong purfue and follow the fame. What is he liuing fo ignoraunt, that knoweth not our life paffeth quicklyer awaye than the lightening that commeth before the thunder clap, and in the darke clowdes giueth moft fhort light: and that our fight (the lightening paft) comming into the darke is blinded more?
the

the man truly that is loft in this worldlye broyle, and entered into the fea of miferies: that that fenfuall appetite and fhort defire fheweth him, feemeth light vnto him, but in a moment (wretched creature he) he findeth himfelf in darkeneffe. What part haue we of any good thing in this fhort courfe of life? where is our good beginning? where the excellent middeft? or where the perfite end? In that day (O miferable man) that thou art begotten in thy mothers wombe, in the felfe fame day death imbraceth thee to ouerthrow thee at his will. Our firft originall is begun in darkneffe and corruption, the firft paffage that putteth vs forth to the light of this world, bringeth vs forow and lamentation. We are borne naked, fubiect to difeafes, vncleane, and haue neede of all things, and of euery bodies helpe. Afterwardes, vnleffe we would feeme ymages of ftone or timber without vnderftandinge, wee muft be taught, ruled, and inftructed, which bringeth vs difeafes, troubles, paynes, forrowes, and griefes. And in this while how many neceffities doe affault vs? how many bufineffes doe oppreffe vs? the elements offende vs with heate, colde, and barreneffe. Difeafes neuer forfake our bodies, and the troubles of this world neuer letteth vs reft an houre. To be alone it grieueth vs: to be accompanied it troubleth

vs:

vs: to liue long it werieth vs: to haue little misliketh vs: and sufficient contenteth vs not. The thought of death on the one side assaulteth our life: and on the other, the passions of the minde to forsake our goodes, friends, wife, children, and the worlde, doe still pricke vs. O what troubles and afflictions, what terrors and passions, abideth this our confused bodie: which the most part of our time is replete with anger, rancor, and malice, but often voyde (rather euer) of iustice, mercie, and pittie. And lastly, what doth one man for another? He causeth that by force the good is troden downe with the euill. The foole taketh away the reputation of the wise: the lyer plucketh out of his seate him that alwayes telleth troth: the noble Gentleman well brought vp is ruled by the vndiscrete and rude Cloyne. What more? vertue alacke dieth, but ignoraunce liueth. Wherefore our state is in more daungers and troubles than his, that flying the fiercenesse of fower Lions to saue himselfe, leapt into a Well with greater daunger. As writeth the great Philosopher *Tiabonus*.

A Parable of the Worlde.

A certayne lusty yong man trauelling throughe a desert countrie, wandering to and fro amongst the

OF MORALL PHILOSOPHIE. 61

the thicke and huge woodes, happened one day to come into a great large playne, where not farre from him he ſawe trauerſing in the way fower great and terrible Lions: whereof he being marueilouſly afrayd (to beholde ſo horrible a ſight), tooke him to his legges and ranne for

life: and bicauſe he was not able to runne ſo farre right out, as the Lions had force to followe him, by good hap in running he was ware of a Well in the middeſt of the field, about which grew certain wilde rootes of little trees, and being come to the Well he caught holde with
his

his handes of the thwigges of the fame, and fo caft himfelfe into it, hanging by force of his armes vpon the thwigges, not falling downe at all: and throwing his legges a croffe to the fides, he ftayde himfelfe with them, and the ftrength of his hands to kepe him from falling downe. While hee ftoode thus vpon his feete and force of handes, looking downe into the Well, he fawe a terrible Dragon that with open mouth gaped for his fall. This youth brought nowe to fuch a prefent mifchiefe, rayfed vp himfelfe perforce fometimes, and looked out of the Well to fee if thefe devouring beafts were gone their waye: and feeing them ftanding hard by him, with great forrowe and paine he hunge ftill on force of his armes fcant able to continue. A newe mifhappe (and worfe than all the reft) affaulted this iolye youth. Two beafts of colour white and blacke came to gnaw the rootes of thefe thwigges, the tops whereof he gladlye helde faft in his handes to fuftaine himfelf aliue withall: so that nowe he fawe prefent death on euerie fide prefented. Remayning thus in this daunger (brought to forrow and difpaire), cafting backe his eie, he fawe a little hole behind him wherein there was a pot full of honie, layd there by chaunce by fome fhepehearde paffing by that waye. And forgetting quite in what termes

of

of life he ftode, he beganne with one hande to taste of it, holding himfelfe by the other, and fo long hee attended to thys little tafte, that forow ftroke him on the necke. For the two beafts had gnawen a funder the rootes when he hedlong fell into the Well and died.

What is fignified hereby, or who can other-wife interpret it, but thus :—The Well repre-fenteth the world. The foure Lions the foure elements, which feeke ftill to deuour man. The Dragon with gaping mouth, what was it elfe but the graue? The two thwigges or boughes, tem-porall goodes and loue to which we are wholly inclined: both which by the two beaftes are gnawen a funder, the one white, the other blacke, which are vnderftanded for the day and night. But the pot with that little fweete honie, to which we are giuen, not regarding our daunger, betokeneth no other but the fhort pleafure of this worlde, which retayneth vs, and fuffereth vs not to knowe the daungers and troubles of this moft miferable world, and of our thrall and troubled lyfe.

The Seconde Part of Morall Philoſophie, ſhewing the wonderfull abuſes of this wretched Worlde.

MANY and diuers are the ſayinges of our wyſe and auncient Fathers ſpoken to exhort man to quietneſſe, and to make himſelfe wonderfull in behauiour, wyſe and ware in theſe wordly thinges, and pacient of life. That noble Romaine that fought and laboured to bring the people and communaltie to loue their Magiſtrates and ſuperiours, tolde them a pretie tale (to write it happilye in this Booke for him that knoweth it not) howe the handes were angrie with the bodie, and thus at variaunce would not for malice giue meate to the mouth: as thoſe that thought themſelues inferiour to no other member, and thought ſcorne to take ſuche paynes, and the other members not. By reaſon whereof vſing this
abſtinence

abſtinence of ſelfe will a while, refrayning to doe their office in giuing meate to the bellie: the bellie ſuffering lacked his ſuſtinance, the handes alſo beganne to leaue the ſkirmiſhe, and knowing then their lacke and hurt (for preſeruation of both) repenting themſelues, they returned to their office, and beganne againe to feede the mouth. And thus vnited both in one, they preſerued eche other. With this pretie tale he made the people ſenſibly to vnderſtand what became them, and how they ſhould behaue themſelues to their ſuperiours, for their muſt needes be Magiſtrates and inferiours, Maiſters and ſervaunts. An other likewiſe tolde a tale, that manye yeares paſt there was a Horſe vſed to feede in a goodly paſture, where hee alone was Lorde and Maiſter within himſelfe. At length by chaunce there came within his dioceiſe a mightie growne Hart, who tooke his herbage there as his right alſo, and did eate and feede beyond all reaſon or meaſure. Inſomuch that this horſe diſdaining his beaſtly attempt, chaſed this Hart from the ground full many a time & oft. And perceyuing he could not for all that ouercome him, bicauſe his hornes were of as much force as his feete, he was madde for anger. It happened ſo onē day a man came through this paſture, and paſſing by, the horſe came

came neare him, and tolde him his whole mifhap, praying him to helpe him. This man that was more wife and fubtill than a beaft, tolde the horfe that hee alone coulde not doe this feate, and fhewed him plainly that he muft needes haue faddle, bridle, and rodde: to fpeak of ftirrops, ftirrop leathers, and fpurres, me think it no wordes of Grammer. For when the Latine tongue was onely vfed they had no fuch termes, bicaufe they had no fuch toyes. The beaft to be reuenged of the other beaft did beaftly let himfelfe be ridden, and like a beaft became prifoner to the man. Æfope recyteth alfo many of thefe pretie fables, being verie pleafant, learned, fharpe, profitable, and full of Moralitie, as you fhal heare in this deceytfull framed practife deuifed by a Moyle, betwene the Lion king of all beafts and the Bull, which was neuer made and inuented by the wife Fathers to other ende, but to fhadow and couer the life of man from the foule fpottes of vice: as fheweth you this prefent hyftorie following.

In India, in thofe worthy and iuft times adorned with vertue and wifdome, euery one of thofe royall princes (as Lordes of noble manners and behauiour) retayned with them in their princely Courtes men no leffe learned than vertuous.

tuous. Among which a king there was (called in their tongue) *Diſtes*, who deſired much to reade hyſtories, and to imprint in memorie the goodly and profitable examples to direct him and his withall. O noble time and happie yeares: in his reigne I ſaye liued in this *Diſtes* Court this noble Philoſopher *Sendebar*, ſo excellent in his compariſons and examples, as no man that went before or after him coulde once go euen with him, much leſſe exceede him. This worthy Prince rapt with the excellencie of this rare (yea odde) man, moſt willingly ſpent ſome time in diſcourſing with him: and this wonderfull Philoſopher alſo with deepe and profounde ſentences ſhewed his worthineſſe. But amonge all the beſt thinges hee ſpake, hee alwayes admoniſhed the Prince to haue a good eie to his Court, and a ſounde iudgement to iudge hys people: and chiefly that hee ſhoulde not loue fauour, nor eſteeme for friendes (endeuoring himſelfe all he coulde to knowe them) double tongued men, lyers, tale bearers, and vitious liuers. And to the ende his Maieſtie ſhoulde ſoone feele ſuch mates as it were at hys fingers endes, he made him a longe diſcourſe of their maners and practiſes, with theſe examples which you ſhall heare, woonderfull and learned.

Beholde

*Beholde the pageants and
miferies of the court of this Worlde.*

There was a Heyward or neteyarde that had the keeping of a great herde of Cattell in a large common, as Gotes, Sheepe, Mares, Kyne, Horfes, and Bullockes, And it happened that a Bull amongft the herde (called by ye herdman *Chiarino*) became in looue wyth a iolye yonge Heighfare, that had diuers trimme markes and fpottes on her fkinne, and was fauoured and belyked alfo of the Herdman—who for hir beautie and fayreneffe named hir likewife *Incoronata*, and many times did crowne hir with a garlande of fundrye fortes of flowers. Ill fortune willinge it, and hir deftinye with all, this fayre yonge Heighfare playing and leaping from hill to hill, unfortunately fell and brake hir necke, and with hir fall dyed. This herdman fimplye fleade hir, and with hir fayre fkinne made him an open caffock fauadge fafhion. Now I leaue you to imagine the rage and madneffe of this Bull, lacking his fayre yonge heighfare, that like other Bulles wandered vp and downe to feeke hir. In this raging beftiall loue of hys, the herdeman foolifhly caft vpon him the caffock made of the heighfares fkinne, which this Bull feing runneth fiercely vnto the herdeman, lowing
and

and fnuffing extremely, in fo muche as if the herdeman had not hyed him quicklye to have caft it of his backe, the Bull had forthwith panched him. The cloyne being mad with *Chiarino* the Bull that had fcared him thus, threwe his hedging bill at hym, and hitting hym full on the knee he cutte him fuch a gafhe, as he had beene as good almoft haue howght him. So this poore Bull with his wounde was left in the fielde, not able to go after the herde. The herdeman after the tyme of gifting hys cattell came out, and that the feafon of the yeare did hafte him home to preferue the beaftes from the fharpe and bitter wether of the mountaines; he brought them into the playnes againe, and delivered vp his account of them all, fhewinge infteade of the heighfare his caffock made of hir fkinne, declaring hir death and the Bulles departure. Saying that the Bull beinge in loue with hir, (and in his chiefe pride) ranne his waye, and ftrayed fo farre, that he went quite out of fight and coulde never be fet eye on agayne—fo that the owner amazed with that tale quieted himfelfe. This poore *Chiarino* lefte all alone and fickely, limping went feeding vp and downe, and fteppe by fteppe halting on (paffing thorowe many mountaines and hilles) in many dayes he hapned to come into a folitarie (but fertile) country, inhabited

habited with infinit number of wilde beaftes: and meeting there with good pafture and better ayre, in time he waxed whole and founde as euer he was, fauing that age had ftolen upon him, by meanes whereof he had quite forgot *Incoronata:* to weete the crowned heighfare. Yet continuing thus without any make of his kinde, he rored and yelled amiddeft that valley & caues, whofe lowing ecco rebounding backe with terrible founde, impreffed a merueylous feare in all the herde of wilde and fauadge beaftes. The Lyon that was Kinge of all the reft, hearing the hollow and fearefull noyfe of this mighty Bull, not acquainted before with the like noyfe: notwithftanding his hardineffe, yet was hee fore afrayde and amazed both, and durft not once for fhame faye I am afrayde. In the ende parplexed thus, he refolved to fende a fpye, and calling to him fecretely a wilde Bore, he fent him ftraight to fee what newe and ftraunge thing that was. This wilde Bore running through thickets, thornes, bryers, and hedges, at length came neare to the Bull. And when he fawe fo goodly a beafte, with his fharpe hornes fo pointing out, and with his parted hide (halfe blacke, halfe white) and blafed ftarre in the foreheade, fo well fhaped with all—hee ftoode in a maze, as one ouercome with feare, and fo much the more, bicaufe at that
inftant

inſtant the Bull put forth three or foure terrible lowes. So that the poore wylde Bore was driuen for feare to hide himſelfe in mudde, all ſaue his head onely. Now when he eſpied his time he retourned to the Lyon, and tolde him the qualitie and condition of thys moſt terrible beaſte. I do not tell you now what feare this Lyon had, that princelyke kept his denne, as kinge in deede, of all the reaſt: and that was a Pallace for the counſayle, a chamber of preſence for his Gentlemen, wherein they gaue themſelues to diſport. But of this kingly feare was ware a ſauadge Aſſe of longe appointed eares, and priuie to the ſame alſo a Moyle, brother to the Aſſe, which both detirmined to vnderſtande the cauſe. The ſhee Aſſe, Aunt to the Moyle, and mother of the Aſſe, chaunced ſodeinly to heare certaine whiſperings amongſt them, and one ſoftly to ſay to the other, It is no marueyle that the Kinge cometh not oute of hys denne. It is no marueyle neither that he goeth not ahunting, hawking, fyſhing, tournieng and iuſting other whyle as hee was wont to doe. The other anſwered, It is certayne that he is afrayde of that great and mightie Beefe, and that he ſuſpecteth his kingdome ſhoulde be taken from him. Doeſt thou not marke his croſſe aunſweres, howe wyde from the matter? hee is ſo full of choller that he wyll ſpeake to no mã,

neyther

neyther fuffer any to fpeake to him: fo as hee is not to be delt withall by any. The fhee Affe vnderftanding the effect of their talke by dyfcretion, ftepping in betweene them both, fhe would needes make the thirde, and faye hir minde too. He that is well cannot keepe him fo. The Lyon taketh you both for hys friendes, therefore feeke not I praye you that that pertayneth not to you. What a goodyere haue you to do to meddle in his matters? are yee out of your wittes, or wearye of your liues? or what wilbe, attende you on Gods name to your bufyneffe. For hee that is bufye in that he knoweth not, nor toucheth him not, and that concerneth not his Arte; if any mifchaunce lighteth on him, he hath but that he hath iuftly deferued. As I will tell you hereafter a tale of an Ape, and what hapned to hym, bicaufe he woulde needes meddle with a craft he had no fkill of. But before I beginne to tell you I will make a little digreffion with two wordes.

It hath bene an olde and true opinion, that for the feruante to fearch his maifters doings it is both naught and vncomely too: but to defire to know the Princes caufes or affaires is of all other yet moft daungerous. And naturally who fo is giuen to be a fearcher out of other men's doings, he can neuer be reckened good nor honeft. Now giue eare vnto the tale.

A

*A tale of an Ape medling in
that he had no ſkill.*

There was an Ape in our Maiſters woodes, which made manie pretie toys and deuiſes with his handes, for I that carried home the woode from thence ſawe it, and therefore I can be witneſſe of it. But one day being buſie to meddle with an Arte he had no ſkill of in ſteade of a fiſhe he caught a frogge. I ſay therefore that a laboring man of oures went one daye to the woode, and hewed out a lode of woode, which laying on my backe I caried home. It fortuned one daye that he cloue certaine logges or billets not very bigge: and to make them fitte for burdens he hewed them with a long axe, riuings them with wedges out of hand, that the woode opened, ſo that giuing fower ſtrokes with the Betell he layde them on the ground in peeces. Nowe this bleſſed Ape got him up to the top of an oke and looked diligently after what maner this labourer hewed his woode in ſo ſmall pieces, and was verie deſirous (as it ſeemed) to proue it with his owne handes if he coulde likewiſe doe the ſame, and he had his deſire. The woode cleauer hauing clouen one halfe aſunder, left it euen ſo, and went and layde him downe in the ſhadowe to take a nappe: ſo that the wedges and axe remayned in the woode.
Straight

Straight commeth doune this foolifh Ape from the Oke, and ketcheth holde on the fteale of the Axe, and tampered fo long withall that at length he gate it out of the logge: but euen with his ftriving the axe comming out at a twitch vnawares layd him alongeft on the blocke, and one of his legges vnhappily flipt in the clyft, which clofing togither, helde his foote as faft as might bee, fo that for extreeme paine he cried out as he had been gelt. The cleauer of woode that lay not farre of, hearing this noife and lowde crie, ranne to the place, and faw this foolifh beaft caught faft in the logge. Which then too late efpied his beaftly follie; that he tooke vpon him to meddle in things that pertained not to him, when he faw this churlifh Cloyne lift vp his armes with a Bat in his handes to pafhe his braines a peeces: which he full dearely bought with the loffe of braine and life.

It is not good therefore I tell you plaine for you to deale in Princes matters, to fearche out their meanings & intents. If needes yee will, marke well my wordes; and faye I tolde it you. Vpon my lyfe yee bothe in the ende fhall feele the fmart and payne thereof. The Affe perfwaded by his Mothers wordes left off his enterprife: but the prowde Moyle fayde, I intende to know
them,

them, and therefore I will get mee to the court.
And I will you knowe, deare Mother, that
manuell craft is one exercife, and to knowe to
behave themfelues in Court is an other Arte.
Thy wordes in parte are good, to caufe them
refrayne from doing things they can not bring to
paffe. But to me that muft remaine in Princes
Court, I maye not go fo plainlye and fimply to
worke, but muft vfe euery one with Arte, feeding
ftill their humor; to deale in others matters with
deceyt, and in mine owne to have a fubtill witte,
deuifing ftill all I may to be chiefe about the
Prince. And that that now I haue tolde you, I
haue long fince determined to doe. In Princes
Courts he that proceedeth not ftowtely in his
matters, befides that he is thought a Coward, they
take him for a foole. What? Know not you
that fortune fauoureth ftill the prowde and
ftowte? think ye my ftowteneffe will not fauour
me, accompanied with the malice of vnderftandinge, and with the pride of reputing my felfe
of noble bloud, which preheminences obtaine
happie ftate in Court? And he that hath the
name to bee wife, fubtile, fharpe of wit, and with
that to be of noble houfe: hath made him already
a Cloke for finne, and a garment for his naughtineffe. That that I haue fayde I fpeake with
iudgement, and for proofe thereof I can alledge

you

you infinit examples. The Pecocke though his faire tayle couer his fowle feete, yet it is not faide that he fcrapeth in dunghill at all, but he is reputed the faireft Fowle of two feete. The flefhe of the Tortoife that is fo good and holefome for man is not readily folde, but rather lotheth many becaufe of his vglye fight. If I doe but looke well into Princes Courtes, none go great thither, and thofe that come to greatneffe clime by diuers degrees. Who for vertue, another for ftrength, and fome (be it fpoken with reuerence of thofe beaftes that haue vnderftandinge) for malice: others by continuall feruice, and numbers by other meanes. He that rifeth thus in greatneffe, and is noble and vertuous, it feemeth he goth into his proper naturall houfe: but he that commeth to that greatneffe with malice, and fayned appearance, he may make iuft account I fay that they are but lent him.

¶ Yea marie nowe thou commeft to vnderftande me, therefore and thou be wife go not to the Court how foeuer thou doeft. For if Fortune fhould make thee great, whether it were by Arte, fubtiltie, or deceit: the Lordes and Peeres that are fine and cunning, and knowe all the points of malice, would doe to thee, as a Judge of the beaftes did to the Woolfe. And hearken howe.

A

A tale of the Woolfe concerning breach of promiſe.

A Woolfe was taken in a ſnare that a ſhepeheard had pitched at the foote of a hill (where euerye morning he founde the haunt and tracke of the Woolfe's feete) and at that time there paſſed by another ſilly ſhepeherde, whom the Wolfe called to him, and made a bargain with him, that if he would loſe him he woulde neuer take any of his ſhepe, & thereupon gaue him his faith. The ſhepeherde newly come to keepe ſheepe, like a foole beleeued him, and loſing him in deede let him goe. The Woolfe being at libertie ſtrayde not farre but he had gotten a fatte Weather by the neck: the ſhepeherde ſeeing that, complained, and appealed to the Judges, and tolde them the pleaſure he had done him, and what the Wolfe did promiſe him. The Woolfe being brought before the Judges, denied that he promiſed him ought: and if they would needes make it that he had made him a promiſe, he ſayd that in that place where they ſay he had promiſed him, he would go from his worde againe. The Judges agreed, and went togithers to the place. The Woolfe being come to the foote of the hill, ſaid to the ſhepeherd: was I here? yea anſwered hee.

hee. And here then fayde the Woolfe before thefe Judges I doe vnfaye it againe. Naye fayde the Judges (knowing his malice) it will not ferue thee, vnleffe thou wert faft tied in the fnare euen as he founde thee. The Woolfe glad to be releafed of his promife (being indeede a fubtile beaft, but yet not drawing fo deepe as the Judge vpon the fodeine) beaftly fuffered himfelfe to be fnared againe as the fhepeherde found him. O, now thou art fafe fayde the fhepeherde, keepe thee there, denie it nowe a Gods name, I giue thee leaue, thou fhalt mocke me no more I warrant thee. Whileft this matter was doing thus, the other fhepeherde commeth in the nicke that firft had pitched his fnare, and fo tooke the Woolfe for praye (as of right hee might) and forth with he flue him with his fheepehooke. So that now you may heare how they fare that liue upon deceyt. Go not therefore I faye, if thou meane to clyme to high degree by fuch vnlawful and difhoneft meanes. Then fayde the Affe vnto the Moyle his brother as followeth.

Brother Moyle our Mother hath reafon, and fure fhe telleth thee true. Thou promifeft largely to thyfelfe. Thou feekeft when thou art caught not to lofe thyfelfe, but to catch others, with no profit to thee but hurt to others : and this is not thy

thy waye to deale. Therefore I my felfe perfwade thee now to tarie, and bidde thee not to go. She fayth true anfwereth the Moyle. But fhall I telle thee brother Affe? A fimpler beaft in the worlde than thou, liueth not. Thou proceedeft fimply like a good goofe. Thou careft for no more fo thou haue three or fower thiftels to gnaw vpon, and a little water to drinke ferueth thy turne. I pray thee tell me: are there not in the Kinges Court many meaner in all conditions than I? if Fortune haue fauoured them why the goodyere fhould fhe not alfo fauour mee? if I had not manye times feene (fayde the Affe) a little Affe eate a great bundell of ftraw, I would yeelde to thee, and confirme thy opinion. But woteft thou what? a little Axe ouerthroweth a great Oke. The arrowes for the moft part touch the heigthes, and he that clymeth vp to the tops of trees, falling hath the greater broofe. But I fee deare brother Moyle thou fhakeft thy heade at me, and that thou little forceft my wordes: and fure I were a great and monfterous beaft to perfwade myfelfe to obtayne that, which our Mother coulde neuer reache vnto. But fith it booteth not to perfwade thee, and that thou art felfe willed and bent to goe to the Court,(compelled thereto by a naturall inftinct, which for the moft part driueth euerie one headlonge forwarde,

warde, and that thou canſt not ſhunne it) I will yet ſhewe thee what fauour and helpe I can: but by the waye take this leſſon.

For the firſt thing thou ſhalt flie ignorance, which euer ſitteth ſtill and doth nothing, and hath two great eares as thoſe of mine thou ſeeſt, but hir feete take part after the Griffin, and part after the Aſſe. One part ſignifieth that the ignorant are familier Aſſes, & the other that they are greedie of honor, and of the profit of good deſeruing beaſtes. Thoſe long eares ſignifie the ignorant, which will heare all others doings, and beleeue they knowe all thinges. Thou muſt alſo be true to thy maiſter, and when thou art once retained in ſeruice, thou muſt not betraye thy Lorde for any golde or corruption in the world. For many times thoſe that are in fauour with Princes, and neare about them, are ſought vnto to practiſe to poyſon them, to kill them, to doe them ſome miſchiefe, or alſo to robbe them of their treaſure, and to ſubvert their whole ſtate. For no reſpect in the world, whileſt thou art in ſeruice, (nor after) ſee thou deceive him not of a mite. I do aduiſe thee alſo to be pacient. For theſe Lordes and States I tell thee for the moſt part are fantaſticall, and I marueile not at it at all: for in deede the Princes matters and affaires

doth

doth fo occupie and trouble their heades that God knoweth they are full of paffions, and can yee blame them? Therefore fometimes, will they nill they, they looue and hate againe. And when thou perfwadeft thy felfe (by reafon of a fewe fmyling lookes they haue ouerwhile giuen thee) that thou art in high fauour, then they feeme not to knowe thee. And thou mufte alfo looke after recompence of thy feruice, though vnhappily thou haft perhaps beftowed fiue and twentie yeares time, and thy youth withall, and yet notwithftanding haft not beene the better a rufh for al this: and another in foure daies is made riche. For thus thou fhouldeft but wrappe thy felfe in care to thy vndoinge and yet the thing nothing remedied. And what? they will not fticke to playe thee many of thefe pranckes. Therefore he that cannot beare it paciently, lifteth vp his head, and a flie lighteth on his nofe, and byteth him with thefe and fuch like Courtly graces, & fo goeth his way: fo he that loofeth his time and yeres. Pacience therefore that oft goeth to fleepe with Hope, bringeth thee at leaft to fuche ende as thou art not ware of, and fome time it carieth meate in mouth & getteth thee fomewhat. Feare generally muft be thy right eie to guide thee with. Thou muft feare the enuie of Courtiers, for they will make thee
ftumble

F

ſtumble and laye thee flat on the ground vpon thy noſe. And the more thou groweſt in fauour with thy Maiſter, and that he giueth thee, and make thee fatte in purſe: ſo much more take thou heede to thy ſelfe, and looke about thee. Now marke well what followeth.

The vnthankfulneſſe of Maiſters.

Buriaſo (one of our corporation) was a certayne beaſt that if thou hadſt knowne him, thou wouldeſt rather haue taken him for a ſlouenly beaſt than a man. He brought vp a Soowe and made ſo much of hir that he himſelfe fedde hir with one hande, and with the other he clawed hir. And when this Soowe had often times brought him Pigges, and that good ſtore at a farrowe, he ſtyed her vp and fatted hir, and when ſhe was fat, (forgetting the loue he bare hir) he ſticked hir, and in time eate hir. There are ſuch like Maiſters that clawe thee with one hande, that is, they giue thee faire wordes: with the other they feede thee, to weete, they giue thee draffe. And when thou haſt ſerued them (which is vnderſtanded by the bringing foorth of Pigges) a time and ſpent thy youth: and if Fortune be thy friende, then they giue thee, and make thee riche: If thou die before thy good happe, farewell thou, ſo much is ſaued.

If

If thou liue long, and art growne fatte, some blast of displeasure may call thee to *Coram*. So art thou chopt vp, the lawe proceedeth on thee, and shortly all the fatte and grease thou hast gotten before melteth into the Princes Cofers. Howbeit, I may tell it to thee (be it spoken without offence of beastes of vnderstanding) there is good prouision made to the contrarie now adayes. For what so euer becometh of themselues they make all sure that they can: let the carkas go where it will, the fatte and grease they haue gathered is betimes disposed to others for feare of that they looked for. And thus all thinges are preuented by polycie. I say no more. This is the worlde, and so it goeth. Keepe this in minde and harcken further.

If fortune fauour thee so that thy Maister make such account of thee, as he commeth to aske thy counsell in anye thing: doe not as many Counsellors doe, and those that are in estimation with Princes: which thinking to please them, giueth them counsell according to the profite they finde for them, and according to the Princes passion, I maye not saye, will, and right. But bee thou bolde to say truely and vprightly, not looking in any bodies face. If thy Maister shoulde happen to frowne vpon thee, and that he were angrie, in

anye

anye wife holde thy peace, and replie not againe
as others doe, neither fhake thy heade as though
thou miflykedeft, but get thee out of fight as
thou wert not hee. Neuer be afrayde of bend-
ing his browes, or of a frowning looke, as longe
as thou ftandeft vpright, that is: that thou
proceedeft truly and honeftly in thy doings.
Sometimes they giue thee faire words, and do to
thee as the fowler that catcheth Thrufhes that
cried out for colde of his handes amongeft the
boughes: and the Thrufhes that were in the cage
to make a noyfe, fayde that he cried for that he
was forie they came to ftoope to the Birdlime.
No fayde a little Birde looke to his handes, and
let his eyes alone. Take alwayes heede to the
doinges and not to the wordes. Knoweft thou
not of the Quaile that hunge out of the windowe
in a Cage, and a fparrow-Hawke feeing hir,
ftooped downe to the Cage, and fayde to hir,
Daughter mine, be not afrayde, make no noyfe,
for I bring thee good newes: and began to tell
hir ftraunge and pleafant fables, and in the meane
while with hir talentes fhe beganne to teare the
wyers of the Cage. The Quaile leauing to give
eare to hir bablinges, feeing hir woorking well
ynough, began to be frowarde, and to beftirre
hir. Inafmuch as hir Maifter hearing hir flut-
tering in the Cage (knowing there was fomewhat
about

about hir) ranne to the windowe and fo faued hir. Truft not therefore I faye the words of fuch, but beleeue their doings, and alwaies fay & do thou well: Giue good counfell, and be alwayes prayfing of thy Maifter. And if thou fee him take vppon him anye enterprife for his profite and reputation, commende it, and exalte it: affift him, and encourage him to it. Thou muft be wife alfo thou reache not to farre, that thou take not more vppon thee than thou art able to difcharge, but alwayes keepe thee within boundes, if fortune fhould neuer fo little fauor thee. For the fauor of the Maifter is a hill full of goodly flowers, and wonderfull fruites and plantes. But in this hill there dwelleth moft cruell and terrible beaftes. Some fpitteth forth furie, fome poyfon, one fpitteth fire, another fmoke: fo that thou muft alwayes bee armed to defende thyfelfe, or elfe that thou may not be offended.

The Moyle being weried with the cumberfome wordes of the Affe his Brother, cutting off his talke, as one whofe iudgement with ambition was corrupted, he tooke his heeles, and on his waye to the Court he flingeth to this princely King and Lion. And being come vnto his Maiefties prefence obferuing all maner of duties

and

and reuerances pertinent to fo royall a throne (as his fubtill and craftie Moilefhip knew well ynough to doe) euen forthwith he crept into his bofome, and got into his fauor, faying thus. The fame of your Royall Maieftie which runneth through the world, hath made me not onely to come to humble myfelfe, and to doe my dutie, but alfo to offer your highneffe my feruice: putting him in remembrance alfo that many yeares agoe (in their firft yong flourifhing age) the Affe his brother and he were verie familier with his Maieftie : and in maner all one with him. And fhewing him that he was able to doe his Maieftie feruice in many things, he kiffed his feete, and offered him armour and horfes to ferue his Maieftie and the Realme: adding thereto, that it woulde pleafe his highneffe to accept his poore offer: faying that a little toothpike doth feruice to the greateft Prince, which he alwaies occupieth in his mouth, being reckened one of the chiefeft places a man hath.

The Moyle's words greatly pleafed the King, and turning to his Lordes hee fayde. Sure my Lordes mee thinketh he hath a deepe iudgement & capacitie, and as I remember in their very youth his brother and he had excellent wittes, and fee I pray you now how trimly he is come forwarde : I
promife

promife you he hath fpoken verie clarkly. Surely he is able to doe vs good feruice at all times when we call him. And to conclude my deare Lords, vertue cannot longe bee hidden, albeit for a time by fome euill accident it be oppreffed. Flame and fire alfo couered with violence, when it burfteth out againe, fheweth the greater, and maketh waye where it commeth. Beholde how orderly hee came to me. And though we cannot knowe his inwarde minde, and that it were not that it fheweth: yet is it fitting for a noble Prince to entertaine him that commeth, not knowing him at all. Although the Needle pricketh, yet a man occupieth it to ferue his turne, and is as neceffarie as a Knife. Wee will place euery one in his rowme. The firft feate is for the Elephantes, the other for the Camels; the Apes in their place, and fo forth, to vfe eche one according to his degree and calling. For the nailes may not be placed where the teeth are, nor the teethe where the eyes ftande, much leffe the eyes in place of the heeles: but let euery member doe in his place his office pertayning to him. A man to feede Serpents, were a ftrange fight and perillous. For he fhoulde not only ftande in danger to haue his hande deuoured of the Serpent, but to be flaine foorthwith alfo with his fpitting poyfon. Our common weale is like vnto a bodie which

diuerfly

diuerſly doth occupie diueres meanes. The eares goe not, the feete heare not, the nailes crye not, neyther doth the tongue ſcratch or giue any helpe, as doth the office of the nayles. In thoſe Cities where theſe tame beaſtes doe dwell: they make not Rattes to ketche Hennes, nor Hennes ketche Hares, or Garden wormes ketche Flies, nor Flies ketch Graſſhoppers, but euery one doth his office. The Catte taketh Miſe, the Grey hounde the Hare, the Foxe the Hennes, the Hounde the Foxe, the yong the olde: The ſparrowe Hawke flieth at Quailes, the Goſhawke at Pheaſants, and the Falcon at Partridges. I haue a ſmall Court, and a little Realme, but for thoſe fewe beaſtes of heade that I keepe, they are able to doe ſeruice, in reſpect of other Princes, which kepe a rabblement of raſcals & miſerable wretches, with little honor, and great ſhame. I better like my little and fruitful countrie, than a greater being barren: yea, & I am one of thoſe that loue a good ſeruante, though he be a ſtraunger, as I doe thoſe of mine owne countrie. The fruites of our ortcharde are good, and thoſe that are broughte farre of are not yll. If we ſhoulde feede of no other but of our owne fruites, we ſhould ſeldome fill our bellies: ſaying, I will none of them bicauſe they are none of ours. Then turning to the Moyle, with a certaine
                                                                            louing

louing afpect, he followed on his tale. The worthinefs of the minde and vertue, is that that is to be efteemed. That fure is the knowne fhielde and armes of the true Gentilman, and not the greatneffe. The King in deede of right ought to imbrace men of fuch vertues and qualities, rewarding euery one according to his merits, and not to fhew partialitie to any, and to banifhe out of his court all thofe that feeke for *fingularum comodum*, never to repute them for his friendes, nor to accept them for fervauntes. After thefe and a fewe other wordes hee fpake, he tooke his leaue of his Lordes, and withdrewe him felfe into his withdrawing chamber (as all Princes of like eftate are wont to doe) calling the Moyle to him, and fecretely they communed. Who when he faw the King make of him, and that he layde his faourable hande vppon the croope of his malice he wagged his tayle, aduancing him felfe in his Affe like maner, and finely couched in Rethoricke his cloked flatterie: and when he fawe his time, he fpared not to fpeake, and thus he fayde.

Of the Turkie Cocke and what happened to him.

A Turkie Cock (one of the faireft, of the braggeft, and alfo the ftatelieft in all our quarters)

quarters) was taken prifoner in the battell of
the Pigmies, and was folde to the King of
Pheafants with condicion to be ranfomed. Who
feeing fo fantafticall a beaft with fo great barbs,
which fometime were a pale blew, fometime a
fkie colour, now changed from that to white,
and then to black againe, he wondered to fee
thofe fodeine chaunges: and more beholding
his fwelling and raifing up his fethers, putting
forth that horne of flefhe, he fayde he neuer
faw before fo goodly a woonder. And talking
a little with him, hee founde him of a bigge
voyce, of fewe wordes, but refolute, fo as hee
made much of him. And wote ye what? thither
came a number of beaftes of his countrie (vnderftanding of his captiuitie) to ranfome him. But
he being high minded, and reputing himfelfe
the chiefe Birde of the dunghill (as true he
was) would neuer fay he was a prifoner, but
that he was amongft the Phefants for his pleafure, and thus difpifed their fauor and the helpe
of them all. On a time there came a friend of
his to him, and fecretly offered to giue him
(that no man fhould know it) fo much golde as
fhould redeeme him out of prifon. But he refufed it, and woulde none of it, bicaufe he
would not feeme to be a prifoner. In the ende
(neceffitie enforcinge him, and remembring his
cafe)

caſe) hee was contented to be counſelled by that faithfull and louing friende of his, and cloſely tooke the money (that in fine doth all) and payde it, and ſo departed. For if he had continued in that fooliſh reputation of him ſelfe ſtill, and had dwelled in his obſtinacie, he had perhaps dearly bought the price of his follye. It may peraduenture ſeeme to your Maieſtie that I paſſe the boundes of modeſtie, if I ſhould open to your highneſſe my meaning hereby. I come as your Maieſtie's humble and faithfull ſeruaunt, and true friend, to tell your Maieſtie that I am ſorie to ſee you go no more abrode a hunting, a walking, and ſporting yourſelfe at your pleaſure as you were woont, but that you keepe your Pallace ſtil with malancholie, which was not your woont I knowe. Well, I ſtande nowe before your highneſſe readie to ſpende my life and goods in your ſeruice and quarell: and if I might knowe your griefe, I make no doubt at all but I woulde labour ſo, that your Maieſtie ſhould be ſatisfyed, and lyke of my ſeruice. If you be troubled for any matter concerning the ſtate, or any other thing of importaunce: your highneſſe muſte impart it with a fewe of your faithfull ſeruants, and ſuch as you truſt beſt. And although they be of the meaner ſort, yet they maye ſerue your Maieſtie with hartie looue

and

and good will, and doe their beft indeuour. I
haue prefumed vnder you Maiefties good licence
to faye thus much, bicaufe I recken myfelfe to
be one of the faythfulleft feruaunts your Maieftie
hath euer had, or now retayneth.

The Lyon, as King of beaftes, and that knew
before of the wilde Bores report the nature and
propertie of this mightie beaft the Bull, mooued
not a whit at thefe wordes, but wifelye hid that
inwardly which hee openly vnderftoode; and
with large wordes and new deuifes fayned diuers
his perticular accidents, faying that he was not
well at eafe, and founde himfelfe fubiect to his
ordinarye ague. And thus the King and Moyle
difcourfing togithers (a happie chaunce for the
Moyle, and an yll happe for the Lyon) the Bull
that was harde at the Court gate gaue three or
foure terrible lowes that the Lyon fhooke agayne
to heare him as one that was more afrayde now
than he was before, by reafon of the great noyfe
and rebounde of his voyce: and not able any
longer to hide his griefe, he fayde. This voice
fo bigge and terrible runneth throughe my
whole bodie, and in counfell I tell it thee,
(knowing thy troth and fidelitie to me) I promife thee I am afrayde of my Kingdome: and
my reafon is this. That feeing the voyce of this
fearefull

fearefull beaſt is ſo great (as thou heareſt) it is lyke his bodie is aunſwerable to the reſt, which if it be, I am in no ſafetie. And now without further ceremonie thou knoweſt the whole cauſe of my ſodeine chaunge and feare, therefore in this caſe I would be glad to heare thy opinion and iudgement.

Mightie Prince, if no other noueltie or occaſion haue cauſed you to refrayne your pleaſures but this voice which I haue heard, me thinketh it is but ſmall and not to be accounted off. Your noble courage ſhould not be afraide of anything before you know it, and what it is, and whether it be to be feared or not: as I will let your Maieſtie knowe by this tale I will tell you ſeruing for the purpoſe.

Of the Foxe and his fooliſh feare.

A foxe with all his familie chaunged his hole, and got him to another, and harde by the ſame, there was a little cottage, where dwelled a .xxv. Muleters with their Moyles, and euerye morning betimes they came to lade them. You muſt vnderſtande that the noiſe of theſe ſundrie ſortes of belles and other trappings that they put aboute theſe beaſtes, made all the countrie
                                          ringe

ringe with that mad noyſe. The Foxe hearing the ſounde of thys yll fauored noyſe ranne quickly to hide himſelfe in hys hole, where he lurcked ſtill till the noyſe was gone: which was ſuch, that it feared the Pullen, and ſcared him from his pray. One day this Foxe being on the ſide of a hill, hearde againe this fearefull noyſe of belles, and lifting up his heade to looke about him, there he ſawe theſe bleſſed Moyles comming with their belles, and laughing to himſelf, was aſhamed of his ſimplicitie. The ſame ſaye I vnto your Maieſtie, that my opinion is, that this your Maieſties feare is ſuch a like fantaſie: and bicauſe your Grace ſhould be informed with ſpeede of this matter (aſſuring your Grace to kepe your griefe ſecret) I doe offer my ſelfe, if it ſtande with your pleaſure to goe abrode into the Countrye, and to diſcouer the thing vnto you. And ſo ſoone as I ſhall haue knowledge of the beaſt and of his qualitie, I will forthwith aduertiſe your Maieſtie howe it ſtandeth, what the matter is, and how this geare goth about. And you ſhall know it euen as it is, I will not miſſe a iotte, leaſt you ſhould be informed contrarie of ſome timorous beaſt, taking one thing for another. Therefore I beſech you ſir comfort yourſelf, and let him alone that knoweth it: and thus he tooke his leaue, and
trotted

trotted from the king. The king highlye commended his counfell and aduice, and willed him to difpatch that he had promifed.

This worfhipfull Moyle was fcant out of fight, but the Lyon beganne to haue Hammers in his head, and to imagine a thoufande ftraunge deuifes, and grewe in choler with himfelfe, fufpecting and fearing both at one time: and fayd. Well, what and he double with me? yea, and how if he beguile me with his cloked colour to doe me good? fure his foothing words doe not like me, mee thinketh he is to full of them. May not hee tell him with the terrible voyce, that I am afrayde of him? and out of doubt for as much as I can imagine, he cannot but be a beaft of a marueylous ftrength: and adding thereto the others treafon, it is another maner of thing than to be but afrayde only. For betweene them both they may vtterly vndoe mee. Many other mifhappes fall out in this bucke, that if I had not this thought (feeling my feare) might happen. And peraduenture too this beaft is enimy to the Moyle, and wil fet him vpon me, to thende that I fhoulde reuenge fome injurie done him: and if he be as vnhappie as he feemeth for, out of doubt hee will not fayle to put a flea into his eare. Sure I fhall be driuen
to

to flie and haue the woorfte. O wretch that I am, what haue I done? alacke I fee I haue done amiffe, I have taken a wrong Soowe by the eare, and fo going in the darcke I muft needes fall. And thus the Lion out of one doubt leapt into two or three more, and ftoode betwixt life and death, with no leffe hope than great feare. Hee went vp and downe his Pallace like one halfe lunaticke, fretting and chafing, now aboue, then beneath, ftill looking for the Moyles coming, which had broken his appointed houre with the Kinge: yet at length looking out at a windowe (which opened to the playne fieldes) he efpied the beaft comming with a wondrous ioy. His Moylefhip brauely yerked out with both legges, and liuely fhook his eares and head. He brayed and flong as he had bene madde. The Lyon as though he had not bene grieued at all, returned againe into his place, and looked for the Moyle. Who arrived, was receiued ioyfully, and with good countenance of the whole court. The King after thefe graue folemnities and ceremonies done, retired into his withdrawing chamber with the Moyle: and vnderftanding by him that this beaft the Bull was faire, gentle, and pleafant withall, (and that for no refpect he fhould once feeme to fufpect any thing in him, but if it had bene

his

his Maiefties pleafure he would rather have brought him to his prefcence to haue done his dutie to him) hee reioyced much, and for very loue and kindneffe imbraced and kiffed him an houre long togither. And hearing by him that this Bul was wife, and of good capacitie, and able well to execute; hee fent him backe againe with charge to bring him to the Court, at leaft to vfe all meanes and perfwafions he coulde poffible to bring him thither. The Moyle putting on a newe paire of fhooes to doe the Prince feruice, galloped as he had flowne, and ftraight he was with the Bull, whom he founde lyinge in the fhadow, chewing of his cudde: and the Moyle lying downe by him began to talke in this maner.

O faire Bull, and more than beloued brother: knowe thou I am Secretarie to the King of all vs vnreafonable beafts, and am fent to thee from the Lyon moft puifant and mightie, not only of men, but of ftrength aboue all other vnfpeakable. And as a friende I come to tell thee, that this gronde thou feedeft on, and dwelleft in, is not thine, but pertaineth to his Maieftie. By reafon whereof he hath manye times put himfelfe in armes, and affembled his force, with minde to giue thee battell, and chafe thee out of his
Realme,

G

Realme, and peraduenture to take thy life from thee alſo. But I that am to him as I am (it maketh no matter:) was a meane vnto his Maieſtie (as it is a part of all honeſt beaſtes) and tooke vpon me this iourney to thee, and haue promiſed the King in thy behalfe (I knowe thou wilt not deceyue mee) that thou ſhalt come vnto his Maieſtie, adding further too, that if thou hadſt knowne his Maieſtie had bene at hand (as he was indeede) I was bolde to ſaye thou wouldeſt haue come to his highneſſe, & humbly haue done thy dutie to him. Aſſure thyſelfe he is a King that honorablye entertaineth, rewardeth, and requiteth any ſeruice done him by his faithfull ſeruants, and he is not alſo forgetfull of his friendes good willes. And if thou wilt be but ſuch a beaſt as thou oughteſt to be, I warrant thee thou ſhalt ſet thy foote by the Kings and bee no leſſe thought of than he, and will he nill he thou ſhalt be as well fedde euery day as hee. If thou wilt not come aduiſe thee, I haue ſayde, thinke vpon it: thou art olde ynough, there fore thou knoweſt or ſhouldeſt knowe what thou haſte to doe. He is King here and will bee King too. If thou wilt not ſhewe thy ſelf a ſubiect, the Kinge is to doe as he thinketh good, and ſo I leaue thee. The Bull that had no more the white fome in his mouth and had loſt his luſtie courage,

courage, wanting his yong and wonted force, confidered of it like an aged bodie, as hee had bene a gelt Oxe that had drawne in plough a xij yeares, and aunfwered many wordes confufedlye, running from one thinge to another, and thus they went debating and kneading of the matter togithers a good while: the Bull ftanding rather in feare than hope; which feare this Moyle with hys true reafons brought out of his heade againe. The Bull perfwaded by the Moyle was contented to go with him, relying ftill upon his promife. Who gaue him his worde that he fhould by this iourney (in goinge to fhewe his duetie to the King) haue no maner of hurt, neither in word nor deede: and this promife alwayes kept, he fayde he woulde willinglye abide with the Kinge. Then the Moyle bounde his promife with a folemne othe and that with as great an oth as a Moyle might fweare by: and that was by the eares of the Affe his brother. And then touching their feet togithers (I would faye handes in beaftes is vnderftanded) they kiffed in the verye mouth euen with their tongues, and fo went on the neareft way. The King ftanding in his ftately Tarras, (mounted in the higheft place of his Princelie Palace) looking rounde about the Countrie, thinking it a thoufande yeares till he fawe this mightie Bull: beholde he fpied
the

the Moyle comming and the faire Bull by his ſide, marching demurely with his harde horned heade, that in ſhow he ſeemed a great Lorde. Then ſayde the King to himſelfe. O, what a goodly proportioned beaſt is hee? My Kingdome without his force were nothing. And euen in

that moment at the firſt ſight hee fell in loue with him. And nowe come to the Kinges preſence, this Bull kneeled downe, kiſſed his hande, and ſaluted him: and did ſo finelye and cunninglye excuſe his negligence in comming to his Maieſtie, that the Lordes ſtanding rounde about

about the King were rauifhed with his wordes, they did fo pleafe them. The King bade him ftande vp, and willed him to tell the caufe why he kept fo long in thofe fieldes, and what hee ment to braye and rore fo terribly. The Bull tooke vpon him the oratores part, and ftanding afide from the beginning to the ende he tolde him the whole difcourfe of his miferies. So that the whole auditorie pitying his mifhaps became his friends. This Bull in his Oration, fhewed him felfe to be a great Bacheler in Rethoricke, a great Maifter in Arte in grauitie to expounde things and a marueylous high hill of eloquence. The King wondering at his yeares, commanded ftreight ftables fhould be provided for his Lordfhip, and gaue him an infinite number of feruaunts to wayte upon him, making him Prince of Bulles. Dukes of Beefes, Marqueffe of Calues, and Earle and Lorde great Maifter of Kyne: and with a wonderfull great prouifion he furnifhed hys rackes yearly, and made hym of his priuie counfell. After he had imployed him a while, hee knewe his worthineffe and difcretion : fo that in the ende he made him Viceroy & greateft Lorde of his Realme.

This Moile alfo that liued in Court in feruice of the Prince, more than a fewe good wordes,
courteous

courteous entertainement, and familiar acceſſe he had to the King hee could neuer get landes nor poſſeſſions: howbeit he obtained many pretie ſuites of the Kinge, nowe for one man, than for another. Further, he was ſo bolde and familier with him that hee woulde not ſticke to giue him worde for worde, nor forbeare him an inche. And paſſed many things by the Bulles meanes, which his mightie Bulſhip gaue him gratis, for that he was as a ſworne brother to his Moileſhip. In the ende this Moyle growen thus great began to looke hie, and prouinder pricked him ſo, that like a beaſt (forgetting himſelfe) he muſt needes take vpon him to reproue his Maieſtie of parcialitie, and ignoraunce; and hauing no bodie that he might truſt to breake withall he was ready to burſt for anger. Wherefore he was forced to ſeeke oute the Aſſe his brother, and to make him priuie to the matter, knowing he had none ſo ſure a friend to him whom he might truſt but he. When they met, he beganne to tell him at large his whole griefe and trouble, complayning of the ingratitude of the King all at once, that he had ſo long followed his tayle, and had neuer any thing of him worth his trauell; and if I had done no more but brought him out of the feare he was in, and to bring the Bull to his preſence. And here hee poured out to the Aſſe a worlde
of

of wordes, fayings, and deedes. The Affe that heard him all this while, began now to fpeake.

I tolde thee ynough that thou wouldeft be to bufye in matters: in faith brother thy braine fwimmeth nowe. Thou muft not be fo fonde to take all flyes that flye in the Court: Thou fhouldeft haue confidered this in the beginning brother mine, (but thou wouldeft not be ruled). And haue perfwaded thy felfe that this fhoulde happen to thee and woorfe. Thou wert a verie beaft, a beaft thou haft fhewed thyfelfe, and a beaft thou wilt continue ftill, but it fkilleth no matter, as thou haft brewed fo bake, and there an ende. If thou wilt not be called by the Kinge to deale in his matters, why doft thou (foole) put thy hande in the fire, and meddleth with that thou has naught to doe? Thou that mighteft haue liued quietly at home & at eafe: what the goodyere ayleft thou to clyme to the toppe of trees? See nowe what thou haft done, and whereto thou has brought thyfelfe: quite out of fauor with the Prince. Neuer fharpe thy tongue if thou wilt not haue it cut thy hande when thou occupyeft it. What knoweft thou whether the Bull lay this heavy burthen on thee, knowing now thy double dealing with him in his comming to the King? Well doe as thou wilt, if thou carie a Snake in thy bofome, what

can

can I doe withall? Mee thinketh this thy mifhap is much like to that that happened to the holye man in the other mountaine by a theefe of that countrie: and bicaufe I would haue thee knowe it to ferue thy turne another time, thou mayft heare it.

In the top of *Pirinei* Mountaynes, harde to *Pampilona,* a Citie of *Nauarra,* in a mountayne called *Verrucola dell amiraglio* (where the Deuill left *Malagigi* the notable coniurer when hee brought him to the iourney of Roncifualle) there dwelled a folitarie man giuen altogither to the contemplation of the high and celeftiall things of God, who was vifited for his holyneffe and doctrine of all the countrie. So it fell into the King of *Canetteria* his heade to go fee him alfo, and thither he went. Who when he founde him deepe in iudgement of high myfteries (as he was moft ignoraunt in bafe and mean things) he gaue hym great treafure to buylde and fuftaine him without trauayle. An olde long practifed and beaten theefe hearing of this richeffe, imagined ftreight with himfelfe to ketche two Doues with one Beane; and one nyght he toke his iourney towardes this holy man, and when hee was come to him, pitifully bewayling the yll lyfe he had led, he prayed the fielye foole to keepe

keepe him company in his prayers, and to teach him the good and holy commaundements of the lawe. And forthwith he gaue himfelfe to fafting and prayer. So that this holy and fimple man thought he would haue loft his wittes, and thus with his cloked deuotion by little and little he made himfelfe maifter of the houfe and riches. One night this ftowte theefe caryed awaye a great fumme and value, cleering the houfe of all that was ought woorth (as a Barbers bafin) and bought him a Hogge. This holy deuout man ryfing in the morning, and miffing all his necef- faries, hee wondered with himfelfe, but moft of all hee mufed that all his golde, filuer, and things of value were fhrunke awaye. Yet hee had fuche a heade that he ftraight thought vppon the malice of his vnhappie fcholler, lamenting much the loffe of this ftrayed, or rather alto- gither loft man. But to heare of him agayne he wandered through many a countrie, carefully feeking vp and downe, at leaft to meete with him, though hee might not recouer his goodes, and it grieued him fore to be in the middeft of his forow, for the loffe of the one and the other. This good man being in good hope yet, met in the waye with two wylde and fauage Gotes, which were at deadlye foode togither, and tried it out by the heades for lyfe and death, to which fraye came

alfo

alſo the wylde Foxe, that ſtepping in betweene them both, lycked vp the ſtreames of bloude that fell from their harde horned heades, and tending ſtill this bloudie feaſt, not regarding the daunger he was in they fiercelye meeting their bodies togither, cruſſhed this Foxe betweene them, both ſtrayght to death, who deſeruedly payde his proude attempt. The holy man ſeeing thys chaunce, kept on his waye, and came at length to a great towne: and bicauſe it was night, bichaunce he came to be lodged in a pore old beade womans houſe that playd the Bawde, whych had laide hir egges for hir ſelfe long time before, & then was glad to haue others to lay egges in hir houſe, of which ſhee otherwhile liked to feede on and to take ſome little profit. But at that preſent time the yong faire Henne ſhe had in hir houſe at halfe of the profit, ſhe had a Cocke by hir ſelfe, and would be troden of no other. Now the Bawde ſeeing ſmall profit come of hir egges, ſhe tooke on lyke a mad woman. And the yonge Henne keeping hir ſelfe ſtill to one Cock, ſhe was not able to liue ſo on it. This made the woman madde for anger, inſomuch as ſhe detirmined one daye to giue him a remedie for this: and the fooliſh Henne hauing appointed hir friende and Louer one night, and prepared a certaine drinke to breath him in his iourney, and to make him
luſtie

luftie, it happened fhee vnwittingly chaunged it, and in lieu of hir firft and coftly potion, fhee placed where hir Louer fhould lie a receyt of *oppium*. This Cocke fleeping foundly coulde by no meanes be awaked: fo that the poore broken Maide went up and downe the chamber like one ftraught of hir wittes, and thought to go out for fomewhat to wake him, faying that he that gaue this potion had fure chaunged Violles: and going hir waye abrode to feeke remedie, the Bawde thought ftrayght to difpatch him. And hauing prepared already a Quill which fhe had fylled with fine venimous beaten powder, fhee went and put it to the mouth of this fleeping Cocke, and blewe at one of the endes to make it enter perforce into the body. But it happened farre otherwife than fhee looked for. For euen at that inftant there came fuch a blaft of winde from him that had the *oppium*, that fhe hauing hir mouth ready to blowe, receiued with the force of his winde the whole powder into hir owne bodie, which was made fo ftrong that forthwith fhee fell downe dead. And thus weening to haue deliuered the yong Mayde from him, to haue gotten the more gaine to hir felfe, fhee quit hir felfe of hir owne life. As man fhoulde neuer for any vile corruption relieue one to hurt another. For neyther doth Gods lawe nor the lawe of nature

nature beare it. And in the ende the worlde will hate such wicked meanes, though for a whyle and at the beginning it seemeth to fauor them. That this horrible fact and mischiefe was misliked the world doth know it, testified by so many written authorities: shewing that hee which gaue himselfe ouer in praye to vice, and shee for hir wicked fact, were both buried togithers in one graue. The whole Planets assembled themselues togither to consult vpon condigne and solemne punishment: bicause they would not suche wickednesse shoulde passe without memorie, testomie, and perpetuall record of eche others deede. And all ioyntly concurring togithers in consent, agreed to frame a notable Monument, as now followeth. They turned the Louer into a Moyle, and the deade Woman continuallye rode vpon him through wild and sauage countries, still laying on him with a rodde without ceasing. This holy man departed from his lodging, and the night following he came to such another, in maner greater, or at least the like. A yong maried wife intised by an olde Bawde fell to naughtinesse, and still as opportunitie serued the yong man hir Louer came into the gardein of hir pleasures. The husband being ware of hir trade, fayned to go forth, and saw all the becknings and promises: so vpon a sodain he returned into hir house and
without

without any word at all tied his wiue's belly to a naked pillar, and laid him downe to flepe behind the fame where hir Louer muft needes come in : who walking at his appoynted houre, and miffing of his purpofe, went ftraight to the Bawde, and made hir go into the houfe, which bichance had the keye giuen hir of the fore gate by this yong wedded wyfe. And when fhe came in, finding her bound, fhe vnlofed hir, and ftoode hir felfe tied in hir roume, and fent this pleafaunt wife awaye to fetch a good night. In the meane time the hufbande of this yong woman awaking, defirous to knowe how all things went, he called his wife many times, but the Bawde would not aunfwere for hir bicaufe fhe would not be knowne. The Goodman rifing up in the darke in a rage fayd, wilt thou not aunfwere me? with that he flue upon hir and cut of hir nofe. The Bawd was whifht all this while, and dare not fpeake for hir life. The yonge woman that had bene feafted abroade and fweetelye taken hir pleafure, returned home, and feeinge the olde Bawde thus vnhappilye dreffed for hir fake, it grieued hir verye fore (yet gladde hir felfe had efcaped the daunger) and fo untying hir, bounde hir felfe againe, and fent this wretched Bawde home without a nofe. The Bawde departed thence, the yonge woman called hir hufbande, and

and making pitifull mone ſhewed hir innocencie: and that this is true ſayde ſhee, beholde my face (is as it was at the firſt) made whole againe by God (reſtoring me my noſe) bicauſe I am true to thee, and to let thee knowe thou haſt done mee open wrong. The fooliſhe huſbande ranne for the candell, and found hir noſe faſt to hir face (which he beleeued he had cut off) as if he had not touched hir: and aſking hir forgiueneſſe, ever after he loued hir antierly, and thought hir honeſt. The olde Crone and Bawde returned to hir houſe with hir noſe in hir hande, and hir face all beſmearde with bloude: yet fortune fauored hir in this, that ſhee was a Barbers wyfe, and hir huſband ryſing early in the morning before daye to ſhaue the tayles of the Monckyes of Portingale (for there there groweth heare on their Buttockes, and no where elſe) called to hys olde wyfe for his Combe caſe with razors and other trinckets. Nowe ſhe being thus handled as ye haue hearde, (loth to ſhew hir ſelfe) put it to aduenture, and giuing hym all his conceytes within the caſe, ſhe reached hym the razors in his hand, the blades not put into the hafts. The poore man haſtie of his worke, in the darcke haſtilye took the razors in his hands, and all to cut hys fingers: and then for anger (feeling his fingers cut) he threw them frō him with great violence.

violence. With that this craftie olde Bawde cryed out amaine, alas, alas, my nofe. And taking one of thofe razors fhe al to bloudied it and ftraight fhewed him (hir hufbande coming with the light) the bloud, hir nofe, and razor. The hufband aftonied at this, to fee this in maner impoffible happe, fhee ftanding ftowtely to it, caufed hir friendes and kinsfolks to be fent for, & pitifully complaining to them they altogithers went to prefent this chaunce to the Lordes and rulers of the towne, and made hir hufbande be punifhed. This holy man (as one in deede that fawe this practife) loth to fee the innocent hufbande fuffer for his wifes falfe accufation: went to the feffions at the day of his araynement to witneffe a troth for the feilye man. And as he was bent to fpeake in fauour of this poore Barber, he fodeinly efpied that olde beaten theefe that had robbed him, and whom he went fo long to feeke, who was euen newlye punifhed for an olde offence he had done. This good man forgetting to follow the barbers caufe, and to doe that good he came for: cried oute vppon the Judge for iuftice agaynft the theefe (as hee that in deede had more minde of hys golde than of deuotion:) and befought him he might haue fome part of his owne that was left, fince he coulde not poffible recouer the whole. The Moyle that

all

all this while had hearde the Affes long difcourfe, replyed ftraight and thus he fayde.

O I perceyue your meaning well ynough (good brother Affe) and I knowe I take yee right. If this holye man had ferued God and not caft his whole minde on this worldlye pelfe, he had not had that loffe he hath, nor bene troubled as he is. If this carren Bawde had beene at home at hir houfe ftill, fhe had kept hir nofe on hir face. And that other Bawde to, if fhee had not minded to haue killed the Cocke of hir yong Henne, fhe alfo had not died. Laftly the theefe had not fuffered death if he had let the olde mans goodes alone: and my felfe (to fay truly) fhoulde not fuffer nowe fuch griefe, if I had but onely followed mine owne bufineffe. I graunt that if I were as I was at the firft, I would not once ftirre a foote to meddle in anye bodies matters but mine owne. But well, well, what remedie now? fince I am in for a Birde, and cannot get out, and being ready to burft for fpight I beare the Bull that he is thus made off, and fet vp: by the Maffe I will ende it one waye or other, by hooke or crooke, or it fhall coft me the fetting on, runne dogge, runne deuill. Sure as a clubbe I will rayfe fome flaunder of him, to eafe my hart burning withall, and to bring him if I may out of credite. And this
cockle

cockle that I will fow may perhaps be profitable for the King. For many times we fee that men raifed to high degree, commonly practife things hurtful to the Prince and ftate: or elfe that the fubiectes otherwhile gouerned by him they miflike, doe ftreight rebell againft the Prince. If I fet in foote, I tell thee it were well done of mee, that the Kinge might not in time receyue as much hurt of the Bull, as the Bull hath receyued goodneffe of him. The Affe lift up his head, and girned at his brother to fee his ftubborneffe: and fayde vnto him. O brother mine, I am forie for thee. I fee thou art in health, and yet thou takeft Phificke to bring thee to an Ague: for vnder the colour for letting fall thine eares in token of humilitie, thou wilt fling out apace. Better fit ftill than rife and fall. Put vppon thee honeftie and vpright dealing, let them bee euer thy beft friendes and countenance: and lift not up thy hart fo much with paffion, leaft it happen to thee, (not thincking of it) as it did to him that fhooting at rouers up and downe in the woodes (fuppofing no bodie to be there) was fhot at againe with his owne fhaft, and fo hit in the breft died ftraight. Thou playeft feeft me feeft me not, and perfwadeft thyfelfe that none will fpie thy wicked practifes, when in deede thou fhall be payde home and neuer knowe who
hurt

hurt thee. But I wonder how thou dareſt once take vppon them to offend ſuch a mightie beaſt. He is wiſe, of great ſtrength, and hath great credit, beſides that he is in fauor, and doth what he liſt: and what he doth, the King doth. O Maiſter Aſſe ſayde the Moyle, Nowe like a foole thou ſpeakeſt. Thou knoweſt nothing if thou beleeue that the greateſt perſons onely can reuenge and none others. Seeſt thou not that ſometime the ſimple and ignorant doe not regard nor aſteeme the good and vertuous: and many times doe them ſhrewde turnes and diſpleaſures? The Commons robbe the Gentlemen. But what more? the little ſometime eateth vp the great: and the Coward killeth the valiant. And bicauſe I haue hearde thee a while, and haſt alledged many fables and examples: thou ſhalt now liſten to mine another while, and ſo wee will conſult what is to be done. Jeſu thou makeſt this Bull wonderfull great, and mee but a poore beaſt and of no account, but I pray thee heare me, being poore and little as I am.

Of the Eagle and Beetell, and what commeth of ſelfe will.

In the cliftes of Mount *Olympus* there haunted a yong Leueret, feeding continually in that place: and an eagle ſpying, marked hir forme where

where fhe fate, and at a trice came downe to feafe on hir. This pore Leueret feeing hir felfe thus diftreffed vpon the fodeine, called on the Beetell that was makinge certayne little Balles, I can not tell what, and bade him helpe hir. The Beetell fiercely turning on the Eagle, bade hir get hir thence, and let hir alone, for fhe was his. The Eagle beholding the foolifhe Beetell, how he ftoode on his feete ftowtly aduancing himfelfe fmyled, and laughing ftill fedde on the vnfortunate Leueret till fhe had deuoured hir all, not weyghing the Beetell one of the woorft and leaft feathers on hir backe. The Beetell looked vppon hir, and put his finger to his mouth, and threatning hir went thence attending his balles agayne, as who fhoulde faye: tyme will come when I will bee euen wyth thee. Within a whyle after the Betell carying this iniurie in minde, fawe thys Eagle in loue, and dodging hir to hir neaft, hee came thither fo oft, that at length he founde egges, and lifting up his tayle hee beganne to rowle them vp and downe (the Eagle being abrode) and rowled them quite out of the neft, euen in maner when the yong Eagles were almoft readye to bee hatched, and with the fall the laye at the foote of the rocke broken, and quafhed all to peeces. When the Eagle returned

turned to hir neaſt, & ſawe (hauing a verie good eye) hir children in a hundreth peeces, ſhee pitifully lamented, the teares trickling downe hir cheekes. The little beaſt that in a hole ſtoode to ſee the ende of this tragedy, ſeing the Eagle take on thus heauily, ſaid vnto hir: nay, nay, it makes no matter, thou art euen well ſerued: thou wouldeſt not let my Leueret alone, and with that he ſhronke into his hole, that the deuill himſelfe could not finde him out. So that my good Maiſter Aſſe and deare brother, a man muſt beware of will: for all thynges may be brought to paſſe, and nothing is hard to him that determineth to doe it. Well yet heare another and then woonder as thou wilt. It booteth not to ſtriue agaynſt the ſtreame.

There was a Rauen that in the top of a great old tree, in a hollow place of the ſame (where none could find out hir neaſt) did euer lay hir egges. Beholde there came out of a hole at the roote of the old rotten tree a Snake, which leape by leape got vp to the toppe of the tree, and ſucked theſe egges when they were newly layde: and woorſe than that, what prouiſion of vitailes ſoever the Rauen had brought to hir neaſt, the Snake ſtill deuoured, ſo that the pore Rauen could neuer haue hir
prouiſion

prouifion fhe prepared agaynft foule weather. The foolifhe Rauen got hir to the Foxe hir coufin to afke him counfell, and when fhe had told him all and more, fhee refolued ftrayght to flie on the toppe of the Eagles heade, and to pecke out hir eyes: and therefore fhee defired to knowe the Foxes iudgement. Beware faid the Foxe, do it not: for it will not fal out as thou thinkeft. Doeft thou not remember what our elders were wont to fay: that it booteth not to ftriue agaynft the ftreame, nor preuayleth to be reuenged on him that is ftronger and mightier than himfelfe? but malice and treafon onely muft ferue that turne. Therefore lyften a little, and thou fhalt heare this notable chaunce.

Firft of felowfhips heare mee but foure wordes by the waye, and then fay on that that muft be fhall be. The Bull was euen predeftined great, thou a Moyle, and I an Affe. He that is odeyned to be a King, thoughe hee be a Plowe man, I beleue fure he fhall be King, and that heauen doth direct all things aright and not otherwife. The examples are verie good, but yet how things will fall out the ende fhall trie it. Now on Gods name, fay what thou wilt.

There

There dwelled a great Paragone of India (of thoſe that liue a hundreth yeares and neuer mue their feathers), a bird of the water, aire, and earth, in a great thicke cloſe knot of Roſemarie vppon a pleaſaunt Lake, placed beneath amongſt the little hilles spred ouer with herbes and flowers. And always in his youth he liued (as his nature is) of fiſhe, the which with ſome deuiſe hee tooke by moone light with great ſweat and labor. And nowe being aged, and not able to plunge into the water with his wonted force, he was driuen to flie in the aire and feede on
Crickets,

Crickets, which beyng fewe in number, he was almoſt ſtarued for hunger. But one day ſtanding by the riuers ſide all ſadde and malincholy, loe there commeth a great Crabbe wyth hir legges ſpred abrode to the bankes ſide which ſayde: Sir Fowle how doe you? in faith quoth he, naught at home: for we haue yll newes abrode. I pray you what are they ſayde the Crabbe? Certayne fiſhers ſayde he that within fewe dayes with ſome engines and deuiſes will drie vp this Lake and take vp all the fiſh. But I pore wretch, that yet other while had one, how ſhall I doe? I would I might ſaue them (ſince I am like to loſe them) for the benifite that I haue had ſo long time, and that I might take them out of the Lake, & flying carie them to ſome other ſurer place. The Crabbe hearing ſo yll newes, called to Parliament all the Fiſhes of the Lake, and told them this matter. The fiſhes foreſeeing the daunger at hande, had preſent recourſe vnto the wylde Fowle for counſell, to tell him howe it ſtoode wyth them: and ſayde vnto him. If this be true, out of all doubt we are in great daunger: therefore giue us the beſt counſell thou canſt, as well for the loue thou beareſt to this Lake, as for the ſeruice we looke to do to thee, honeſt Fowle. The Paragone that knew there was good paſture and a

fertile

fertile foyle, caught holde, and bitte ftreyght: faying. The great loue I beare you (quoth hee) dear brethren myne, for that I haue been bredde, fedde, and brought vp in this Lake, euen to crooked age, maketh me truly to pittie yee, and fure I am and will be ready to doe yee any good I can. Therefore in my opinion (and yee will be ruled by mee) you fhall doe beft to gette you hence, and tarye not their comming, for they wyll fpare none: all is fifhe that commeth to nette with them. And bicaufe I am practifed in the worlde (as he that goeth in euery place) I can tel you there are a thoufand places fairer than this, better, and a cleerer water, and were marueyloufly more for your profite and healthes: and if ye be contented, I wyll tell you where and how. All at once yeelded to him, and greatly commended him, (O foolifhe fifhes to beleeue fuch a beaft) prayinge him to difpatche the matter wyth as much celeritie as might be. He willed then fome of them to get vnder his pinions, and to hold faft with their billes by the fethers of his tayle, and fo to trayne them on, hee diued fo farre vnder water that they might conueniently faften themfelues in order to flie with the Fowle. And when they were mounted on his backe he tooke his flyht fayre and foftlye to the toppe of one of thofe high mountaynes,
and

and fetting them downe on the ground he eate them al at his pleafure. This manner of fifhing continued a while bicaufe it went forward day by day as he beganne, ftill filling his bellie. But the fhe Crabbe that was rather malicious than not imagined that thys Fowle had wrought fome deceite, and euen then there was a Tenche that fhe loued well ready to goe wyth the Fowle as the reaft had done before, and this Tenche was fo plumme and fatte that fhee might well ferue him for a good meale. In the ende the Crabbe fayde. O Fowle my deare brother, I would thou wouldeft carye me to the place where the other fifhes are: and hee was contented. So he gate vp on horfebacke as it were, and with hir feete clafped the Fowle about the necke, and he ftreight mounted into the fkyes, as one that ment in deede to let the Crabbe fall and breake in peeces: and euen then hee efpyed for the purpofe a heape of ftones where he thought to woorke thys feate to let hir fall. The Crabbe beholdinge the garbage and offal of thofe deade fifhes, feeing the ymminent daunger fhe was in, ftreight opened his mouth and feafed on the neck of the Fowle, holding as hard as fhee could for hir life: and fhee kept hir holde fo well, that ftreight fhee ftrangled him, and the Fowle fell downe deade, the Crabbe on his backe aliue
without

without any hurt at all. The Crabbe returned home to hir Lake, and tolde all the mifchiefe of the Fowle, and in what daunger fhe was in, and howe fhee had freed them all from his deuouring throte. Which vnderftoode the fifhes all wyth one confent gaue hir many a thanke.

The Foxe telling his tale, came to giue this counfell to the Rauen, that he fhould goe into fome neighbours houfe and fteale a Ring, but fteale it that he might be feene take it, hopping from place to place, fnatching here and there till he came into the Serpents hole. For by this meanes being afpied with the maner, euery bodye woulde runne after him, and then he fhould let it fall into the Snakes hole. They to get the Ringe againe would digge into it, and feeing the Serpent, they fhould by this meanes come to kill her. The Rauen lyked the Foxes opinion, and robbed from one a Jewell of good value, and caried it thither, whither all the yonge people ranne after him, and digging the hole, the Serpent came out amongft them, and they flue hir. And thus with one little reuenge he quited many injuiries done him. The Affe that knewe his fubtile practifes well ynough, aunfwered. And fo am I of thy opinion, fpecially if one deale with a foole, or with one that will

put

put a vifer on his face, and that imagineth none can make it fo faft and fit as himfelfe, and that trufteth altogither to his money, efteeming no bodie, and liues fitting in his chaire without any care. The Bull doth not fo, for I haue alwayes knowne him in his affaires no leffe fubtill than wife, and likes to heare euerye bodie, but fpeciallye to followe the counfell of graue men in his matters. And touching this matter I dare boldly faye to thee and affure thee, that the Bull hath a great confidence in me, bicause I brought him to the Court vnder the fafe condite of my worde, (although it needed not) and the other that I made hym, will make him beleeue me in anye thing I faye: and therefore let him come when he lift, I haue done his errant well inough I warrant ye. He reckeneth himfelfe fafe with me but I will playe him fuch a part as the vicious and wicked Foxe played another Lion (as the ftorie following reiciteth), being like to haue bene deuoured of him.

Of the Foxe and the Lion and of the Foxes deceit to kill the Lion.

There was a maruelous drougth in *Arabia Petrea*, in that yeare that the hote burninge windes were, and as I remember it was euen
vppon

vppon the making of the Leape yeare in that
countrie, and being the firſt time alſo of it, ſo
there was no water to be had any where, but
onely a little ſpring in the toppe of the Mountagne
called *Carcobite*. At that time there lay by that
ſpring a braue and fierce Lion, which as we poore
beaſtes went to the water to quench our thirſt,
ſet vppon vs, and deuoured vs, or at leaſt ſlue vs.
So that he made a Butchers ſhambles greater than
anye Butcher maketh at Chriſtmas againſt any
feaſt. Fame blewe forth this ſtraunge death and
cruelty, ſo that the beaſtes compelled to aſſemble
diſpatched ambaſſadors to the Lyon, and offered
compoſition, to giue him daylye ſome praye to
ſatisfie him with, and that they might not all die
for lack of water. The Lion accepted the condicion, ſticking to their offer, as one that had
aduiſed him ſelfe well, conſideringe that if he
had not done it, they had all dyed for thirſte, and
hee for famine, and therevpon agreed. The
beaſts drue lots, and on whome the lotte fell, hee
went his waye, to gyue him ſelfe in pray vnto the
Lion. So long theſe lottes continued that at
length it lighted on the Foxes necke to be
ſwallowed vp of this deuouring Lion, which
ſeeing no remedie but to die hee muſt (at leaſt as
he thought) he deuiſed to reuenge the death of
the reſt, and to free his owne. And forth he
                                                              runneth

runneth apace vnto this Lyon, and protrating him felfe at his feete, beganne to enlarge his olde and faythful feruice done heretofore to his auncient predeceffors, and tolde him alfo how he was fent Ambaffadour from the companie of the beaftes to fignifye to him a ftraunge hapened cafe anew at that inftant. And this it was. That the lot fell on a fatte Wether to come to paye his tribute, and by the way another ftraunge Lion met him, and tooke him quite away, faying that hee was farre worthier to haue the Wether than you, and that (prowdely) hee woulde make you knowe it. If you meane to maintaine your honor, I will bring him to you, and there you fhall determine it betweene you by the teeth and nayles. The Lyon madde at this, little fufpectinge the flye Foxes wiles and craftes, was ready to runne out of hys wittes, whan the Foxe beganne anewe. My Lorde he hath dared to faye (with fuche arrogancie) that he will chaften you well ynough, and let you knowe you doe not well, and that you fhould do better and more honorably to goe into the fielde, and there to get praye, than to tarye by the fountayne, looking that other fhoulde bring it vnto you, and as it were to put meate into your mouth. And at the laft, he fayde plainly you were but a flouch and fluggardly beaft. Come on, come on, fayde the
                                                            Lion,

Lion, fhewe me this bolde and daungerous beaft, bringe mee to him where he is without any more adoe. The Foxe that knewe a Welle where they drue up water with ropes, that the beaftes could not drink of it, brought him to the Welles fyde, and fayde. Sir, the Lion your enimie is within the Welle. He luftily leaped vp ftreight vpon the Curbe of the Welle, and feeing his ymage in the water he fierfeyle caft himfelfe into the Well, fuppofing to haue encountered with the Lyon his enemie: by meanes whereof hee plunged himfelfe into the bottome, and drowned ftreight. Which newes brought vnto the beafts, auouched for troth, they ioyfully imbraced this craftie recouered Foxe. Therefore faid the Affe, thou thinkft thou goeft in clowdes, & handleft thy matters in fuch fecret that they fhal not be knowne. But if through thy fpight and malice the Bull come to his death, what haft thou done? To hurt him that is the bountie and goodneffe of the world, it were to great a finne. Thinkeft thou the heauens beholde thee not? Beleeueft thou thy naughtyneffe is hidden from Gods fecrete knowledge? O maifter Moyle, thou art deceyued, thou knoweft not what thou doeft.

Good brother Affe fay what thou lift, I am felfe willed in this I tell thee, and out of doubt I will
bring

bring him out of the Kings fauor, or I will die for it: and tell not me of honeſtie or diſhoneſtie, Tut a figge I am determined. Happie man happie dole. Sure I will trie my witte, and ſee the ende and vttermoſt of my malice.

¶ The thirde parte of Morall Philo-
fophie defcribing the great treafons
of the Court of this
Worlde.

CAN not too muche exhort you (good Readers) to take fome paine to continue the reading of this Treatyfe, knowing how much it wil delight and profit you, hauing fomewhat vnderftanded alfo by that yee haue read before, befide that ye fhal vnderftand in reading this that followeth. Where you fhall know how much a wife Courtier may doe, and a double man, whofe ende was aunfwerable to his naughtie minde and lyfe. Which God graunt maye come to all fuch enuious and fpitefull perfons, that in Princes Courtes) (and thorowe Chriftendome) delyght in fo Vile an Arte, and to commit fo deteftable treafons. And now giue attentiue eare and you fhal heare.

Beholde

Beholde the wicked practifes and deuilifh inuentions of a falfe trayterous Courtier.

This worfhipfull Moyle when he had repofed himfelfe a fewe dayes, and had liuely framed this treafon in his head, hee went to the Kinge, and fhewed him by his lookes that hee was melincholye, penfiue, and fore troubled in his minde. The King that fawe this perplexed beaft, and dearelye louing him: woulde needes knowe of the Moyle the caufe of his griefe. Whom this fubtill Moyle finely aunfwered, and with thefe wordes.

Moft puiffant and mightie Prince, I haue euen ftriued with myfelfe to hide the caufe of my inwarde forrow, which in deede is fo much as it can be no more. And albeit I haue bene many dayes in comming to your Maieftie, feeking to eafe fome part of my trouble: yet I could neuer finde any deuife or meane to releafe my heauye and wofull heart of any one iotte therof. And this is onely growne (O noble Prince) of the great loue I beare your Grace, bicaufe it toucheth not onely your highneffe in perfon, but there with the whole ftate of your Princely Monarchie. And I that am your Maieftie's vafall and fubiect, and a louer of the conferuation of your Realme and

and Kingdome, and bounde (will I nill I) to difcharge my bownden dutie to your Honour, which the loue your Maieſtie doth beare me doth ſo commaunde. Truely the trembling of heart that I haue ſuffered hath bene extreme, night and daye continuallye vexing and tormenting me, when I haue thought of ſo daungerous a caſe. The thought that pricked mee on the one ſide was to doubt that your Maieſtie woulde not credite me, bewraying to you the daunger : and not diſcloſing it, I had not diſcharged the dutie of a true ſubiect and faithfull ſeruant to his Lorde. Compelled therefore to open (as is the dutie of euery ſeruante) all that that any way may fall out to the hurte and preiudice of the Maiſter, I come moſt humbly to ſignifie to your Grace the caſe as it ſtandeth.

A verie faithfull and ſecret friende of myne not long ſince came vnto me, and made mee promiſe him, and ſweare vnto him with great othes that I ſhoulde not tell it in any caſe, bicauſe he is a man of great honor and dignitie, and worthie to be well thought of and credited. And he tolde me that the Bull had ſecret practiſe with the chiefe of your Realme, and that he had oft priuie conference with them. And amongſt other things he tolde them all the great feare your Maieſtie had of him, diſcloſing to them alſo your
cowardly

cowardly hart and fmall force. And he went fo farre forth in termes of reproche and difhonour of your highneffe, that if his counfell, fauour, helpe, and good gouernment had not bene, as he faid: your Maiefties Realme (not knowing whether you are aliue or dead) had ben at this prefent brought to nothing. And further more he did exhort them to affemble togither for their profit, and to choofe him for their King. Saying, if they would doe this for him, he would take it vpon him to driue you out of your kingdome: and he being King woulde fo exalt them and fhewe them fuch fauor, that they fhoulde not finde him vnthankfull, befides that he would acknowledge the whole benefite proceeding from them. And moreouer (the worft is yet behind) the more part of them, I fweare to your highneffe by the heade of my brother, haue promifed with fpeede to put it in practife, and continually they deuife the way to performe it. So that inuincible Prince, take not Negligence for your guide, but preferre and entertein Diligence to preuente the traiterous prepared daunger, and to forefee the happie wifhed health of your Royall perfon. I was hee that made him promife your Maieftie fhoulde not offende him, nor once touche him when I brought him to the Court, I am he that euer lyked and loued him as my deare brother. But yet

yet am I not he that will fuffer or conceale fo highe a treafon againft my Lorde and Prince. Tract not time, moft noble Prince, in wondering at thefe thinges, but prefently put your felfe in order for your fafetie: (fo fhall you meete with your enimie, and be ready for him) leaft your Maieftie by flouth vnawares be taken tardie, as was the flow fifhe which was taken in a Lake with two others in companie. And this is a certaine and true tale that I will tell your highneffe.

Of three great fifhes, and what is fignified by them.

Almoft vpon the borders of Hungarie there was a certayne Lake that bredde fifhe of a marueylous bone, and that of monfterous greatneffe as was to be founde or hearde of in the worlde. The King bicaufe of the wonder of this Lake would not fuffer it to be fifhed at any time: but that himfelf when it pleafed him euery certaine yeares did draw it drie. The King forgetting the Lake a great time, and leauing his wonted fifhing, three fifhes grew therein of a monftrous bigneffe and vnfpeakable hugeneffe, the which feeding on the leffer eate vppe the ftore of the Lake, leauing it in maner without fifhe to what it was before. Now, as ftill it chaunceth, euery thing is knowne,

knowne, the deuouring of thefe fifhes was brought to the Kinges eare, infomuch as hee determined to goe fifhe the Lake for the three deuoring fifhes to eate them, that the frye might increafe. Order giuen to his fifhers, hee went vnto the Lake. My Lord you muft know that euerye where there is of all fortes, fome reftie, fome liuelye, fome knauifhe, fome good, fome naught, fome madde, fome fwift, fome flowe, and fo forth. I meane that of thefe three fifhes one of them was malicious and fubtill: the other of a highe minde and very flowte: and the third was flothfull and timorous. An olde Frogge that ftoode many times wyth thefe fifhes in difcourfe, to talke and play at fundrie other paftimes (the whiche knewe ouer night the drawing of the Lake) went the fame night to feeke out thefe fyfhes, and tolde them of the daunger at hande: and euen as one would haue it, they were at the table with three great Eales, although it were late, (for then Fifhes fuppe) and yet for all this newes, they ftirred not a whit, but made the Frogge fit downe, and they beganne to carrowfe when it was about midnight. So that within a whyle hauing taken in their cuppes, (bidding well for it) their heades waxed heauye, and fo to fleepe they went: Some at the table, fome on the ground, fome in one place, fome in another. At
the

the dawning of the day the Fifhers began to fpreade their nettes, and to compaffe the Lake drawing all alongft. The Eales hearing the noyfe got them into the mudde, that the verie mappe of Navigation could not haue difcouered them. The fubtill and malicious fyfhe hearing a noyfe, ranne ftreight into a dytch and entered into a little ryuer where hee was fafe from daunger of the nette. The other was not quick, for the nettes had ftopped his paffage, and bicaufe he was ftrong and ftowte, hee made as though he had bene deade, hauing his mouth full of ftynckinge mudde, and fo floted with the waues vp and down, And the thirde was called of the Frogge ten times that hee fhoulde rife and awake : whooe, but all in vayne. He punched him for the nonfte, and iogged hym agayne to make him awake, but it woulde not be. And he, tut lyke a fluggarde, aunfwered hym. I will ryfe anone, anone : I pray thee let me alone a while, let me lye yet a little curtefie and then haue with thee. Still the Fifhers went on apace with their nets, and let go the water : and when they faw this great Fifh aboue the water, floating as I tolde you, they tooke him vp and fmelled to hym, and perceyuinge hee ftoncke they threwe him from them into the Lake agayne, and caft him into the fame place where they had already drawne
their

their nettes, and fo he fcaped with life. They happened on the thirde, which was as a man would fay a certayne let me alone, and drowfie fifhe, and they tooke hym euen napping. And when they had him (thinking they had done a great act to ketch him) they caried him in hafte to the King (but by the waye I doe not tell yee of the bragges they made in ketching thys Fifhe) alyue as he was. Who commaunded ftreight he fhoulde bee dreifed in a thoufande kyndes and wayes, for that he was fatte, great, and mightilye fedde. Now your Maieftie hath hearde the tale of the flowe and fleepie Fifh, I leaue it to your highneffe iudgement and determination, to forefee the daunger, reaping the profite: or to leape into it vtterly ouerthrowing yourfelfe.

The King fet a good countenaunce on the matter, althoughe thefe newes touched him inwardly, and feemed as they had not altered him at all, and with great modeftie and courtefie aunfwered the Moyle. I make no doubt of thy true and faithfull feruice to mee, bicaufe I knowe thou canft not fuffer fo much as the fhadow of the daunger of my eftate & kingdome, much leffe the hurt of my perfon. Although many Princes and Lordes in fuch cafe thinke themfelues yll ferued: yet it is meete
and

and right that the good bee rather ledde by vertuous inſtinct, then caried away from the right through diſpleaſure receyued. I ſee thou willeſt mee good, & am ſure that the loue thou beareſt me, maketh thee ielous of the maintenance of mine honor and eſtate. Yet it hardly entreth into mee, and me thinketh it ſtraunge (ſaue that thou telleſt it me, I could hardly thinke it, much leſſe beleeue it) that ſuch wicked thoughts ſhould breede in the Bulles breſt to me, ſince by proofe I knowe him in many things both good, faithfull, and honeſt in his ſeruice: and hee knoweth beſides my goodneſſe to him, howe I receyued him courteouſly into my Court, and that he may ſaye hee is made Lorde in maner of my kingdome.

Sacred Prince (ſayd the Moyle) I beleeue in deede that the Bull thinketh himſelfe well intreated of your Maieſtie: (and good cauſe he hath ſo to doe) and that hee meaneth no hurt to your royall perſon for any diſpleaſure he hath receyued of you, or for any conceyued hate he hath towards you. And I thinke ſure he taketh not vppon him ſo fowle an enterpriſe to other ende, but bicauſe prouinder pricketh him, and maketh him luſtie to fling and play the wanton, and for that he is well he cannot ſee it, and that maketh him to deuiſe ſome miſchiefe, weening

to

to have all in his hands, faue the very title of
the King, and that this little, (hauing all the
reft) which is, alfo the moft, is eafie for him
to obtaine. I fuppofe your Highneffe hath
vnderftoode me: nowe take what way you lift.
I knowe well ynough that an Affe loden with
golde may fleepe more fafely amongft theeues,
than a King that trufteth trayterous officers
and gouernours appointed for the ftate. And
let your Maieftie bee fure of this, that that
which the Bull can not compaffe nor reach
vnto by his owne force and others, he will
certainly practife by deceit vffing fuch meanes
to bring him to it, as the Flea did to bring
the Lowfe to that paffe he brought him to,
and that he had long purfued as followeth.

A tale of the Flea and the Lowfe and how the Flea was reuenged of the Lowfe.

There lodged an old Flea in the chamber of
a great Prince, and there dwelled with him alfo
a gentle Loufe. The one continually fed vpon
little white doges of fyne longe heare, and after
hee had fylled himfelfe he retired with fafetye
all the daye, and walked at pleafure. The Lowfe
that was ftronger of bodie, and bit harder, many
times draue hir from hir pafture: So that the
poore

poore Flea was madde for anger fhee could not be reuenged. It happened that the Prince tooke to wife a beautiful yong Ladie one of the moſt delicateſt and fineſt morſels that euer Prince taſted of in the world, and in that chamber was his wedding bedde. The Flea drawne to the wedlocke bedde with the ſweete ſauour of hir bloud conueyed hir ſelfe ſtreight betweene the ſheetes, and in hir firſt ſleepe ſhe ſweetely fedde at will on this angelicall foode. Nowe ſhee bit hir yuorie thighes, then ſhee gnawed hir breeſt of congealed milke, anone ſhee ſucked hir delicate and ſoft throte, another while ſhe pretie playde hir, pinching that ſweete carcaſe, and when ſhe had filled hir bellie ſhee leaped away, and went to take hir reſt, ſhunning the day light. The Lowſe attended to fedde on Dogges fleſhe (for at that time it was the order, that Fleas fedde of men, and Lyce of Dogges) and liued in Gods peace. The Flea, whome extreme rage did gnawe to bee reuenged of the Lowſe, went to ſeeke him out with this cloked brotherly loue, and ſayd vnto him. Brother, though no cauſe mooue me to deale friendly with thee, hauing receyued continuall diſpleaſures and wronges at thy handes, yet I cannot refrayne but I muſt doe ſomewhat for thee, ſince ſo good occaſion is offered me : and I am the willinger to doe it,
bicauſe

bicaufe thou fhalt knowe I loue thee, and wyfhe thee well. Thou fhalt vnderftande I feede euerye nyght on the moft fweeteft bloud in the world: and woteft thou who it is? it is of the beautifull and delicate yong Lady newly epoufed. If thou wilt go in my companie I am contented to carye thee thyther with me, and will gladly impart my ioyes and welfare to thee: and henceforth let peace for euer be concluded betweene vs. Agreed quoth the Loufe. And with that they louingly imbraced eche others: the Flea inuiting the Lowfe, and the Lowfe accepting hir bidding. With this newe cloked reconciliation togithers they went, to the great ioye of the Flea, not for the atonement made betweene them, but for the opportunitie of time that had fo fitted hir to make hir reuenge: and the more it gladded hir to, that hir owne force and might being infufficient to encounter with his ftrength, yet fleyght and policie fupplanted and exceeded hys force. The nyght was come, the Prince and his Ladye were layde in bedde to take their reft, the Flea and the Lowfe lyke brethren leaped on the bed, and when they fawe them at reft, and faft a fleepe, they difpofed themfelues to feede, and lyke ftaruelynges in maner famifhed they layde on lode, fo that they rayfed great brode fpots like pimples, as red as a Rofe. Thefe vermins being
now

now in the only gardein of fweetneffe, continuing their byting euer in good earneft: this tender Ladie forced with their cruell and vncourteous bittes awaked perforce and foftly called hir Lorde and hufbande and tolde him. I feele myfelfe terriblye bitten this night with fome vermine, and yet I know not what it is that thus hath difeafed me. Hir hufband ftreight called vp his men, and bade them bring light. The Flea fo foon as fhe efpied light, like an olde practifer, at fowre leapes conueyed hir felfe away, and fo efcaped. The poore Lowfe that was no great horfe to leap, was taken tardie, and not able to alledge for his purgation, as a dumbe creature receyued the lawe, condemned to die, and was committed to be preffed to death between the Maydes two nayles, where for his obftinacie and prefumption fhe thruft out his blood and milke that he prefumingly had fucked of fo noble a Ladie. Your highneffe alfo maye take this example of that olde lame creature, crooke backed, yll fhaped, and deformed, which with all thefe impediments (drawing one fteppe after another) went as farre as he had his limmes and helth, though with longer time, and crept at length vnto his iourneys ende to doe any bufineffe he had. This Bull wanteth not time to further his pretence, hee will put his hande into
the

OF MORALL PHILOSOPHIE. 141

the Pye, and fet in foote when hee feeth his time. And for this time I will occupy your Maieftie no more but two words only of the Flea, which hearing the cracke of the fillie Lowfe laughed awhile at the reuenge that others toke of him for hir: and to hir felfe fhe fayd. Ah firra, gramercy my good witte yet. Thou haft done that on a fodeine for mee, that all the ftrength I haue could not bring to paffe in a long time: and nowe yet with another mans hande I haue pulled out the Crabbe out of hir hole. I am euen with him I warrant him.

Why

Why what shall wee doe then? if the case stande as thou settest it forth, what way shall we take? I will heare thee willingly, and follow thy counsell: with this condicion though, that in this interim my Realme and person be not touched, or that I sustaine perill or losse.

Inuincible Lorde, to haue any member festered and rankle, and plainly to see that if it be not cut off it will corrupt and infect the whole bodie, and in cutting it off the bodie remayneth safe and free from infection: what is he so madde that will not cut it off? The shepherde findinge in his flocke (I speake more resolutely) a scabbie and infected sheepe, doth not only cut off his legge, but riddeth him out of the way, bicause he shall not infect the flocke.

Sure this sodeine matter maketh me much muse, sayde the Lion. For one way draweth me to loue him, and that is the credit I repose in him, the long experience of his good gouernment, his vertues and wisedome, and bicause I neuer founde cause in him to detect him any way. The other thing that presseth me much, is feare: which is a great burthen. I would faine, therefore finde a way betweene both, that shoulde be betwixt loue and hate, or betwixt
feare

feare or truft, and this it is. To call (if thou thinke good) the Bull, and to examine him well and ftreightly. And if I finde him anything at all blotted with this humor, I will chaftife him with banifhment, and neuer imbrue my handes in his bloud, proceeding lyke a great and noble Prince. This determination lyked not the Moyle, as he that was fure to liue like a wretched beaft, and that his malice by this deuife fhould appeere: and ftreight he aunfwered the King. Your Maieftie hath euen lighted right on the moft ftranglingft morfell, and the hardeft Nutte to cracke: if you meane to follow that you haue propounded. For he careth not to throwe at his enimie, that beleeueth he is not feene: but ftandeth to beholde if it light right. But if he beware once he is feene, then for fhame he fticketh to his tackle, and followeth on his blowe, leaft he fhoulde be counted a foole and coward, both in his doings. And by fuch like meanes I haue oft times feene a little fparckle kindle a great fire. O my Lorde, he that fayneth he hath not bene offended, maye at his eafe and leyfure be reuenged. Contrarie to thofe that neuer bring any thing to paffe that they would, when they fpit that out with their tongue that they thinke in their heart. Therefore I am determined (if your maieftie will like my opinion)

to

to worke another and peradventure a better way. I will home to his houſe, and as a friend I will feele him to the bottome and grope his minde: and he as my verie friende alſo (and that aſſuredly truſteth me) will laye himſelfe open to mee, I am ſure of it. Such paſſioned mindes will eaſilye break out at the firſt, and they cannot keepe it in but out it muſt. They are beſides that great boaſters and vaunters. For they thinke they ſtande in deede in that degree and termes of reputation and honor that they imagine themſelues to be in, and they make large promiſes, and build Caſtels in the aire: and at euery worde they ſaye they will make thee great, and bring thee into fauor, and when time ſerueth thou ſhalt ſee what I will ſay and doe both. It will not be long to it. Well, well I know what I ſay. So that with ſuch lyke Phraſes and deuiſes, it ſhall proceede rightly. And thus in theſe traines appeere yet tokens euident inough and very notable. If he haue not capacitie and iudgement to conceyue mee, and that he euen croſſe not my meaning: I that have an ynckling of the thing already, I will be with him in euery corner, I will not miſſe him an ynch. If he rayſe men, what order he hath giuen, and whether his houſe be armed or no, yea, and I will drawe out the matter ye ſhall ſee finely out
of

of his naughtie fantafticall head. And if he go fo priuily to worke that I cannot fee him where he goes, nor know what he doth, as I am fure I know perfitely all his practifes: I will bring him to your Highneffe, and when he fhall appeere before you, you fhall eafilye finde him, for his heade is not without feare, and his fight very dull, and he will not come to you with that cheerfull countenance he was woont to looke on you before. He will be verie fufpicious and not continue in a tale, and I know your Grace fhall perceyue his malicious and fpiteful practife by many tokens euident ynough. And what knoweth your Grace whether the penne of his hart will not write all his thoughts in his forhed? as many times it falleth out vnhappily, contrarie to the difpofition of his thought that hath offended.

This fable filled the Lions heade full, and he bade him not flowe to bringe his matters to paffe. The Moyle when he fawe this geare woorke with the King, and that his brayne was fwollen for fufpicion, fayd to him felfe, Nowe good man Bul is caught, we haue him euen as we would. So forthwith without delay he went to *Chiarino* (the Bull fo called) and he was as pale and melincholye as it had rained on him. O your Moilfhip is welcome fayd the Bull: Jefu what hath become

become of your Lordſhip ſo long? In fayth you haue beene longed for at the Court, that you haue bene thus long abſent. But I doubt me we ſhal heare worſe th'an that ſeeing you thus leane and miſerably conſumed away. But I pray you how cōmeth it to paſſe that I finde ye in this wretched ſtate? you wil not maruaile I truſt I am thus inquiſitiue. For you muſt vnderſtande the loue I beare you, and partlye the dutie I owe you, (where I may pleaſure you with my countenaunce or auċthoritie) are not to be put in Salt nor Oyle to doe you good, and to helpe you if you bee in anye daunger. Leaue off this ſadneſſe of fellowſhip, and tell me your griefe, and I will vnfolde it well ynough be it neuer ſo intricate, and ſpare me not I praye you but be bolde of mee. Tut, giue me but halfe a looke, and then let mee alone. With theſe wordes the Moyle made aunſwere.

Truly faith hath left hir habitation on the earth, and bountie reigneth no more in any land: neyther doe I thinke your wiſdome can doe more or leſſe, that the heauens and celeſtial motions doe diſpoſe you to. Lorde, what a marueylous thing is this? that to come to fame and renowne by degrees of honor, it bringeth a thouſand daungers with it. We neuer (or ſeldome) doe well,

well, when we followe our owne humor or counſel. And he alſo that out of the bookes of the ignoraunt taketh forth any ſentence to ſerue his turne, muſt of neceſſitie repent him when he ſeeth his folye. All the ſtories of the worlde affirme, that a lame man can neuer go vpright. The Sages alſo agree, that the higheſt places are moſt daungerous to clyme. Therefore it is beſt euer to beare a lowe ſaile: not to hie for the Pie, nor to lowe for the Crowe.

Thy talke brother Moyle (ſayde *Chiarino* the Bull) me thinketh it verye troubleſome and ydle and without any maner of reaſon. It ſeemeth a folde of wordes that the angry hart diſcouereth, and that hee is not in good peace with hys maiſter. How ſaye ye? aunſwere me but to this.

My good *Chiarino:* thou art inſpired with the holy ghoſt, the Deuill is within thee thou haſt ſo rightly hit me. It is true the King is angrie and ſuſpecteth ſomewhat, but not thorow me I aſſure thee, nor by my meanes. Now thou knoweſt verie well the promiſe I made for thee, and the beaſtly othe I tooke which bindeth me in deede to my worde: and let it go as it will, ſure I will not breake my promiſe with my friende that I loue, for anye reſpect in the worlde, let the

worlde

worlde runne on wheeles as it lift. Therefore I will tell thee if thou hadſt not beene warned of it before. And hearken how.

Two Gotes my verye friendes, and of great iudgement came to ſee me, weening to bring me pleaſant newes, not knowing that we two are tyed as it were by the nauels together being both as one in friendſhip. And they tolde me for certaintie that the Lion our King is marueylous angrie, that he ſmoked againe at the mouth, making ſuch verſes as the cattes doe when they goe a catterwauling in Januarie, and in that furie, he ſpit forth theſe wordes. Euer when I ſee that Bull before me I am ready to fall for anger. An vnprofitable body, and no goodneſſe in him at all: brought into the world but to fill his paunch at others coſt. I can not be well, he doth vexe all the partes of me he doth ſo much offend me. Well, I will take order for this well ynough, and ſith he doth me no ſeruice by his life, I will profit my ſelfe by his death at leaſt. When I heard theſe wordes ſpoken, thou mayſt imagine whether my heares ſtoode vpright or no, and I could not hold but I muſt needes ſay. Well, well, ſuch Lordes, in faith they are lyker Plowmen than thoſe they repreſent. I ſee they ſtie the Hogge to fatte him vp, and ſo to eate him. O this his ingratitude and crueltie, (I
cannot

cannot hyde it) and his fo great beaftlyneffe
togither hath taken mee by the nofe, as if I had
met with the Muftarde pot. For thofe good
qualities of thine, for that league that is betwixt
vs (although I were fure of his Graces indignation) and bicaufe me thinke thou are betrayde,
I could not choofe but come and tell it thee.
So that good *Chiarino,* thou are great and olde
ynough, looke well to thyfelf, thou needeft not
be taught, thou art wife ynough, and there an
ende. Thou art paft a Steere, and a Bull full
growne, nay rather a fat oxe. But heareft
thou me, Gods my bones not a word for thy life:
for if thou doeft, all the fatte lieth in the fire,
and the pottage maye be fpilt and caft on the
Moyles backe.

Chiarino ftoode awhile on the ground like a
mazed beaft, as one that had bene drie beaten,
being fronted with fo malicious a deuife. Then
he layde his hande on his heart, and bethought
him of all his bufineffe and matters: as of his
gouernment, office, liuing, auchoritie, and regi-
ment: and knowing himfelfe as cleere as a
Barbers bafen, he hit the matter rightly, imagining (as it was) that fome had wrought
knauery agaynft him, and fayde. Well, go to:
there is nothing breedes more occafion of mortall
hate

hate than the vyle and flye practifes of the peruerfe and wicked. Our Court is full of anxious perfons, which ftirred vp perhaps with fpite to fee the Prince favor and lyke my feruice (being a corefey to their heart to abide it) doe wickedly practife and deuife fuch mifchiefes. They feeing (as I fay) the graces and benefites the Prince beftowed on mee, making mee honourable, and heapyng great thinges vppon mee, doe procure by indirect meanes to make his Maieftie turne his copie, and me to chaunge my wonted maners. Sure when I loke into the matter and aduife it well, it is me thinkes a thing not to be credited and makes me not a little to wonder that hys Grace without caufe is thus deceyued: yet in the ende truth I knowe wyll take place. God will not long fuffer fuch practifes. Neyther Lawe wyll in any wyfe permit that a man fhall haue iudgement before he be heard. Since I came firft as a beaft into his Highnes feruice, I neuer did anything that my confcience fhoulde accufe me in. But yet I haue as great caufe to bewayle my mifhaps come to me, as he that putting himfelfe to the fea, (and might haue gone fafe by land) was thrown on a rock and drowned: and all through his owne feeking. All they which bufie themfelues thus in Court, and run from table to table, making themfelues great with

this

this man and that man, still whispering in their eares, must (notwithstanding that the Prince rewarde them, or that he bee very well serued of them, and lyke them) looke to be touched at one time or other and vnhappilye to fall into the Princes disgrace, and perhaps to remaine so a good whyle out of favour. And this onely riseth by these double reporters and tale bearers, or by the enuie of Courtiers, which is mother of all vyce and iniquitie. I dare boldly shewe my face euery where, for anye offence I euer did the King. And if I had committed a fault throughe ignoraunce, and not of wyll: me thinkes I should not be punished neyther for the one nor the other. The counsell that I alwayes gaue him, hath euer fallen out well, and to good purpose. And if perhaps they haue not all taken such effect as they ought: he must thinke Fortune will play hir part in these worldly things. And this I saye for purgation of my vpright and honest meaning to his royall Maiestie. I am sure the Kinge will but proceede with iustice, following the steppes of the iust: the which will laye no violent handes on any beast but wyll first inquire, whether the cause be iust, who are the accusers, whether hee be a lawfull man that doth such a thing, and if the qualitie of the offence agree

with

with the conditions of the accufed, wyth fuch other lyke circumftances and ceremonies pertinent to matters of fuche importaunce. Hee that gathereth vnripe fruite, repenteth him of the marring it. Beholde the fruites eaten in Court: in the mouth paffing fweete and lufshious, but in the bodie God knoweth verie bitter and hurtfull. Lorde, howe manye doth the foolifhe vayne pompe of the worlde deceyue and abufe? I maye rightly take myfelfe for one of thofe that fcant hath tafted of the fhadowe of his fweetneffe, but I am euen filled with poyfon. The heauens beget beafts, and they ioyne togithers: but I would I had neuer ioyned with it, fince I fhall leaue it fo quickly, foole that I was, that I coulde not knowe the difference betwixt him and mee, and difcerne his nature. Go you and ferue in a ftraunge countrie a Gods name. See what difference there is betwixt hym and mee. I muft weare the yoke, and he muft breake it. I am borne to labor, and he muft fit ftill. When I haue meate giuen me I eate, and tarie not his rauening. Flies may liue abrode in the fieldes, and yet they flye into mens eyes: fo that fometime wyth death they paye for their coming, or at leaft are driuen awaye with hurt and mayme. And to conclude, I feede on the graffe, and

fill

fill mee, and hee feedeth on daintie flefhe, and fareth well.

Thefe thy wyfe reafons O *Chiarino* fincke not into my heade fayd the Moyle (as he that woulde needes make him beleeue he gaue him a remedie for his griefe, and prefented a cup with poyfon). Make no more wordes, for thou muft put to thy hande to redreffe it, and not to lament it. For yll ftande wordes in place where deedes are requifite. To fhewe his griefe fayd the Bull, and to breake his minde to his friend, me thinkes it is partly an eafe to the heart and a lightning of the minde to him that is afflicted. And fo much more is this in me bicaufe I fee my felfe in great daunger, and like to be vndone. And although the Lion delighted not in my hurt which I may fuffer, (and as thou fayft liketh him) yet the iniquity of my enimies notwithftanding wil fo preuaile againft me, that the King will giue no eare to my innocencie. And I am fure (for I fee it in the element) that the like will fall on me, that lighted on the Camell with an other lyke Lion: which tale followeth, and this it is.

In *Thebaida* (a countrie fo called) before diuifion of caues were made betweene the great and little

little beaftes, men abode with beaftes manye times in one hole, and liued lyke brothers: and men were then fo fcant that they coulde haue no other men to waite vppon them, infomuch as they tooke vnreafonable beaftes to feruice, as it is written of *Olofar* King of Knaues, which at that time did neuer other but lie alongft on the ground, and was fo floth full that he fuffered the Snakes to come and rubbe his feete to prouoke him to fleepe. Now this ydle beaft dwelled neare vnto a Caue where inhabited togithers three beaftes, to wit: A Woolfe, a Foxe, and a Rauen. I praye yee all what a foolyfhe fraternitie was amongft thefe three: and it might be fayde. The beft taketh vp the worft. This layfie knaue bichaunce got vppe one morning betimes at Cocke crowing, and hee fawe this that I will tell you now. Certayne Merchaunts paffed by with a marueylous number of Camels loden. And as a fodeine one of them fell downe for wearineffe, not able to goe anye further. Infomuch as the Merchaunts vnloded him of hys burden, and caft it on the reaft, to ech one fome, till they had it all on their backe, agayne amongft them, and fo left thys Camell behind them to the mercy of the wylde beaftes. The Wolfe, Foxe, and Rauen, chaunced to come that waye, and they fawe this poore Camell come as one that had neuer a whole ioynt in him, and

as

as it were halfe deade. The Camell recommended him felfe vnto them, and tolde them by what meanes he was brought to this miferable mifhappe. Thefe three were forie for it, and tooke compaffion on him, and as they might caried him to their Caue, where they refrefhed him with fuch confeƈtions, as were fitte for the place and tyme. And thus they kept him ftill in cure till he recouered, and patched him vp agayne. They three feeing fo goodly a morfell of flefh as this Camell was, thought it beft to prefent hym to the king, which was an olde Lion, and his palace not farre from them. The Camell hearing them faye we will preferre you to the Lion our Emperor, King, Prince, Archduke, Duke, Marqueffe, Erle, aud chiefe Lorde ouer vs, to be his page of his priuie Chamber, lyked no whitte of that eftimation and aduancement, and woulde not vnderftande the matter. Howbeit they made fomuch of him, and clawed him, that they brought him on fayre and foftly (as his pace is not faft) and he went as though one ioynt would not hang by an other. When hee was come to the Kings prefence, he humbly kneeled downe, & exhibited to his grace in writing the caufe of his coming to him, as he was before inftruƈted by the Rauen, and kiffed his hande. The Lion hearing himfelfe called inuincible,

moft

moſt puiſlant, moſt noble, right honorable, great Clerke, Suffragane, and Archking, ſhewed him ſelfe very gentle, thoſe royall termes ſo pleaſed him, and woulde not deuour the Camell as the rauening Woolfe had beckened to him, and as that ſubtill Foxe had wincked on him : but he made hym of hys Chamber, and treaſorer of his houſe. And moreouer, beyonde all their expectation, he did aſſure him wyth ſafe conduct, and made marueloufly on hym, ſtroking him a thouſand tymes vnder the chinne, and receyued him into ſeruice. This Camell that was fedde nowe with the Chariot horſes, and fared as they did, grew quite out of faſhion he was ſo full fedde, and his Cote was as ſleeke as a Mowles ſkinne. So that they that knewe him before, and ſaw him then, ſpighted him out of malice, and gaue him many an yll looke. Yea, thoſe chieflye that brought hym firſt to the Court, were they that looked moſt awrye on him.

It fortuned one day that the Lion being a hunting in a great wylde Chaſe, met with an Elephant, who beleeued and was ſure hee was the greateſt beaſt of the world, and looked in all and for all to be the greateſt King, as he was in deede the greateſt bodyed beaſt. Inſomuch as after hote wordes, they grue to luſtie ſtrokes: in the ende the Elephante ſtrake the Lion into the thigh

with

with one of his teeth, that he pierſed it quite through. So that he was forced to ſet one of his ſtubbed feete on the backe of the Lion to plucke it out, that he made him haue the ſquirt for wo he ſo ſqueaſed him, and ſaid: *Cedo bonis.* And the Elephant departed his waye for the kinglieſt beaſt of beaſtes. This battayle fell out yll for the Lyon, ſo they caried him home vpon a wheele barrow after the faſhion of the countrie, and there hee was ſtreight miniſtered vnto with ſouereygne Balmes, and within ſhort time galantly healed. The Lion continued hys dyet a while at the Woolues prouiſion, and his mealeſ were ſo ſlender that he became as leane and drie as a Kixe: that if one had put a candle light into his bodie, it would haue giuen light as through a Lanterne. After this foughten fraye betweene the Lion and Elephant, not a beaſte of them durſt once ſturre to hunt, and the Lion him ſelfe was more afrayde than before leaſt he ſhould meete with ſuch another banket. Yet being this leane as he was, and ſuch a dearth beſides, he was ſorier for his ſeruaunts, than for himſelfe. The Rauen, the Woolfe, and the Foxe that were all three in maner famiſhed, one day vnder good licence and coulour they painted theſe wordes vnto him. The benifites receyued from your Maieſtie, moſt excellent Prince, before
the

the Elephant had thus mifvſed you, maketh vs greatly to pitie your caſe. Therefore we are all determined to our vttermoſt powers to go out to prouide you of vittayles ynough and more than ſhall ſerue you. The Lion gaue them agayne wordes of *Sgratis vobis*, and that hee was rather bounde to them, with many other ceremonies: yet in the ende hee prayed them if they would doe anye thing to relieue him, that they woulde doe it quickly without delay. Theſe worſhipfull beaſtes layd their heads togither, and conſulted on the matter, and hauing imagined many and ſundrie wayes and deuiſes, and not knowing which waye to bring this geare about: the Rauen that alwayes bringeth euyll tidings, ſayd thus. My maiſters this Camell is not of our league & fraternitie, neyther commeth anything neare our maners and faſhions, nor liueth not of that that we liue of. Beſides that he is ſuch a ſtalking foole, a monſtrous gorbellied beaſt, bigge as a houſe, and a laſie lowtiſh thing: & we are wiſe, malicious, valiant, and ſtrong. So that betwixt our peruerſe fantaſie and his fooliſh vnderſtandinge there is as much difference as betwixt water and lande. Were it not beſt to ſhew the King that in this neceſſitie hee myght doe well to eate him, and the rather for that he is verie good fleſhe, and fatte as a crammed capon.

capon. If any will obiect and say he doth all in the Court, and manigeth the whole affayres of the Realme, O beware what ye doe. Then may we anfwere. What lacke or myffe fhall the Realme haue of any fuch paunches? What wonders or feruice doth he more than others? How faye ye, how lyke yee my opinion: faye I not well? Yes fayde the Woolfe. And I like it the better bicaufe of his heigth and ftature. For I warraunt you, a good fkeyne of threede and fomewhat more will not meafure his length he is fo tall, but all the better for vs. For there is fo much meate on him that when the Lion hath eaten all the flefhe (which will fill him, truft to it) and taken his pleafure, the fhauing of the bones will ferue vs well eyght dayes. The Foxe was of contrarie opinion: and wifhed rather they fhould driue a nayle in the heade of him, to ridde him out of the waye, fo that dying of himfelfe they were fure no bodie woulde come and eate of him, and much leffe fufpect that hee were made away. And thus fayde hee we three fhall have meate ynough to chawe on, to ferue vs gallantly for a moneth, and fare lyke Lordes. Tufhe as for the Lions good grace, let his King-fhippe fhift as he lyft, neuer take thought for him: Gods Lord is not he King? he may take and leaue where he thinkes good. O thou foole
fayd

fayd the Rauen, art thou fo fimple as to beleeue that fo huge a carkas as he will dye for fo little a pricke or hurt? No, no, thou thinckeſt thou haſt a Henne or Partridge in hande that are foone nipped in the heade, and difpatched ſtreight. I tell it thee for this, fayd the Foxe. Sure the King will not giue eare to it, nor heare a worde fpoken agaynſt him: and all bicaufe he gaue him hys worde, and promifed him he would not touch him. And what? thinke ye the Prince can with his honor go backe from his worde? no, he may not, and I dare warrant you he wyll not. The Rauen that was the wyfeſt in the towne, and a Doctor in *furtis*, like a fubtill Carin tooke vpon him the burden, with his malice to get out of thefe bryers well ynough, and fo togithers they went to the Princes Pallace, and after they had done their due negligences, pulled of their cappes, and giuen him *bona dies*, they fate them downe in their feates. The King feeing them come to him at fo rare an howre, beganne to playe on the bridle, and fayde to himfelfe. O bellie, now prepare thy felfe, good newes and God will. And turning him to the Rauen (that was reaching with his bill as though he would haue fpoken to the King) he afked him. Ah Sira, how is it with you: what faye you to me worſhipfull Maiſter Carrin? Haue you

you prouided vs of vittayles as yee informed vs? Maifter Rauen blufhing lyke a black dogge, fet a good face on the matter, and boldly aunfwered him.

Moft mightie Prince the Prouerbe fayth. Who feeketh fhall finde. Like as he can not fee

that hath not eyes, nor heare that hath not eares: So wee poore wretches that ftarue for hunger, thruft vp betwixt the doore and the wall, we I fay can not fee one another, and haue loft all our fenfes. And being thus blinded we cannot feeke, and not feeking yee may well
thinke

L

thinke that we are all ready to faint and fall downe right. But yet we haue founde a waye not to famifhe: and to bee plaine with your Grace at a worde, we woulde haue you kill the Camell, and the Woolfe, and the Foxe, and I will be readye to affift you. He is rounde, plumme, fatte, and as full as an Egge, fo that he will ferue you a great while, & alfo he is none of ours at any hand, neither yet is he called to any feruice for his richeffe: for I haue knowne him a very beggar ywis. The Lion cut of his tale and deuice on a fodeine, and more than halfe angrie he faid to him. Get thee hence out of my fight thou and thy wicked counfel, vile ftinking beaft that thou art, that doeft nothing elfe but plucke out eyes, a beaft without difcretion or fayth. Doft thou not remember what I fayd to the Camell? Doth he not liue under my protection and warrant? The Rauen lyke an olde theefe let him go on and faye his pleafure. And though the King grounded himfelfe on juftice, and fought to perfourme his worde and promife paft him, yet he ftirred not a whit, no more than the wilde Bore amongft the thicke bufhes and briers, nor once hid himfelfe for all his heate and hote wordes, but took hart of grace on him againe. And as one that knewe he ftoode on a fure grounde, and that hee fpake for

the

the Princes profite (a good ftaffe to leane on and make a man bolde I warrant ye, for it maketh many a bitter fray with honor, and putteth him oft to flight: and iuftice is more corrupted for commoditie, than honor doth caufe it to proceede with equitie). He replied to the King, and told him a trimme tale with thefe wordes. Victorious Prince, your opinion is no leffe good than iuft, and I lyke it well that your minde agreeth with the greatneffe of your crowne: but I ftande in great feare that this your carnell holyneffe will fall out verie hurtfull for your Kingdome. Sure generall honeftie banifheth from euery one murder: but priuate profite calleth it againe. We your obedient vaffals and fubiects, humbly befeeche your Maieftie on the knees of our hearts, that of two hard choyces ye will take the beft, or as they fay, of two euyls the leaft. Caft not away for Gods fake to faue one vnprofitable member, fo many profitable and neceffarie members, making them vnprofitable and not neceffary. Your life ftandeth yourfelfe and all vs vppon, and importeth all. If he liue, you die: if he die, you liue, and we to ferue you. My Lorde I faye, honor for others that lyft, but profit for your felfe. Your Maieftie once gone, your fubiectes and Realme are lyke to come to naught. Your preferuation is ours alfo.

alſo. It is of neceſſitie one Well muſt be clenſed to cleere the reſt. And though in deede your word and aſſurance hath tied your handes, and that in that reſpect you woulde not breake iuſtice: let mee alone with the matter: I will worke ſuch a feate for him, that I will make him come and offer himſelfe vnto you and laye his necke on the blocke, and yet he ſhall little thinke my meaning. And when you haue his heade on the blocke and cannot finde meanes to choppe it off, in fayth you are worthie to ſtarue: and then at your perill be it for me. You ſee you are famiſhed and we ſtarued, and howe lowe you are brought. Follow my counſell, and I will deliuer him you faire and fatte: ſo ſhall ye ſaue your-ſelfe and vs too.

The King gaue very good eare to his profer, and bade the Rauen hie him, yet with prouiſo alwayes his honor might bee ſaued, and then worke with what arte or deceite he woulde he cared not, handle it as he liſted, neither would he deſire to be priuie to it. The Rauen repaired to the conſiſtorie with his companions, and deli-uered them his deuiſe and opinion. I woulde my maiſters ſayde he wee did deuiſe to ouertake this gorche the Camell, for the King ſtandeth in it no more, he is conſented it ſhall be ſo. They all ſhronke in their ſhoulders, and helde their
heades

heades awrie, and referred it ouer to his charge, as he that had made the promife to the King. Sirs if my companie like ye, I will doe thus. Wee muft haue the Camell with vs, that hee haue no time to preuent the fodeine mifchiefe. All we foure will goe togithers to the King, and looke what profer I make, the fame ye may eafily make without daunger I warrant ye: And after vs out of doubt this fat morfell will offer him felfe to of neceffitie (if it be but for good maner only) and I trow the King wyll vncafe him, and make him leaue his fkinne behinde him. And when they had called the Camell, they went togithers to the King. The Rauen, (the cunningeft fpeaker of them all) with lamentable wordes beganne to fay vnto the king. Sir thefe many yeares I haue enioyed my life vntill this prefent of your fouereigne bountie, vnder your Maiefties good peace and protection, and waying now the extremetie of your Maieftie, it is more than time I fhould fatisfie your goodneffe to me in part, though not in all. But when I loke into myne owne weakneffe, alacke I fee my myferie great, not finding anything in me worthie to prefent you with, or fitte for your hyghneffe. I am forie to fee your Grace aliue halfe dead. Alas that fuch a king fhould perifh for famine. I haue not great thyngs to offer you, and thofe

not

not worthy of your Maieſtie, but yet with willing minde I preſent my bodye to you, take and feede my Lorde of this my poore and ſimple carcas, die not ſir for hunger: for it better lyketh me to die for you. O it is but meete my Lord, that that which is profitable in you ſhould be ſaved, and the vnprofitable in me loſt. And here he proſtrated him ſelf at the Lyons feete, and made him way for his necke and fleſh, lying ſtill as he had bene deade. The Wolfe no ſooner ſawe the Rauen flatte on the grounde, but alſo with a Phiſicall hyſtorie ſayd, and repeated the ſelfe ſame word by word, and chopped himſelfe ſtreight vnder the Kinge, that he might take his pleaſure of him if he lyked him. This maner of humilitie and offer lyked not the Foxe a whit, and ſteppe by ſteppe he came to make his oration, creeping as the Snake to the charme, or the Beare to the ſtake. Now when the Camell ſaw him make no more haſte, he ſtepped in before him and occupied the place: and kneeling downe he ſayd. My Lord thoſe that ſerue faithfully diſpatch their ſeruice quickly: lo, I am here for you, relieue your famine. The craftie Foxe that ſtoode aloofe ſayde, although my fleſhe be naught and an vnwholeſome morſell for your Maieſtie, yet you may if you lyke taſte it, and ſo he looked downe, and layde himſelfe on the grounde. The
Lion

Lion feeing thefe beaftes on the grounde like drunken chickens, thanked them one by one, faying to the Rauen, that his flefhe was full of yll humors, and if it had bene good he would haue neuer haue offered it to him: and to the Woolfe alfo he fayde, that his was to tough to digeft, and at once hee put his deuouring mouth to the throte of the Camell, and fet his griping talons on him, and tore him in peeces before a man would haue fayde I am here, when the poore wretche thoughte he fhoulde haue efcaped with the reft. O God that fayth affured in wordes commeth to bee broken in deedes: euen fo auerice becometh enimye to all honeftie. But the beft was, the Lyon fent the other beaftes packing to the Gallowes and they would, for he would not giue them a bytte to relieue them with, fo they died miferably for hunger. Sure a fit death to aunfwere fo wicked a life.

This tale I haue tolde thee fayd the Bull, bicaufe thou fhouldeft knowe thefe courtlike fables, deuifes and practifes of vaine and wicked Courtiers. I knowe them all, and I am fo much the better acquainted with them, becaufe I fee them daily vfed againft the good and vertuous, and well difpofed minds. And one no fooner maketh waye for vertue, but they ftreight fet
thornes

thornes in his way to prick his feete. But I will not hazard my life in going about to maintaine the place and credite I haue about the Prince. If the loue thou bearest me be true I praye thee doe but giue me a watch worde how I may faue my felfe, and helpe me with thy counfell in this diftreffe, for I promife thee I cannot counfell my felfe. And for any other to counfell me in fo harde a cafe, I cannot fee any light at all, bicaufe me thinkes I fee fome beaftly part playde me, and I am ready to burft for forrowe: and the worft of all that I fee no ende to bring mee to any fure hauen. So that I praye thee helpe to faue me: and this thing I craue of thee, bicaufe it is fitte for euerye body to feeke for his helth.

Thou haft fayd better than a Crabbe that hath two mouthes fayd the Moyle: and furely to feeke for thy health is but reafon, and a lawfull excufe. For he that cannot faue his life by force, is to be borne withall if he worke for his life by fubtiltie or malice. Howbeit aboue all thinges euery little enimie is greatly to be thought on and looked vnto: now iudge thou then howe much the great is to be feared. And hee that will not efteeme this and beleeue what I faye, it fhoulde happen to him that happened to the male and female Linnet in making their neaft.

A

*A man hath no greater enimie
than himſelfe.*

Alongeſt the ſea ſyde, in a fewe rocks and clyffes full of wylde Herbes, certaine Linnets were wont to lay and breede: and breeding time beinge come to laye their egges, the Cocke began to make his neaſt there. In ſo much as the Henne ſayd to the Cocke: me thinkes it were better for vs to go ſeeke ſome other place to hatch our yong ones, (bicauſe this is not certayne, and beſide that perilous, as it is often ſeene) that we might yet once bring vp our poore little fooles to ſome good. What ſayth the Cock, doeſt thou miſlyke of this ſeate, and is it ſo daungerous as thou talkeſt of? Here paſſe no people, here it is hote, no windes at all, and an infinite ſorts of Herbes doe growe here as thou ſeeſt: ſo that wee ſhall haue meate at all times at will. O my good ſweet Honie huſbande quoth the Henne, it is not fitte for vs God knoweth. For in ſuch like ſeats is euer great daunger, vppon any rage of the ſeas to loſe them all, that it is: therefore I pray thee let vs auoyde the daunger. Wilt thou doe as the Pigeon that being aſked of a Pie why ſhe returned to the Douehouſe to laye hir egges
(where

(where all hir yong ones were ſtill taken away) aunſwered: my ſimplicitie is the cauſe and hath euer bene of my griefe. Thou that haſt great experience and haſt pyſſed in ſo many ſnowes, wilt thou not take it yll to bee handled likes a Coddes head in thy olde dayes? and that it ſhoulde bee tolde thee he knewe it, and would not knowe it, he beleeued it not, he did it not, and ſo forth? but the foolyſhe huſbande hauing no capacitie to conceyue his wyues words, went his way, and flue vp to the top of the tree, and the more ſhee ſpake, the worſe heade had he to vnderſtande hir. So he ſtoode ſtill in his owne conceyte, thinking hee had bene handled like a tame foole, if he had followed his wyues fantaſie. O how noble a foole. O what a cockes combe. All is one: ſhe might ſay what ſhe would, but he would doe as hee liſted, and follow his owne fantaſy. And ſo he dwelled ſtill in his opinion, and made his neaſt, and ſhee layde hir egges and hatched them. A man hath no greater enimye than himſelfe, and that beaſt ſpecially that knowing he did amiſſe, did rather continue his obſtinacie to his hurt, than for his profit once to accept the counſell of his wyfe or friende: And laſt of all ſhe tolde him a tale of proteſtation.

In the fiſhings of the Sophie there was a worlde of

of Fowles that kept about it to feede of thofe
fifhes, and amongft them was a Torteife of the
water that had ftreight friendfhip with two great
and fat Fowles, who diuing vnder water droue
the fifhe all about, and they no fooner appeered
almoft aboue water, but at a choppe they had
them in their mouthes. The Lake was full of
cliftes, I cannot tell howe but by certayne earth-
quakes, and by little and little it beganne to
waxe drie, fo that they were faine to voyde out
the water to take out the great number of fifhe
that were in it, that they fhould not die in that
drougth but rather eate them vp. The fifhes
therefore of that Lake meaning to depart out of
that countrie, came one morning to breake their
faft togithers, and to take their leaue of the Torteife their friend. The which when fhe faw
them forfake hir, fhe wept bitterly, & pitifully
lamenting fhe fayd. Alas! what fhall I doe here
alone? But what thing can come worfe to mee
than to lofe the water and my friendes at one
inftant. O poore Torteife that I am, wretched
creature I, whither fhould I go to feeke out
water, that am fo flowe to go? I like not to
tarie longer in this countrie. O good brethren
helpe me, I pray you forfake me not in my diftreffe. Ah vnhappie was I borne in this worlde,
that I muft carie my houfe with me, and can

put

put no vittayles into it. In others houſes alacke there is place ynough for their neceſſaries: but in mine I can ſcant hyde myſelfe. A, woe, woe is me, howe ſhall I doe? if ye haue any pitie on me my brethren, & if ye haue taken me for your friend, helpe me for Gods ſake. Leaue me not here to burſt for thirſt. I woulde gladly go with you, and that you woulde gladly put me in ſome Lake, and I would followe mine olde trade as I haue done, therefore deare Fowles helpe me. Theſe wordes did penetrate the heartes of theſe great water Fowles, and taking no leſſe pitie on hir, than looking to their owne profite, they ſayde vnto hir. Deare Mother Torteiſe, we coulde not doe better than ſatisfie thy deſire, but alas what meanes haue we to carry thee hence into any Lake? yet there is an eaſie way to bring it to paſſe, ſo that thy hart will ſerue thee to take vpon thee to holde a peece of wood faſt in thy teeth a good while. And then we, (the one on the one ſide of thee, and the other on the other ſide) will with our bylles take the ende of the ſticke in our mouthes alſo, and ſo carye thee trimlye into ſome Lake, and there we would leade our liues and fare delicately. But in any caſe thou muſt beware thou open not thy mouth at any time, bicauſe the other birdes that flie vp and downe will gladly play with thee and laugh

to

to fee thee flie in the ayre, thou that are vfed to tarie on the earth, and vnder the water. Therefore they will tell thee marueylous wonders, and will be verie bufie with thee, and peradventure they will afke thee : Oh pretie fhe beaft, whence commeft thou I pray thee, that thou are flying thus, and whither wilt thou? But take thou no heede to them, fee them not, nor once harken to them I would aduife thee. And if they prattle to thee, faying, Oh what an enterprife of birdes, good Lorde what a peece of worke they haue taken in hande. Whifhte not a worde thou, for thy life, nor looke not that wee fhould aunfwere them. For we hauing the fticke in our mouthes cannot fpeake but thou muft needes fall, if the fticke (by talke) fall out of our mouthes at any time. Well, now thou haft heard all, how fayeft thou? will thy minde ferue thee, haft thou any fantafie to the matter? Who I? yes that I haue, I am ready to doe anything : I will venter rather than I will tarie behinde. The Fowle founde out a fticke, and made the Torteife holde it faft with hir teeth as fhe could for hir life, and then they eche of them tooke an ende in their mouth, and putting themfelues vppe, ftreight flue into the aire : that it was one of the foolifh-eft fightes to fee a Torteife flie in the aire that euer was fcene. And beholde a whole flight of
birdes

birdes met them, feeing them flie thus ftraungely, and houered rounde about them, with great laughteres, and noyfes, and fpeaking the vileft wordes to them they coulde. O here is a braue fight, looke, here is a goodly ieaft, whoo, what bugge haue we here faid fome. See, fee, fhe

hangeth by the throte, and therefore fhe fpeakeft not, faide others: and the beaft flieth not, like a beaft. Thefe tauntes and fpiteful wordes went to the hart of the Torteife, that fhe was as madde as fhe coulde bee: fo fhe coulde no longer holde but aunfwere fhe would (at leaft as fhe thought) and

and when fhe opened hir mouth to fpeake, downe fhe fell to the grounde, and pafhte hir all to peeces: and all bicaufe fhe fhoulde haue fayde, I am an honeft woman, and no theefe. I would ye fhoulde knowe it: Knaues, Rafcals, and rauening birds that ye are. So that cotemning the good counfell was giuen hir, or to fay better bicaufe fhe woulde not beleeue them fhe payde hir folly with death. And now I returne backe againe whence I came.

The Birde loft hir yong ones bicaufe the fea rofe high, and the furging waues caried them quite awaye. Now bicaufe fhe would lay no more in any fuch daungerous place, fhee affembled all hir parentage and kinfefolkes, and came before the Crane (Queene of all Fowles) to cite hir hufbande, and tolde hir the whole matter. The which when fhe fawe the little difcretion of hir hufband, fhe rebuked him, and wifely tolde him howe great follye it was (yea rather madneffe) to put himfelfe and his a feconde time in open & manifeft daunger, being fallen into it once already. Shewing him by example a tale of the Curbe, that being angry with the Well ranne agaynft it, thinking to make a hole in it, but in fine it brake in tenne peeces. Learne therefore fayde the Crane not to ftriue with thofe
that

that are greater than thy felfe, if thou meaneſt not to haue the ſhame and loſſe. Therefore builde thy neaſt no more alongeſt the ſea banckes.

I thought good to tell thee this diſcourſe, ſayd the Moile to the Bul, to ſhow thee that thou canſt not be in ſuretie to fight againſt a Kinge, and to prooue thy ſtrength. But thou ſhouldeſt go with a leaden heele: that is to ſay, with wiſedome, and malice. The Bull aunſwered. The beſt way I can take in this matter me thinketh is to go before his Maieſtie, and not to make any countenance that I am troubled or offended, but euen after myne olde woonted maner: and then ſhall I eaſily perceiue whether he haue ought in his minde againſt me, and that he ſtomacke mee. If at my firſt comming he doe not to me as King *Lutorcena* did to *Biſenzo* hys Captaine, who hauing him in ſome ſuſpicion, with his owne handes, threw him to the grounde, and ſlue him.

The Moyle liked not this determination, (perceiuing hys reaching heade to preuent his mallice) imagining that the King knowing his wiſedome, and feeing in him no alteration, would ſtreight thinke himſelfe abuſed, and then were he vtterly ſhamed and vndone both. Therefore fearing his fault hee ſayde vnto him. My Lorde

Lorde *Chiarino,* and brother deare (I will giue thee a watche worde to ferue thy turne at neede) when thou fhalt come before the Kinge, if perchaunce thou finde him very fufpicious, and that he caft his deadly eyes on thee, and bende his fhort eares, ftanding vpright to heare what thou fayeft, or if any worde thou fpeakeft maketh him caft vp his heade, or hang it downe: then (truft me) beware of him that he playe thee not fome part, therefore carie thy eyes before thee, and looke to his fingers, and ftand to thy defence lyke a worthie Champion. For when he fhall fee thee prepare thyfelfe with fworde and buckler to refift him, euen at that inftant he will chaunge his mind: and fo by this meanes thou fhalt fee what he will doe. The Bull tooke his (as friendly) counfell, & went forthwith to the Court. The Moyle alfo departed from him, and with great ioy flingeth to the Affe his brother, and tolde him I haue difpatched this matter. I haue done his errant I warrant him. I knowe he knoweth his payne by this time, feeft thou? Well I fayd and did fo much, that at the laft I brought him to it. And though I had great labor to bring it to paffe, yet better late than neuer. My fubtill and malicious practifes at length yet are brought to good purpofe I thanke God. Oh what fame fhall I get, fhe
fhall

shall be full of eyes though I haue seene light. Sounde thy trumpet once Ladie Fame through all the countries round about, farre and neere: and if my practise fall out right, thou neuer foundest in thy life so goodly a double treason. O what a perfite counsellor should I be, how trimly coulde I bring a spouse to bedde? be of good cheare brother, the Bull perswaded by me goth to Court to seeke out the King, if he see him sturre any thing at all; and the Lion also hath my Coccomber in his bodie, and in his heade the toyes and deuises that I haue tolde him, looking for the Bull with many an yll thought. Now beginnes the game. I haue so cunningly handeled this matter betweene them both, that one of them I holde ye a grote will leaue his skinne behinde him, part it betwixt them as they list. But I that haue my feete in two stirropes (as God would haue it) am sure inough from falling. Let them trie it out by the teeth and hornes, I will saue one I warrant thee. I will stande and giue ayme.

When the Bull was come to the King's presence, and that he saw his head full of suspicion, and perceyued in him those signes & tokens that trayterous villeyne the Moyle had tolde him imagining presently the Kings pawes on his backe, and his mouth on his throte

throte, rememberinge the Moyles peftilent counfell, he ftoode ftreight to his defence. And the King on the other fide fuppofed he went to affault him, and being informed before by the Moyle hee thought it fure fo, and that it was true that the Moyle tolde him: therefore without any farther daliance, or tarrying his meaning, he rowfed himfelfe, and on him he goeth, fo that they began a fierfe battayle, howbeit in the ende the olde Lyon wearied the Bull, that he laye deade before him, for fuch is the iuftice amongeft the Nobilitie and worfhipfull Courtiers of beafts. And yet though the Lyon was ftronger than the Bull: dealing wyth defperate perfons he had but a bloudie victorie. The cafe was fuch, and fo fodeine, that all the Court was fullof forowe, and the more for that it happened vnlooked for, and neuer a worde fpoken of it before: fo that they were all by this chaunce ftricken with a marueylous feare. The Affe being informed of the terror of the matter was very heauy, and angry with his brother, infomuch as he fayde to him: O curfed brother, thou haft done a horrible and wicked fact. Haft thou not almoft brought the Kinge to deathes dore, caufed thy friend to be flayne, and put all the Court in feare, daunger, and forowe? and woorft of all, thou haft loft thy credite and good

good name, fhamed thyfelfe, and for euer befamed thy houfe and parentage. And if thy wicked practife were knowne, what fhould (thinkeft thou) become of thy life? Oh caytyfe wretch. I faye no more Moyle, but marke the ende, this mifchiefe will fall on thy neck, and thou fhalt gather of thy naughtye feede thou fowedft, naught elfe but prickes and thornes. For thy barren and drie grounde can bring forth nothing but Burres and Brambles. Gods diuine iuftice will not fuffer fuch and fo wicked a dede vnpunifhed. And though prefently it lighteth not on thy heade, the deferring of it will fhowe thee howe much the whip with time doth growe. Oh brutifhe creature thou: neuer to feare God, nor to loue thy neighbour, but alwayes to follow thyfelfe, and to purfue thy beaftly minde wythout regarde? thou mayntayneft thy ambition, & wyth that thou wouldeft fubuert and ouerthrow a thoufand Realmes.

The trayterous Moyle hoong downe his heade all the while, and knewe well ynough that it was true the Affe fayd, and that he miffed not much the marke, yet he helde his peace, and would not aunfwere one worde. So the Affe followed on his tale, and came againe to the matter. I fee my wordes but loft, and worke fmall effect: and I am fure there is no rebuke

more

more caſt away and blowne into the winde, than that that is giuen him, that is neyther capable of it, nor honeſt and iuſt? nay rather feareth no puniſhment for his peruerſe and wicked works. It ſhall doe well therefore (though I be but thy brother by the fathers ſide) to take care of thee, leaſt I ſhould fall into that that a little Popingey fell into with an Ape of *Soria*.

*It booteth not to giue counſell
where it is not followed.*

Betwixt *Dalmatia* and the Realme of *Granata* there is a marueylous great valley full of high Firre trees and Pineapples. It happened once in yᵉ winter ſeaſon that there went a ſhole of Apes togither from one countrie to another, and the night ouertooke them alongeſt theſe trees, ſo that they ſtoode there cracking of theſe Pineapple kirnels, determining to take vp their lodging there for the night. But bicauſe the night was ſomewhat colde, they blewe their nayles and chattered their teeth apace. In this meane while one of the Apes had ſpyed a Glowe worme in a hedge that ſhewed like fire: and beleuing it had bene fire indeede, they ranne all to fetch ſtrawe, ſtickes, and drie Pines to lay vppon hir,

being

being verie defirous to warme them. And when they had layde on all this wood on the backe of hir, they beganne to blowe, and to lay on lode to kindle the fire; but all in vayne for the deuill of ftycke or ftrawe once fmoked much lefs burned, fo that they were ready to goe madde for anger they could not warme them. Certaine Popingeyes dwelt in thofe Firre trees, the goodlieft Birdes in that countrie. Whereof one of them behelde the fimplicitie of thefe Apes at leaft three howres, how they laboured and toyled for life about Moone fhine in the water: So that he mooued with pitie and compaffion towards them, came downe out of the tree, and tolde them. Good wyfe Apes, it grieues me to fee your follye and great labour, and quite without profite, that ye are fo madde to beleeue to fet a fire thofe ftickes with that fhining Glow worme. Alacke poore fooles, yee lofe your winde and time both, befides that euery body that feeth you will thinke yee verye beaftes in deede without wit. For the thing that fhineth fo is not fire in Gods name, but it is a certayne Worme which naturally hath that vile fhining at his tayle, fo that ye are deceiued truly: therefore yee were beft take another way if ye meane to get heate. One of the fhe Apes no leffe tattling than obftinate, commeth towardes him, and putting hir hande by hir fide, fhee
aunfwered

aunſwered him, lyke a madde, prowde, Bedlem foole.

Oh ydle Birde, in fayth thou haſt but little witte to meddle with that that toucheth thee not. What is it to thee whether we knowe or not knowe? who intreated or bade thee come to

giue vs counſell or helpe? If thou doe not get thee hence to ſleepe againe, and that quickly, I will promiſe thee a broken heade at the leaſt and I turne not thy ſkinne ouer thy eares too, heareſt thou me? I praye yee ſee how hee meddles in our matters. Diſpatch, get thee hence

hence I fay, and meddle with thy Birdes with a murren to thee, and let vs alone: leaft perhaps thou wifheft thou hadft, when it will be too late. And with that fhe beganne to fhowe hir teeth, with an euill fauoured looke withall.

The poore Birde when he faw hir make that face to him was halfe afraide, yet leauing hir he went to counfell the others, fuppofing by being importunate to make them knowe their follie: and fo he began to fee and repeate verie oft that he fayd to the other Ape before, fo that that Ape coulde not abyde him any longer for fpight, but gaue a leape or two to ketch him. But the Fowle being wight of winge eafilye fcaped hir: and fure if he had taried never fo little, and had not flowen awaye fo faft as he did, the Ape had not left a feather on his back, fhe had torne him. And like to the Ape art thou, for there is no good counfell will take place with thee, nor no admonitions or warnings that will once make thee beware or take heed. I fhoulde be the obftinate Birde that fhoulde ftill go about to perfwade thee, but in the ende I feare me that woulde happen to mee, which chaunced to a Pie with hir Maifter, being a fetter forth of Playes and Enterludes.

He

*He that diggeth a pitte for others
many times falleth into it himſelfe.*

A maker of Playes, dwellinge in a towne called *Baccheretto*, gaue to a rich Merchant a Pie (which one of his boyes that playde a parte euer in his playes had brought vppe:) that had a propertie to blabbe and tell all that ſhe ſaw done in the houſe. This Merchant had a faire wife, which wantonly choſe to hyde hir ſelfe otherwhile with a goodly yong man hir neighbour. The huſbande was many times told of it, and did in maner perceiue ſomewhat himſelfe too; but becauſe it was but ſuſpicion and no proofe (and if he ſhould haue ſtirred in it had not beene able to haue taken his othe that it was true) he ſtoode betweene two waters, as he that was verie loth to beleeue it. And as in ſuch caſes it falleth out many times, that the ſeruants and familie (for the loue of their Miſtreſſe) doe depende rather of their Myſtreſſe than of their Maiſter, and are readyer to pleaſe hir of both. The huſbande ſeeking diuerſe meanes to come to the light of this matter, coulde neuer get out of them, but ſure ſir it is not ſo, you are deceyued. The good man perplexed in his minde, not knowing what way to deuiſe to boulte out this matter, remembered at the laſt that the Pye
hee

hee had in his Chamber (vpon the windowe) woulde ſerue his turne excellentlye well for the purpoſe, ſo hee brought hir to his wiues Chamber, as though hee had not cared for hir (meaning nothing leſſe) and there he left hir a fewe dayes. When he thought the Meale had bene boulted, hee cauſed the Pye to be brought againe into his Chambre, and ſhee tolde him all things directly as they were done, ſo that he determined to puniſhe hir lewde life. But as many doe, whome loue doth no leſſe ouercome than pitie, he let it alone yet many dayes. All this while he hong vp the Pie in hir cage in the hall, and at night made hir be fetched in, and then he knewe all that was done in the day from point to point, & what had happened. Who was there, if hir Miſtreſſe went abrode, how many poundes of Flaxe the Maides had ſpunne, and how many times the ſeruants had ſet on the Flaxe of the Rock and pulled it off againe: when, what, and how. O what a vile craftie Pye was ſhe. The poore Maydes of the houſe neuer thought ſhe coulde haue tolde any thing in the worlde, nor made any reckening of hir at all. The huſband at the firſt, beganne to groyne and lowre, and to caſt forth certayne wordes and Parables to his wife, the which ſeemed not to vnderſtande him, though ſhee knewe his meaning well ynough, and ſuſpected that ſome of the houſe had opened
the

the matter. Howbeit, not able to burthen anye one particularly, bicaufe fhee woulde be fure not to miffe, fhe flatly fell out wyth them all, and tooke on with them to badde, brawling and fcolding vp and downe the houfe lyke a madde woman all the day long. In continuance of time, whether it was that they ftarued the poor Pye, or how the goodyere it fell out I know not, but the Pye had founde hir tongue & fpake plainely to them, and fayde: giue me fome meate, or I will tell my maifter. When they hearde hir prate thus, imagine you what fport the women had with hir. And bicaufe fhe was a beaft, out fhe tattled at once all that fhe knewe of the men as well as of the women: fo that fhe tolde them how hir Maifter would afke hir how they vfed hir, and what they did, and counterfeited his fafhions and ieftures rightly, afking queftions, and aunfwering hir felfe, euen as if hir maifter had bene prefent to haue afked hir.

The Myftreffe and Maydes gladde they had found out the tale bearer, they came about hir with a light, and fhut to the windowes, and with vifers on their faces, difguifed they daunced fuch a Moreffe about her with Glaffes, Fire, Water, and founding of Belles, beating on the bourdes, fhowting and whooping, that it would haue made the wheele of a Myll deafe, it was fo terrible.
And

And after they had done this returning euerything to his place and openinge the Windowes as they were at the firſt there they left hir alone, and woulde giue hir neuer a bitte of meate. When the Merchant hir maiſter was come home, and that he cauſed the Pye to be brought into his Chamber, ſhe beganne to lay out hir tongue at large, and ſayde. O Maiſter I haue had an yll night todaye, there hath bene ſuch rayne, tempeſts, and ſuch noyſes, and I haue ſeene a number of Pyes paſs by my Cage, but none of them all would tarie with me. O what a fooliſh time was it: and yet in a moment the winde and water ceaſed, and ſo it was daye againe. Bid them giue mee ſome meate that I might dine, for it is eight aclock and I am a hungered. The Merchaunt when hee heard hir ſpeake thus fooliſhly and tell theſe fables, he thought they were but toyes in hir heade, and that ſhee talked at pleaſure, nothing touchinge hir Miſtreſſe matters, and ſo let it paſſe for that tyme. One nyght the Merchant determined to lye out, and ſo he did, and left the Pye in his wyues Chamber. As ſoone as it was darke his wife ſent for hir Louer, and ſtreight cauſed the Pye to bee taken awaye (hir Cage couered ouer) and caried into a Well: and when he that caried hir had let hir Cage downe a pretie deale into the Welle, he vncouered it againe,

againe, tying it faft at the toppe of the Well for falling into it, and being Moone light the fame night, the feruaunt departed his waye without fpeaking to hir, or feeing hir, and fo let hir hange. A little before day the good wife of the houfe made the Cage be couered agayne trimlye, and brought into the Chamber, and fo vncouering it in the darcke, fell afleepe againe (hir Louer being gone) till brode day. The Merchant came home betimes in the morning before funne rifing, and went ftreight to the cage in his chãber. The Pie that hong in the Welle al night, and knew not in what place fhee was in, nor what houfe it was, would very gladly haue tolde hir Maifter all, and thus fhe began. Maifter the Chamber was carried quite awaye tonight, and I was in a great round Glaffe with water at the funnefhine of the daye, all night long almoft, and then the Glaffe and Cage was remoued, but I cannot tell whither: and fo God gyue you good morrow, Maifter. Nowe God giue thee forrow (quoth the Merchaunt) wicked beaft that thou art: for throughe thy foolyfhe wordes I had well nere paide my pore Jone on the Petticote for thy fake. And with that he ranne to the bed and imbraced his wife and fweetely buffed hir. His wyfe that fawe hir time had come now to be reuenged, and to free hir felfe of hir hufbandes conceiued iel-
oufie

ousie, caused the slouenly Wittall her husbande to tell hir all the Pies qualities & tales shee had brought him: which when she had hearde, out on hir whoore quoth shee, kill hir yll fauored harlottry, what meanest thou to kepe that foolish Birde? Hir husband being rather in a rage than well pleased, bicause he would not gladly haue knowne that that his wife had tolde him. Toke the cage and Pie and thrue hir out at the window, & with the Fall the pore wretch died out of hand. Therefore none must intermeddle in thyngs that belongeth not to them, neyther in wordes nor deedes to goe about the destruction of any. For hee that diggeth a pit for others, many times falleth into it himselfe.

The Sea Crabbe disposed to play with a Foole, was contented to be ridden of him, but he like a Cockes combe (not knowing she went back worde) put a Bridle in hir mouth, and it went to hir tayle, and spurring hir forwardes, the Crabbe went backwardes. I am a foole (quoth the foole) to thincke to doe well with thee, since I know not thy nature nor condicion. Now listen what chaunced to an vngracious traueyler, and then consider well of the matter.

Twoo men of the *Mamaleckites* traueyling by the

the way togithers, founde a great bagge full of Golden Wedges, and fo ioyntly togithers they agreed to take it vp determining to carie it to the Citie, and to laye it vp fafe in their lodgings. But when they were come to the walles of the Citie, they altered their mindes, and one of them

fayde to the other. Let vs diuide the treafure, that ache may carie home his part, and doe withall as he thinketh good. The other that was refolved to fteale it, and to haue it al to him-felf, meaning to eafe the good honeft man of his part, aunfwered *ex tempore* for his profite. Mee
       thinketh

thinketh good brother it is not meete that our happe fhould be common, and the friendfhip perticular: but lyke as we met in pouertie, fo let us ioyne in richeffe. Therefore for my part I will not deuide it, but we will enioye it friendly togithers, and the good happe that lighted euenly vpon vs. Howbeit for this time (if thou thinke good) let vs take a peece out to ferue our neceffitie with, to defraie houfeholde expences, and other extraordinarie charges: and for the reaft, it fhall not be amiffe if it runne in common betwixt vs, and we will hyde it in the darke in fome fecrete place fo as we maye from time to time (alwayes as we nede it) take of it at our pleafures. The good fielye man (I will not fay foole) did not thinke of his pretenfed fubtiltie, and that hee went about then lyke a falfe Knaue to deceyue him, but tooke him for a playne meaning man lyke himfelfe, and fayde he was contented it fhoulde be fo. So for companye they tooke eche of them his burthen and the reft they fafely buried vnder the roote of an olde Elme, which the poore neyghbours that dwelled by called vile Knaue, and fo with the little burden of their neceffarie expences, ech of them repayred to their lodginges. Within three houres of the fame night the companion that gaue counfell to leave it abrode, went to the place of the hidden treafure, and fecretely

caried

caried it home with him. When tyme had confumed the honeſt man's money, hee went to the theefe his partener, and fayde to him. Brother I woulde gladly haue the reaſt of my part of the golde that remayneth behinde, let vs goe therefore I pray thee togithers as wee togithers did fynde and hyde it, and we will bring it home betwixt vs: for I aſſure thee I am in great neede. Of mine honeſtie well fayde (quoth the theefe his companion) we are happily met: for I was euen nowe thinking of that thou telleſt me, and I promiſe thee I was comming to thee of the ſame errant. But now thou art come, in fayth welcome, thou haſt ſaued me ſo much labor: come on, gowe, let vs take our horſes and awaye, wee will not dwell long about this matter, I trowe, we will handle it ſo nimbly thou ſhalt fee: and then we ſhall liue merilye without anye care or thought, and neede not feare robbing. Now when they were come to the vyle Knave (the Elme ſo called) where they had buried their treaſure, beinge a great and hollow tree, they began to digge for it, but in faith they might dig vnder the tree till their hartes aked, as deepe and as farre as they liſted for the treaſure was flowen. The theefe then played the Harlots part rightly, that weepeth and lamenteth to the honeſt woman, and beganne to tell him there was no more fayth in in friends, and that loue was loſt. Truſt that truſt lyſt, for by the Maſſe I will neuer truſt agayne. And when hee had often repeated this, hee beganne to throwe away his cappe, to crye out, and beate himſelfe, that he was lyke a madde man, nay a very bedlem in dede. His fellow hat was ſo naturall, though he were ſomewhat lyke a Mome, woulde not bee lowted ſo, but rather laughed to ſee his Knauerie and crafte thinking notwithſtanding that he had ſtolen it (as he had in deede) but yet hee ſtoode in doubt, laughing ſtill. Then the theefe raged like a beaſt (as if he had reaſon on his ſyde) and ſayde. None, no none but thou traytor, theefe, and villen (as thou art) coulde ſteale this. The ſiely man that of both had cauſe to complayne (all hope taken from him to recouer his part) in ſteade of accuſing him, it ſtoode him in hande to excuſe him ſelfe, and to ſweare and forſweare: ſaying I cannot tell of it, I ſaw it not, I touched it not, neither did I once think of it till now. But tut al would not ſerue or ſtaye the theefe, but hee cried out more and more (and that alowde) and called him al to naught, Oh traytor, oh ſlaue, and micherlye theefe, who but you knew of this? What man alyue but thou could once haue layde hands on it? Tarie a little, by Gods paſſion I will tell my L. Mayor of thee.

I will doe thy errant truſt to it: and I trowe he will ſet thee where thou ſhalt ſee no Sunne nor Moone a good while. Harken after.

This brawling and ſcolding continued a good while betweene them, in the ende they went both to the Mayor: who after longe cauillations, intermiſſions, paremptories, exigentes, termes vpon termes, fauors, promiſes, agreements, prayſes, compremiſes, wagers, and a number of other ſuch lyke conceytes and toyes, perceyued his tayle had neither head nor foote. Then ſayd my L. Mayor to pricke out the core of this matter: when ye two hid this treaſure, were there any others with you, or were yee two alone togithers? The Knaue that had occupied his hands as nimbly as he that played on the Phife, aunſwered ſtreight as if he had bene cleere and honeſt in the matter. My Lorde, and if it pleaſe your Honor, with your Graces fauour, the tree it ſelfe and you were there and ſawe it, would witneſſe the matter plainely. For we both I am ſure put it betweene the rootes of the tree, and therefore I beleeue it will ſhowe you the hole which the theefe hath digged. If God be iuſt, I knowe hee will make the tree tell, and as it were poynt with a finger to him that ſtale it, and ſhowe you of him Sir, of him that ſtandeth here before your Lordſhippes goodneſſe

neſſe (and my worſhipfull maiſters) lyke a ſteale counter nowe, for out of doubt he ſtole it. My L. Mayor that had many times put his finger in the fire before, as one well acquaynted with ſuch lyke matters, and that could ſpie day at a little hole, ſayd, well then ye ſtande vpon the teſtimonie of the tree, and ſeeing ye doe ſo, both you and I will be at the doing of it God willing, and I will ſift out to the vttermoſt I warrent ye, feare ye not. They putting in ſureties for their appearance, and a daye appointed for the matter, were diſmiſſed the Court. This determination liked the theefe of life, for he had ſtreight deuiſed a miſchiefe to blind my L. Maior withall. But here I wil make a little digreſſion. He that doth his things without aduiſe and counſell can neuer do well. The counſell is euer found and good that commeth from an olde experienced man, or at least helpeth in ſome part. It is euery wiſe mans part to take counſell in things he goeth about, whereof he is either ignoraunt or doubtfull. He that repreſenteth the Moyle, I hope ſince he will follow no counſell, ye ſhall ſee him ſmart for it in the ende. For it is written. Heare my ſonne my preceptes and counſayles, but the Moile was deafe and coulde not heare of that ſide. And nowe liſten howe.

The

The theefe had imagined a mifchiefe in hys heade, and as foone as hee was come home he fayde vnto his father. O my good luftie olde grey bearde. I will difclose a great fecrete to thee, which till this daye I have kept fecret, fecret in my bofome manye a faire daye, and euer buried it within me, as he that coulde finde no time I tell thee to tryfle. But father, heare ye. To be plaine with you, the treafure I afke of my companion, I myfelfe haue ftollen it, that I might the better releeue thee in thy olde age, and alfo farther and aduance my poore familie, a thing that thou and I both long time haue defired. I thanke God, and my wife forefight (I fhould haue fayd before) it goth as I would haue it, I would wifh it no better. Now if thou wilt be ruled, and haue the thing brought to paffe (being alreadye in good forwardneffe) this cheate will be ours in fpight of the Deuill. And fo rehearfed all to hym that had paffed betweene them before the Maior and the Bench, and adding this withall. I praye thee conuey thyfelfe to night into the hole vnder the rootes of the tree where the treafure was hidde, for it is long, deepe, and large. And when my Lorde Mayar fhall afke the tree: *Quem queritis?* I woulde faye, who caried awaye the treafure? then fhalt thou aunfwere with a counterfeyt voice

voice: *Egus.* That is my companion, and thou ſhalt call him by his name. The old man that was lyke vnto his ſonne in euery poynt, had reaſon to holde of his ſide, after ninetene ſhillings to the pounde: but he aunſwered foure wordes.

Sonne it is good to be merie and wiſe. I care not to take this matter vpon me, but me thinke it is harde and daungerous. A wiſe man will looke ere he leape. I feare me thoſe egges will be broken in the mouth while we are a ſucking of them. It happeneth in an howre that happeneth not in ſeuen yeares. If thys geare come out, we haue ſponne a fayre threede. Conſider it wel, miſhappes are euer at hande. Howbeit, ſo it happen not to me as it did to the Birde that would kill the Snake, I am contented: and now heare the ſtorie how ſhe did.

In the rockes of *Popolonia* there was a goodlye tree, in the which a ſolitarie Birde builte hir neſt: and laying ſixe times, fiue of them miſcaried. Harde by this tree, there dwelled a great and vnhappie Snake, which (as oft as theſe little birdes were in maner hatched and ready to flie) crept vp the tree to the neſt, and deuoured them all, that ſhe was readie to burſt for fulneſſe. So that the poore Syer of them was as angry as a Beare,
he

he was fo full of choler and forrowe. One day hee determined to afke councell in the matter, and confulted with a Crabbe that was a Doctor *in Libris*. Hearing his learning, he faid naught elfe to him, but come and follow me. So he brought him to a Caue where dwelled a certayne beaft (a companion of his) a charmer, an enimie to the Snake for his lyfe, and tolde him his nature, how that this beafte delighted to eate fifhe, and made him carie a little difhe full of them, and go fcattering of them ftill all alongft till he came to the Snakes hole. The charmer hauing the fauor of the fifhe in the winde, followed the fent, and when he was come to the place where the Snake made hir neaft, in a great furie he digged vp the grounde: and finding hir (as one would haue wyfhed it) in hir firft fleepe, hee killed hir. But bicaufe fhee was fo well fedde, he went further groping vp and downe, fearching if there had beene ought elfe to haue lyked him: and hauing thefe Birdes in the winde to, he got him vp to the tree, and deuoured them alfo.

Father you caft beyonde the Moone, and make doubtes where none are: there is no fuch daunger in this as you fpeake of. Too it luftilye, and be not afrayde. I will warrant thee for an Egge at Eafter. What doeft thou thinke I haue not wayed

wayed the matter to the vttermoſt? foreſeene it, preuented it, looked thorowe it, and ſeene to the bottome of it? Yes that I trowe I haue. And if I had not ſeene it done as I would haue it, I would not buye the repentaunce of the lyfe of my deare, ſweete, louing and tender father. Therefore diſpatche, and about thy buſineſſe. The tyde tarieth no man. Nowe is the time that in diſpite of our foes (doe the woorſt they can) wee ſhall haue our purpoſe, and that ſo trimlye, that we ſhall ſwime in wealth, and liue all the dayes of our lyfe after like Gentlemen, and take our pleaſure. So the vnhappie (rather than wiſe) father, daunced after the ſonnes pipe, and forthwith went and conueyed himſelf vnder that hollowe tree, tarying there all night where the treaſure had bene hidden.

In the morning betimes, My Lord Maior, the Shirifes, hys brethren the Aldermen, the Recorder, the counſell of the Citie, my Maiſters the Judges, the Juſtices of peace, with all other of my Lord Maiors and the Shirifes officers attending on him, ſolenymly went to the appoynted place for triall of this matter, and hauing hearde the parties in *partibus* and *spartitibus*, hee reſolued vpon the teſtimonie of the tree, and cried out. What ho, tree (three times). who hath robbed

robbed this treasure? Then this olde man that had lien vnder the tree all night, & had a couple of nuts in his mouth to counterfeit the Matter, aunfwered quickly on a fodeine the name of the good fimple man. When the Maior heard this thing, that within the barks of the trees there were certaine trembling voyces put forth, it fo amazed him, that for the time he was extaticke, & coulde not fpeake a word: feeming to him and to thofe that ftoode by, that it was a wonderful and ftraunge thing. And thus wondering at the matter, to heare the voyce come out of the tree, he was about to fay: Lorde, fee what force truth is off. But with that thought alfo he beganne to fufpect there was fome knauery in hande, and becaufe he would knowe it were fo he commaunded they fhould lay a lode of wood or two about the roote of the tree, & when they had done, that they fhould fet it on fyre: imagining that if there were any yll fauoured worme or vermin in the hollownes of the tree, either he would fire him out, or at the leaft turne hys coate or tayle. And if there were any deceyte, he knewe by this meanes he fhould eafily boult it out: and hauing caufed wood to be brought and layd togither as he commaunded, they ftreight gaue fyre. Now the olde man hauing fyre at his tayle like a Gloworme, and that it began to partch him

(thinke

(thinke what heart he had) cryed out pittifully as lowde as he coulde. Alas alas, alas. Water, water, water. I burne, I burne, I burne. Helpe, helpe, I am fmothered, I am fmothered. Come, come, come. Quick, quick, quick. Open, open for Gods fake. I die, I die, I die. And many fuch wordes he fpake, that he made them all ready to burft with laughing. A firra (quoth my L. Maior) and art thou there in deede. In fayth the fpirite is coniured now, he is fure ynough I warrant him. And fo he caufed the fpirit to be pulled out, that God knoweth looked lyke the verye picture of ftryfe it felfe. Whan he fawe the poore olde Deuill howe he was dreffed, at the firft he laughed, and without any choler did ftreyght examine him. But when the troth in deede appeared as it was, hee payde them home with their owne deuice, and gaue them that they had iuftlye deferved, and delyuered all the treafure to the fimple honeft man. So that nowe thou heareft howe innocence is rewarded, and iniquitie punifhed. Let ftryfe go, and we fhall liue merylie.

Thou mayest nowe turne thys tale to thee, and make thee a fhort cloke, for in footh it is euen fit for thy back, therefore put it on thee. Once againe I tell it thee, that the books which
thou

thou haſt ſtudied are falſe, and the doctrine naught: therefore I can tell thee they will be throwne into the fire. And if thou followe that doctrine, and alleage their authorities; out of doubt thou wilt frye at a ſtake, and thou and thy Doctors will be burned togithers. All will lye on thy neck and of thy childrens: as it did vpon the adultereſſe, and it is not long ſince it happened, as you ſhall heare.

In *Terra Stolida*, in a place called *Vallona*, it is reported there dwelled a riche Farmer, whoſe ſubſtaunce laye moſt in great Cattle: and at certaine times he droue them into other countries to paſture, where he abode with them many moneths. His wyfe that remayned at home, was good and ſquare, and plumme of body, hir brawne as harde as a bourde, and that had hir face before hir as other women: ſo that a great riche man alſo of that Countrie caſt his eyes vpon hir, and entertayned hir in that time of vacation. And ſhe that delighted not to be kept at the rack and maunger, ſuffered hir receipt to runne at large, to fare more daintily. In ſo much as at the laſt (ſinning in gluttonie) hir breaſtes grewe bigge, and hir belly roſe, ſo when time came, ſhee brought forth a goodly Babe, which ſhe carefully put forth to nurſe and thus

it

it grewe: and in fine as hir owne in deede she brought it home and fostered it. Hir husbande being come home that had beene long absent, gladde to see his wyfe and she (in seeming also) no lesse gladde of his comming, (but Lorde what feast and ioye in outwarde showe betweene them) they sweetely kissed, and with louing wordes imbraced eche other. Oh my Conye, welcome, quoth she. Oh my dear Musse (sayde he) gramercy to thee. All wedlocke ceremonies duely accomplished: hir husbande casting his eyes aboute, and seeing this fayre little Boye running about the house. Musse quoth he. I pray thee whence is thys little knaue? what knowest thou not Conye sayde she? it is myne (and this she tolde him as she that could cunningly handle him in his kinde) and so followed on, preuenting his tale. Doest thou not remember that three yeares ago there fell a great Snowe. (Jesu how colde it was) and at the same time I remember the Rauens and Crowes fell downe starke dead in the streetes, and the little fishe dyed in the Welles. Oh what a colde it was, and I tooke it in deede (God knoweth) with throwing of Snowe balles, the yonge maydes of the Countrie and I togithers: and I cannot tell howe, I handled so manye, but well I wote I came home fayre with chylde, and I am sure it

was

was no other but the Snow, and that is ſene by the Boye, that is as faire and whyte as Snow it ſelfe and therefore I called hys name Whyte. And, bicauſe I knowe well ynough yee men are of ſuch mettall, that euen ſtreight yee thinke all the euill of vs poore women that can be, and for that I woulde not put any ielouſie or toye in thy head, I ſent him out of the dores to nurſe thinking afterwardes at leyſure, when thou hadſt knowne thy good wyfe, to ſend for him, and ſo to have tolde thee even plainely from point to point how the matter went, and howe I came by this good, pretie, ſweete, faire, well favoured Boy.

Hir huſbande though in deede he was but an Aſſe and a dremiſhe foole, was not moued a whit at hir yll fauoured tale, nor once honge downe his head for the matter, and made as though he beleued hir : but he knew ſtreight the knauery of the fooliſh inuention of his wife. Howbeit what for the loue he bare hir (bicauſe ſhe was worth the looking on ywis) and for that he was but a rude fellowe to beholde, and thought himſelfe ſcant worthie of hir, and that he had married hir, pyning away for hir ſake : he thought it better to carie ſuch things in hys breſt than in his heade, and the rather peraduenture bicauſe he doubted falſe meaſure, fearing his partners yll
will

will that farmed his grounde at halfes with him: in fine he was contented to bite it in for the time, determining not to be at charges with other mens children. So one day fpying time and place, he caried out of the dores with him this little Boy White: and fuch was his walke that the Boy was neuer more heard of, nor feene after that. The woman looked and looked againe to fee hir fonne returne with hir hufbande. But feeing hir hufbande come home without him, Come fayth fhee to him: I praye thee what haft thou done with my Boy? Hir hufbande that had bought his wyt fo deare, aunfwered hir. A fweete Muffe, the other day vnaduifedly (I confeffe it) I caried him abrode with me, and we walked a great whyle in the Sunne togithers, and thou knoweft how hote it was two dayes ago (alack that I fhould tell it thee) the heate of the Sunne hath quite difolued him. And then I founde thy wordes true which before I hardly beleeued. Alas poore wretch, he fodanely turned all into water, that wo is me. His Muffe hearing this, in a rage flong hir away, and left Conie all alone, fo he neuer after fawe hir.

I haue tolde thee thys fable, bicaufe thou fhouldeft know, and fee both, that all mifchiefe and malice in the ende commeth out, & being disclofed difclofed, it euer receiveth the juft reward and punifhment. What can be hoped for of thee that haft committed fo many and fundrie yll factes, practifed fuch wicked deedes, deuifed fuch abominable practifes, and made fo many fnares to ketch the pore Bull in, that at the length thou broughtest hym to the axe? And moreouer (to giue place to thine iniquitie) haft brought thy friende to his death, the King in daunger, and thy poore kinsfolkes to fhame: and woorft of all, both of you brake your wordes and promife.

Although I be brother to thee by the Fathers fide, I maye not, nor will not truft thee an ynche, nor deale with thee for pinnes. For he that hurteth his friende, wyll not fpare to hurt his brother: and he that hath once deceyued, knoweth how to deceyue againe. But well, once warned halfe armed they fay. I trow I wil beware of thee well ynough. Thou fhalt not colt me be fure, as the merchaunt was colted by an euill companion of his whom he trufted: and this once tolde thee, we will fhake handes and then adue.

They faye there was a great rich Merchaunt that had as much bufineffe as he could turne him to: and amongeft other his fubftance he had many a thoufande weight of yron. His
bufineffe

bufineffe falling oute fo that hee muft needes go to Calicut, (which was a good thoufand myles off) he gaue to his neighbour (a friende of his) his yron to keepe till he came home. The yron taried the maifter many a faire day, and feeing hee came not, he tooke his leaue, and went his waye: but hee that had it in keeping, tooke reuenge well ynough of his departure, and made merie wyth it. The Merchaunt after he was come home, went to his friende and afked hym his yron. But he that was a flye childe, had ftreyght deuyfed an excufe to ferue hys turne, and fayde to him. I would to God you had neuer left it with me. For yee were not fo foone gone, but there came euen the fame nyght an armie of Rattes and Myfe, (drawne thither by the fauor of the mettall) that lay continually at it: fo that in fewe dayes, before I or any of my houfe knewe it (thinke you that heare it how this was likely) they had gnawen and eaten it vp euery whit, and had not left by eftimation vneaten, and not fpoyled, aboue foure ounces. Now imagine you whether this yll happe went to the ftomach of me or no. The Merchaunt hearing fo lowde a lye, could fcant keepe him from laughing, though inwardly it grieued him: & yet foothing him, he made as he beleeued him, and fayd. Sure it is a marueylous matter

howe

howe this fhould come to paffe; and but that I heare you fpeake it, I woulde neuer beleeue it. For doubtleffe it is one of the woonders of the worlde. A fhame take him that folde it mee. I cannot be perfwaded but that he noynted it with fome oyle, or gaue me fome of that foft yron that is made of the water of Steele. But well, let the yron go where it will, and all my ylles withall, although it bee of no fmall weight. I tell you truly I loue you fo muche that I make fmall reckening of my loffe, but rather I affure you I think it well beftowed, fyth the wicked Rattes yet had fomewhat to enterteine them with, and that they pardoned you and your familie. For ye may well know, that fyth they did eate the yron, they had the Woolues difeafe in them: and if that had not bene in the waye to haue relieued them, by my faye you had fmelt of it. But fince it is gone farewell it, no more wordes, as Cobbe fayd to his wife when his heade was broken.

This craftie fellow (but not fo fubtill as he tooke him felf for) reioyced at thefe wordes, fuppofing the Merchaunt had paffed no more for the matter, and fo was pacified: wher vpon he did conuite him the next day to dinner to him, and the Merchaunt accepted his bidding willingly. Howbeit he ftudied all night to ferue him as good

good a turne, and he coulde at leaſt, to be re-uenged at once of his loſſe and mockes, without complayning to the Juſtice of his wrong : and ſure he ſhowed him a right Northfolke tricke, and this was the ieſt.

The Merchaunt ſent for to dinner to hys houſe that had ſtollen the yron, went thyther ſtreight, and was marueylouſly feaſted and made off (but in deede of his owne coſt) howbeit the beſt pleaſure of all was, the Merchaunt made verie much of a pretie little Boye, and he was the onely ſonne and heyre of him that had bidden him to diner: and ſtill he fed the Boy, and made him great cheere. After dinner playing with his ſonne, and makinge much of him as I tolde you before, promiſing (as they doe to children) many goodly thinges : whyleſt the father began to nodde and to take a nappe, the Merchant made the Boy be caried to a neighbours houſe of his, and there he hid him. The father when he awaked, went forth with the Merchant, attending their buſineſſe, and thought nothing of his ſonne, as he that was wont to go forth without any ſuch care. So comming home at night, and not finding his ſonne, out he went all about the towne to ſeeke him, and ſpared not to aſke euerye bodye that he met if they ſaw his ſonne. At the laſt by good happe hee ſtumbled on this Merchaunt, that in deede

deede had ſtollen him (as the other had ſtollen his yron before) and being in great perplexetie he ſorowfullye aſked him of his ſonne. The Merchaunt, all things framing as he wiſhed, (ſauing the giuing of his yron to hym to keepe), aunſwered ſtreight. Yes marrie, I remember I ſawe (not long ſince the winde roſe ſo great) a ſielye Sparrowe catch a little pretie Boye by the heare of his heade, and in that whirle winde ſhee ſnatched him vp, and caried him quite away into the ayre: and ſure by your wordes mee thinkes it ſhould be your ſonne. Therefore ſeeke him no more, for by this time he is in heauen, it is ſo long agoe I sawe him taken vp from the grounde. The father hearing ſo impoſſible a thing, beganne like a madde man to crie oute, and ſayde, O heauen, O earth, O yee people of the worlde: gyue eare vnto this ſtraunge and wonderfull caſe. Who euer heard ſuch a thing? Who euer ſawe ſo ſtraunge a ſight as to ſee little Sparrowes carie children into heauen? Are Children become Chickens or Sparrowes Kytes? What, ſayth the Merchaunt, you ſeeme to haue little practiſe in the worlde, ſyth ye remember not that an Eagle hath taken vp a man and caried him quite away. But Lorde what nedes this wondering: I marueyle at you aboue all men, ſyth you are vſed to ſee greater woonders and im-
poſſibilities

poffibilities than this. For you haue feene Rattes and Myfe gnawe yron, and eate it when they haue done: and I that did but heare it only of your mouth, marueiled not a whitte. By thefe woordes his falfe friende knewe what he ment well ynough, and imagined (as it was) that to be reuenged for his yron he kept his fonne. And feeing no other remedie, fallinge downe at his feete, he afked him forgiueneffe for God's fake, and put him felfe into his handes, promifing he woulde reftore him his yron agayne, and make him amendes for all his loffes. And thus hee came by his fonne agayne, which otherwyfe hee fhould neuer haue heard of.

By this that thou haft hearde (fayd the Affe to the Moyle) of the yll Companion thou fhalt know what thou mayeft hope of booties gotten with deceit: and confequently what thou mayeft looke for of the King, whome thou haft deceyued and betrayed. Which by fwiftneffe of *Time* (that fhortly paffeth ouer many yeares, and that alfo is father of *Veritie*) cannot nor will not fuffer hir to be hidden by any coloured fraude or deceit. So that he will difclofe all by mouth of *Veritie* vnto the King, telling him of thy wretchedneffe: and the matter being knowne, thou fhalt bide the bitter punifhment, and he will be reuenged of thee for the Bull. To this aunfwered the Moyle.

There

There was a faire woman in loue with a Pothecarie, and ſhee could neuer haue leyſure (becauſe hir huſband kept hir ſtreightly) once to ſpeake with him, or with any others to let him knowe it. One night hir huſband euen ſodeinly being verye ſicke, was compelled for preſent remedie to ſend his wyfe in haſte to the Pothecaries. So thither ſhe ranne with al ſpeede, and inſteade of returning with the medicines, ſhee whipped at a trice vp into the Pothecaries chamber to conferre with him of ſecret matters (you know what), and as ſhee was running vp ſhe caſt hir handkircher with hir money downe on the ſhoppe bourde to the Boy, and bade him make ready the medicine in the meane whyle. The Boye that had an eluiſh witte, vndidde hir handkircher, and toke out hir money, and pretily tied it vp againe, hauing filled hir handkircher with the duſt of the ſtreete, of purpoſe to mocke hir, to let hir vnderſtand, that they that came in haſte for ſicke folks did not vſe to ſport them at leyſure on that faſhion: and ſo laid downe hir handkircher againe on the bourde where he found it. When this woman had well paide the Collector vpon hir receit, and that ſhe ſaw ſhee had bene ſomewhat to long in hir account: ſhe came down from the Pothecarie, ſnatched vp hir handkircher,

kircher, and ran home as fhe had bene fcared with fome yll thing. But finding hir hufband fleping (the extremitie of the paine hauing left him) fhe fate downe foftlye by the beddes fyde, and opening hir handkircher, founde hir money turned into verye earth and duft. And euen at that inftant hir hufband awaked, who bicaufe he knew not how long he had flept, he could not tell whether his wife came quickly againe, or taried long: and cafting his eyes on the duft and earth which fhee was looking on, (as fhee that knew fhe was mocked) he afked hir. What duft and baggage is that thou haft there? what are ointments and medicines made of that fafhion? his wyfe ftreight found his malice, and aunfwered foolifhly.

I running haftilye from certaine that were fighting in the ftreetes, my money flipt out of my hande, and being very darke I fought to take it vp, and fo with my handes I tooke all that I coulde finde, thinking with myfelfe in taking vp the duft to get vp my money too; but wo is me, it is fure all gone, and with that burft out in teares. The hufbande fimply beleeued hir, and giuing hir other money fent hir thither againe: and fo with this fecond commodotie fhe fully accomplifhed hir defyre, and fweetly payde the hire of hir pleafure.

Why

Why then doeſt thou thinke with other new and ſtraunge deuiſes yet to occupie the Kings heade? I beſech God he may once pay thee home. But I would aduiſe thee, looke well to thy ſelfe. For thou ſhalt finde great difference betweene ſuch a beaſt as he is, and another fooliſh little beaſt that will eaſily beleeue thee. Vnleſſe thou wouldeſt ſaye to me, that bicauſe thou haſt done the moſt, thou ſhalt haue the leaſt. To this I replie. That one paye payeth all. And a little theft hangeth vp the theefe for many a great robbery. I haue ſayde to thee for this time, and now farewell.

The fourth parte of Morall Philo-
fophie, fhewing the ende of the
treafons and miferies of the Court of
this Worlde.

LTHOUGH yee fynde many good reafones fpoken vnder the fhadow and colour of beaftes without reafon, yet ye are not to maruell a whit: for we alfo that repre-fent reafonable beaftes do oftentimes things without reafon and difcretion both. And thys is excellent to: to fee beafts liue and worke as men. But howe brutifhe a thing it is to fee men lyue and governe themfelues like brute beaftes. Ye muft alfo note in this Treatife one thing, y^t like as men fometime fay thou, or you, worfhipful, Honorable, Noble, or Lord-fhip and fo forth. And doe in deede many times myffe to giue to eche man his right title & dignitie as they ought, and is fit for eche man's calling and vocation : euen fo thefe beaftes
alfo

alſo (for in the ende ye knowe them to be but beaſts) do erre many times, ſpeaking falſe Latine, ſaying thou for you, and maiſter where they ſhould ſay ſeruaunt. Therefore you may not recken of ſuch ſcapes, nor loke after them, though ye ſee them ſtraye a little out of the waye, and take a Goſlinge for a Gooſe, and a Crabbe for a Whale. For it is an olde rule, that both men and beaſts will fault in many things.

The Lyon therefore did amiſſe to kill the Bull, ſuffering himſelfe and his iudgement to be abuſed and ouertaken, by the deuiliſh and ſubtill practiſes of the trayterous Moyle. Inſomuch as when his choler was ouer, and that he had wreaked his anger of him, cruelly putting the guiltleſſe beaſt to death: he then to late looked backe on his bloudie deede, and repented him of his rage, knowing he had not done well to kill ſo wyſe a ſubiect, and ſo graue a counſeller. His conſcience griped him at the hart to thinke he had no lawful cauſe to vſe ſuch crueltie to him. Such inwarde thoughtes drawe deepe, and touche the quicke, and can hardly be holden in and kept ſecrete. So that the Kinges heart burning thus, out he burſt a fewe wordes, which made the Moyles eares glowe: as that peece of wicked fleſh, that alwayes gaue attentiue eare, and looked to be payde home. So that vpon a
ſodeine,

sodeine, to take awaye these thoughtes from the Kinge, and that he should not thinke to much vppon them, besides that to continue him still in his errour: he ranne to the court, and downe he fell on his knees before the Kinge, and with all humilitie he sayd. Most mightie and noble Prince, thou hast brought thy desires now to an ende. The Gods that day did blesse thee, in which they gaue thee honourable victorie, when thou ouercamest so great and stronge an enimie. The worlde, victorious Prince, woondereth, that thou hauing (I meane) cause to reioyce art so sadde and full of pensiuenesse. Oh sayde the Lyon, when I thinke of the cruell and violent death of *Chiarino* without cause, I am ready to eate my fingers for sorrow. And continually I thinke of the great wit he had, of his graue and prudent counsell, indowed besides with many noble gifts and maners. And to conclude, I must tell thee plainely, I cannot comfort my-selfe, nor be in quiet, when I examine the cause of his death. For many things runnes in my heade to perswade me that things were otherwise than I tooke them, and that he had wrong. But nowe I knowe, that that my father sayde so oft is true That a thing oft thought vpon, can seldome misse but it falleth out true.

Your Lorshippe (sayde this wicked Moyle) shoulde

fhoulde not thus forow and bewayle the loffe of him, which made thee lyue in continuall feare and torment. For wife Princes oft times doe both punifhe and cut off many worthie perfones, and thofe whom they dearely loue and efteeme: and why? all for their owne fafetie, and the preferuation of their Realme. And Sir of two euils they choofe the leaft: to kill one, rather than to make a thoufand die. So here is an example. Doe ye not fee my Lord when one is bitten with a venimous ferpent, that ftreight he cutteth off the member that is bitten, not fuffering it to infect and poyfon the whole bodye, by meanes whereof he faveth his life, which elfe hee fhould lofe? The Kinge feemed to graunt him, and the Moyle thought thefe wordes had cleared the Lions hart, and he craftily made much of the worfhipfull Moyle, and like a brother intreated him. The Moyle fate him downe on a forme in the Chamber of prefcence a whyle, and began of himfelfe to think vpon the miferie of Princes of light credit, and of the malice of thefe vile tale bearers, which fet ftryfe and contention betwixt partie and partie, of their tyranie, of their opinions, and fonde fantafies, in thys maner.

Large, great, wonderfull, and infinite are the wayes to offende, and innumerable are the fnares
and

and deuifes that one wicked and naughtie difpofed perfon may deuife and fpread abrode, to ketch a good and true meaning man, to ouerthrow him quite. And there is not fo ftraight a friendfhip but is eafie to be broken, with the hand of naughty proceeding. As I haue proued it. If I coulde write all the thinges that haue happened, the tales that have bene tolde, and the long wouen cloth: I fhould teache Princes howe they fhoulde doe in all their matters, and woulde make them fee the difcretion that many have loft, and what waye they fhould take not to fall into thefe Courtly flatterers. Thofe that beare office, and haue charge ouer others, ought diligently to fearche out the troth of thinges: and not to goe as Flies without heades, and lightly to turne and chaunge as the wauering weather Cock with euery winde. Truely it is a fowle fault in meane men to giue eafie eare to flatterers, but in great perfons it is a farre greater fault, and in Princes chiefly a thing of moft detect and flaunder, and of extreeme crueltie.

Nowe I come to knowe plainlye, what a great burden is layde on the peoples backes, that are gouerned by a Prince of fmall confideration and iudgment: and in what daunger their perfons are, befides the griefe their confcience giueth them for their ftate. O poore people, how many

many thousandes of ye recommended under the scepter of such iustice? Ought not Princes to be like vnto God? and if God will take account of all things at his will (be they neuer so little) why shoulde not the Kinge among his subiectes also doe the lyke? The wickednesse of ministers and officers (if so it were) woulde not then runne on so farre as it doth vnpunished. O little faith to God's lawes. O little labor for a man to knowe himselfe. Where we think goodnesse only harboreth, thence proceedeth all vice and wickednesse: and where wee beleeue troth is lodged, there sleepeth deceyt. Who would not haue beleeued that in this court vertue had remayned? but alas here is the only Court of vice. In outwarde lookes euerie one seemeth to carie troth: but in the inwarde brests is hid all dissimulation and vntroth. Three thinges there are which are vnite togithers, and should neuer be out of the Princes minde: To wit.—To loue God, his neighbour, and to gouerne himselfe. And three other thinges also there are for the subiects to obserue vnto their Prince. Loue, fayth, and obedience. But euery one I see hath forgotten them, from high to lowe. This world then being so full of daungers and deceytes as it is, what man is he alyue so wyse can keepe himselfe from them?

The

The Lyon returned into the Chamber where the Moyle was, hee lycenſed him to depart, and the Moyle with due reuerence tooke his leeue of the King. Now the King left all alone, beganne agayne to lament, and to repent him a thouſande tymes that he was thus ouertaken with the Moyles perſwaſion: and it grieued him ſo muche more bicauſe he remembered the Bulles wyfe counſels, wonderfull behauior, and noble conuerſation. And to baniſhe this inwarde conceyued griefe, that gryed him at the heart, he lyked to be amongſt his Lordes and familiers, whom diuerſely he entertained. And amongſt this rowte was the Lybberd, one of the nobleſt of bloud of his Kynne, and him the King truſted with many ſecrete thinges of his lyfe. This Lybbarde one daye going out of the pallace to walke, paſſed bichaunce by the houſe of the Moyle and Aſſe, and hearde the Aſſe crying out vppon the Moyle, and bitterlye reproouing him for that vyle treaſon he vſed to the Bull: and ſo hee hearde from poynt to poynt euerye acte and deede he did. With theſe wordes the Lybbard felt a thing touch his heart as one had ſpoken to him: and bade him marke well what Gods iuſtice will doe. So that he ſawe certainly the Moyle could not long ſcape the Kings wrath, and that he ſhould dearely buye the Princes griefe, falling into that

ſnare

ſnare he had layde for many others. Nowe as all curious ſearchers doe, that deſire to heare other mens doings, he layde hys eare to the doore, and hearde the Aſſe his brother ſpeake theſe very words vnto him. O thou wouldeſt needes follow thine owne fantaſie: I coulde not rule thee. All is well that endeth well ſaye I. Marke the ende. Thou reiectedſt my counſell, it ſkilleth no matter: I ſay naught but mum. If any miſchiefe light on thee, at thy perill be it: if the King doe puniſhe thee, thou haſt but well deſerued it, and God is iuſt if hee poure it on thee. O goodly act of thine, to betraye an innocent creature and thy faithful friende.

Brother mine (ſayde the Moyle), no more wordes. I praye thee: that that is done cannot be vndone. And it is eaſier to reproue than to amende. When the ſteede is ſtollen it is to late to ſhut the ſtable dore. I knowe *Chiarino* is ſlayne and that guiltleſſe and I confeſſe I was cauſe of his death. But let vs leaue off this vayne talke, and deuyſe ſome waye to driue out the ſuſpition the Kinge hath taken in his heade, that he thinketh there hath bene ſome trechery vſed towards him. The Libbard hauing hearde ynough and as much as ſerued his turne, departed his way and hied him to the Pallace of the Queene mother, whither the King had

ent

ſent him for other affaires of his. After hee had done his meſſage from the King hir ſonne, he tolde the Queene mother al the circumſtaunce of that he had hearde, and of the rebukes of the Aſſe to the Moyle, and of his horrible committed murder. So the Queene mother and he reſolued to kepe it ſecret, bicauſe they would not the Aſſe ſhould haue anye hurt, knowing hee was a good, honeſt, playne, fooliſh beaſt. In the next morning betimes the Queene mother went to the Court to ſee the Kinge hir ſonne, and finding him perplexed, and in heavy caſe, ſhe ſayd vnto him, What ayleſt thou my ſonne that I ſee thee thus troubled, and that theſe many dayes I ſaw thee not mery? If it be for any thing thou haſt loſt, aſſure thy ſelfe that neyther ſighes nor ſobbes will once reſtore it thee agayne. This inwarde griefe doth vexe thy minde, feebleth thy bodie, and tormenteth thee much I ſee. But yet give not waye ſo farre as thou canſt not call it backe againe. Impart at leaſt thy deepe conceyued griefe vnto thy mother, and familier friends, ſuch as beſt doe lyke thee. If any helpe at all there bee, wee will all put to our helping handes. But if ſtill thou doſte burſt out thus in teares and ſighes, thou wilt rather ſhowe thyſelfe a woman than a man. For ſo doe women vſe, for euerye trifle when they liſte to

bring

bring forth a teare. Perhappes it grieues thee thou haſt ſlaine *Chiarino*. Out of doubt I can aſſure thee thou defiledſt thyſelf in innocent bloude: for without any crime, faulte, or liuing offence to thee thou laydeſt thy handes vpon him. His mothers wordes at length drue theſe from him. It is an olde ſaying, and I haue heard it oft. Thinges loſt can never bee recouered: and this thing goeth to the heart of me. Naye ſee mother if I haue cauſe to ſorrowe, that ſince his death, and before, I neuer hard ſo much as an yll worde of my faithful *Chiarino*. Sure if he ment yll to me, it could not haue bene but I ſhoulde haue smelt it out, and it woulde haue come to mine eares one waye or other. And therefore to thee mother alone I confeſſe my faulte, and I maye tell it thee, the only worker of his miſchiefe was his cruell enimie the Moyle: which with practiſes, inuentions, and deuiſes hath supplanted me, and killed him, moouing me to wrath. Ah my ſonne, nowe I muſt needes tell thee agayne, thou haſt bene betrayed and de-ceyued both, and this a truſtie friende hath tolde me. The Lyon would faine haue knowne of whom: but the Queene mother would by no meanes at that time tell him ought. But this ſhe did aſſure him, that there was no newe in-uention nor alteration in his Realme that ſhoulde
offende

offende him in worde or deede: and bade him feeke well, and in fhorte time he fhould knowe all. So the King fince he coulde at that time get no more of his Mother, determined to affemble all the beaftes of his Realme, and to call them to Parliament to confult vppon this matter, and fo he did.

When this generall Counfell was called, where all the great Lordes of his Realme, and the wyfeft of the Commons, with all the foldiours were affembled, he alfo fent for his Mother. Shee looking all the beaftes in the face that were prefent, and miffing the Moyle, caufed him ftreight to be fent for. So he came forthwith. But when he was come to the Pallace, and faw the Parliament houfe furnifhed with all the Colledge of beaftes, then he knewe the Princes indignation, when looking vpon him earneftly he faw his colour chaunge, and that his confcience gnawed him for the death of the Bull. Now the Moyle knowing himfelfe guiltie, began to whet his wittes, and drawing neere to certaine of the great Lordes that ftoode rounde about the Queene mother, hee fayde vnto them. Lorde what ayleth our noble King? what is the caufe of this conuention here? how commeth it he is thus melancholy? What is there any fodeine or ftraunge accident happened in the Court, that

we

we may knowe the caufe? the Counfell hath bene called very fodainly. The Queene mother aunfwered ftreight. Thou needeft not marueyle ywis at the Kings heauineffe. For thou knoweft well ynough (hauing giuen him the caufe) his fadneffe, which with thy fweete fugred wordes haft giuen him bitter gall. Tell me I pray thee, canft thou tell who was the caufe of the death of the moft noble and worthie Knight of our Court? Was it thou perhaps? But the Moyle (as ftowte as Golyas) without any blufhing aunfwered ftreight.

Now I know the faying whiche our olde auncient beaftes vfed in times paft is true: and I am out of doubt of it. That let one doe as much good as he can, his rewarde I warrant yee fhall be little ynough, and that God onely is hee who rewardeth and giveth recompence for anye benifite or feruice done. O what a marueilous matter it is, that he that liueth well in this worlde, cannot continue to liue well, but is compelled to daunce after euery mans pipe: to holde with the Hare, and runne with the Hounde. The true heart I have alwayes borne to the Kinge thy fonne, and founde counfell which (God I take to recorde) I haue euer giuen him, doe not deferue fuch rewarde. For it is knowne well ynough that the Moyle his feruant hath delivered
him

him from many daungers, and prefent death alfo: and refufed no traueyle for his fafetie, and that I make his Lordfhip iudge off. Well I onely craue of his Grace but that hee will inquire of my life and doings. For I knowe my proceedings will appeere better to him than is thought for: and I woulde my troth and honeftie were openlye knowen to the world. And for my part, if the leaft part of that were true that is fpoken of me, and that I were any maner of way to be touched, his Maieftie may be affured I woulde not tarie an houre in the Court, and much leffe haue come before thefe great Lords. And befides that I woulde not thinke my felfe fure in any place of the world wherefoeuer I were, if I had but once receyued fuche a thought in mee, and much leffe if I had committed the deede. Therefore I praye thee noble Ladie, lende not thy eares to the wordes of enuious perfons, nor fuffer his Maieftie to laye handes on my innocencie. For if that feeme a ftraunge thing to you this *a fortiore* were a wicked fact: a fact without reafon, iuftice, and anye maner of equitie. I doe not care to be counted wicked in that cafe, if all the Court doe count me fo. For God himfelfe knoweth well the troth, in whome I only hope, and am fure he will deliuer me from this fufpition and daunger.

This

This Moyle in his wordes feemed to be the
beft beaft of the world, and thofe that lyke
ftraungers heard him, and knew not his Moylifh
nature (a vile traitour Moyle, a whorefon cankred
Moyle, that let a man keepe him in the ftable
.xxv yeares, and make neuer fo much of him:
in the end, for a farewell, and that on a fodeine
(when a man thinketh not of it) he will yerke
out behinde and put him in daunger of his life,)
were very forie for his trouble, and did pitie his
cafe. He that by nature was borne fubtill and
craftie, perceiuing a little parcialitie amongft
them, and that he had reafonable audience: went
about ftreight to intricate the houfe, and fo began
coram populo like vnto this, ftill drawing water
to his Myll,

A tale of the Joyners wife and the Painter.

There was fometime in the countrie of *Cata-
logna* a Joyner of Tharfia, and hee had a verye
faire woman to his wife as any that came into
that citie a thoufand yeares before hir. Thys
faire woman became in loue with a Painter, and
bicaufe the neighbours fhoulde not be priuie of
his acceffe vnto hir: fhe prayed the Painter to
make him a garment to bee knowne from others.
So

So that by hir eye and feelinge (if there were no light) fhe might yet ftreight wayes know him. This deuife and requeft pleafed the Painter well, wherevpon hee made him a white garment paynted with Peacock's eies, and wrought vpon it, and fo with this robe in the night hee went to hir: without calling to any, or knocking at the doore, hee went to a place appointed where he founde hir hidden, and there he fweetely folaced himfelfe to his great contentation. At this compact betweene them for their meeting, one of hir feruauntes had clofely put himfelfe into a corner, and heard all that was fayde and done, who cunningly diffembled that hee knewe ought where his Myftreffe hid her. This Painter with his white robe continued his haunt vnto hir a great while before the feruaunt coulde come to beare halfe of his labor. It hapned yet on a night (as fortune woulde) that this Painter had occafion to goe oute of the towne for certaine bufineffe he had abrode: the feruaunt when he knew it, hied him immediately to the Painters houfe, and bade his wyfe deliuer him hir hufbandes white robe. And when he had it he put it on his back, and fo went to his Myftreffe with all: who when fhe fawe it, and knew it, and beleeued it had bene the Painter (perhaps too, shee lyked to be deceiued) begã to purfue *Venus* fport

sport togithers. His errand delyuered, hee went and rendered thys robe agayne vnto the Paynters wyfe, who good soule knewe not what hir husbande ment to weare that robe euery night. Anone, after midnight as the Deuill would have it, the Paynter came home agayne, whether the sprite mooued hym that he must needes goe coniure the Deuill, or that his busynesse framed not that hee went for or what it was I cannot tell ye, it is ynough home he came: and putting on his white robe on his backe he flong out of the doores agayne in haste, and to the Joyners wyfe hee trudged. But when he came there, he founde all fast shut vppe, and no noyse at all: so that hee was driuen to daunce attendaunce without doores and blowe his nailes, as the Phisition's Moyle that waiteth for his maister, and still chaweth at the bridle. Howbeit the next night hee returned, and at pleasure discouered the countrie. And being hastie in his iourney, what man (quoth she) remember yourself, you rode farre yester night, and you are not yet at your iourneys ende: I perceyue you haue yet a coltes tooth in your heade. Well wanton well, you will tyer your horse: and with such lyke harlottrie louing wordes she entertained hir friende the Painter. The Painter hearing these wordes, beganne to smell a Ratte, and
thought

thought ſtreyght ſhe had taken in more horſes into hir ſtable than two. So he tooke his leaue, and home he went: and when he came home, examining the matter, his wife told him there came one in his name for his robe. Then were they both at an afterdeale, and woorſe than euer they were, for none of them knewe, nor could geſſe what he ſhould be: inſomuch as after he had well fauouredly ribbe roſted his poore innocent wife, he threwe his robe into the fire. So ſhee ſielye woman bare the blame that made no fault. The King therefore ſhoulde not ſo lightly beleeue it, before he be iuſtly informed; that anothers fault bee not puniſhed by my innocencie. My Lords and beaſts, think not I pray you that I ſpeake this for feare of death, but to purge my ſelfe of that ye haue hearde. For death is common to all, and I knowe I cannot ſhunne it, therefore I feare it not. But this I feare, that dying falſely accuſed, my name and houſe ſhould for euer be defamed: and to this I take great heede. The mother of the Lion, that was the very daughter of impacience, coulde not abide to heare any more fables, but caſt up hir head, and turned hir about at theſe words, and halfe in a rage, and in choler, ſayde thus to the Moyle.

If thy deedes were as good as thy wordes, my ſonne ſhoulde not be thus grieued nor offended:

offended: nor the poore Bull had bene nowe deade. But thy double dealings and prittle prattle, who did but giue eare vnto thee (and beleeued thee) not knowing thee, are ynough to turne the Court topſie turuie. As thou diddeſt heretofore to *Pannonia* who come home thou madeſt him beleeue (bicauſe his wife woulde not graunt thy vnhoneſt deſire) that ſhe was naught: ſo that vpon thy wordes he fell vpon hir with his feet, and paſhed hir to death. Then to late repenting his fault, he heaped one yll on another: for he made all his concubines to be burnt. And all this came of thy curſed wordes. Therefore it is beſt for euerye man not to haue thy friendſhip. With that he lift vp his eares, and with open mouth thus aunſwered.

It becommeth not Madame the Kinges mother to heare the cauſes, reaſons, contentions, obiections, and wronges of the ſubieƈt with two eares at once, but with one alone. For your iudgement ought to be vpright & equall, if affeƈtion or partialitie carie ye not away. And if the matter be for *Chiarino:* the Moyle will not for that forget that the King doth yet truſt him, and that he is a true ſeruaunt to his Maieſtie. And be yee aſſured Madame, that to trouble my innocencie, and to moleſt me

that

that to all this Court is ſo true a ſlaue, it is an offence to pitie. Imagine howe the Lioneſſe hart did riſe marueylouſly againſt him, bicauſe ſhe knew the wickedneſſe of the Moyle: and turning to hir ſonne ſhe ſaid. How thinkeſt thou of the boldneſſe of this moſt cruel vncurbed traytor? that as many as heare him think he hath reaſon. See I pray yee howe he played the Foxe. Beholde I beſeech ye his lookes, what kinde of ieſtures he makes. Thinke ye hee cannot hit one on the knee at a pinch and neede be with his heeles? Yes I warrant ye when ye look not for it. O ſubtill beaſt, how he hangeth downe his heade. O what a trayterous looke, ſee his falſe leering eyes. Lorde how terribly he lookes on vs. Dismember my ſonne this curſed beaſt, and henceforth neither for friends, courtiers, nor kynſefolkes requeſtes, euer keepe Moyles any more. The Lion for al theſe words ſtirred not a whitte, neyther once caſt vp his heade as though hee had bene mooued. The Lyoneſſe his mother madde for anger for hir ſonnes griefe: why then bicauſe thou wilt not puniſh a traytor, doeſt thou not beleue me? doeſt thou not credit thy Mother that telleth thee here before them all, and affirmeth to his face that he is a traitour to thee?

Then the King called a certaine fierce beaſt, and

and vgly monſter to beholde, begotten of a Satire and of a Griffin, and he made him take a chaine and chaine the Moyle. The Moyle ſeing ſo horrible a horned beaſt come towardes him, let fall his tayle for feare and ſorrow both, and thus of this helliſh furie he was chained, and caried to priſon, and as ye ſhall heare ſafely kept and examined.

When the Moyle was thus apprehended, the Lyoneſſe went to the Kinge hir ſonne and ſayde to him. The impriſonment of this wicked member hath greatlye reioyced all the Court: knowinge that nowe the tyme is come thys malefactor ſhall bee puniſhed, and receyue iuſt rewarde for his treaſons. God, if thou diddeſt but heare what they talke of hym in Court, of his naughtie tongue, of his carying of tales from one to another, of ſpreading abrode quarrels, contentions, ſtrifes, debates, ſuſpitions in euery place where he commeth, thou wouldeſt bleſſe thee, and thy eares woulde glowe in thy heade. O curſed Moyle. Neuer agree to heare him, neuer giue him audience, but referre his matter to the Counſell, and then let iuſtice proceede. Now I thinke thy lyfe ſafe, and dare boldelye ſaye thy Realme ſhall lyue in peace: ſyth the Moyle is forthcomming, and I hope ſhall be quite diſpatched. And bicauſe I would not haue thee thinke I ſpeake obſcurely:

obscurely: I wil tell thee what reason I haue to speake it. And here the Lionesse reciteth from point to point what the Lybbarde had tolde hir, and how she heard the whole matter of him. The King vnderstanding his fact from the mouth of so credible a person, as that of the Libbarde: then he knewe it to be true, and that he had offended, which yet was not altogither to be belieued, and depended somewhat vpon the Moyle. And thus determined to punish the Moyle, he withdrewe himselfe from the Counsell, as all such princes do.

Nowe when Fame had blowne abrode the Moyles prisonment, and comming to the Asses eares his brother, hee ranne vnto the prison, and his heart panted, and bet marueylously: as that Asse knewe howe this geare was brought about, and he tolde the Moyle. Our playe nowe is like to the playe of the two brethren, that hauing two Balles in their handes, they gaue them ech into other handes, and they were both made of one fashion and bignesse: so that in the ende to choose this or that they saw it was all one, there was no choyce in neyther. To haue thee in prison, alas it troubleth me: and to haue thee abrode also it grieueth me. All commeth to one reckening. And with that for kindenesse he burst out in teares, and wept bitterly. But afterwardes

wardes feing him with the chaine about his necke he quaked for feare, and layde him downe on the grounde, crying out in his Affes maner, and fayde. O brother Moyle, what case art thou in now? Alas there is no more time to reproue thee now, bicaufe there is no remedie, as fewe dayes agoe there was, when thou mighteft haue cancelled all: but thou like an Affeheaded foole, that mighteft haue cleered the countrie (knowing thyfelf to be guilty) why didft thou not take thee to thy legs? Thou defpifedft my counfels to thee, & yet they were good if thou hadft had grace to haue taken them. It is true that is fpoken by the mouth of beaftes that haue vnderftanding. That the falfe and vntrue man dyeth before his time. As me thinketh I fee by the Element will happen to thee. And this for none other but thy infolencie, and naughtineffe: and thy craftes and deceytes hath brought thee to this trouble. O how happie haddeft thou bene if thou haddeft dyed in thy birth? Curfed, and no worth be thy falfe knowledge and enuye of others weale and profperitie: which onely is it hath brought thee to this infamous ende. Then the Moyle relented, and breaking out in teares alfo, aunfwered.

My good brother Affe, no liuing creature howe wife and difcreete fo euer hee be, can fhunne his
mifhappes

mifhappes and yll fortune: and therefore I defpifed a thoufande of thy good counfels, for fo was it giuen me from aboue. And if pride and ambition had not traueiled me ftill I could haue withdrawne mee: but the enuie of others dignitie and eftimation had to much power ouer mee. O blind vnderftanding of mans knowledge. It happened to me as to the fick man, who hauing prepared for him moft wholefome meates, hee refufeth them, and giueth hymfelfe ouer to his will and appetite, takinge them that are hurtfull for him and filleth himfelfe: which doth in deede both hinder his health, and continue his fickeneffe. He knoweth it & yet can not abftaine. I knew well ynough peruerfe vnderftandinge, but I neuer had reafon fufficient to bridle it. Nowe to late I finde my fault, and knowing the daunger I am in, my forrow redoubleth on me: not fo much for myfelfe, as for thy fake, bicaufe thou haft alwayes bene with me. Thou art my brother, and confequentlye they will beleeue and imagine (in deede) that thou art priuie with mee, and partaker of my doings. The Kinges officers therefore may take thee, and put thee on the racke, and make thee confeffe my fault, and when they haue done execute thee. (For fure they fhall neuer haue it of me) and by thy confeffion punifh mee without remiffion or pardon

in

in this worlde. For of thy wordes dependeth my death, and of my wicked gouernment shall growe thy yll, griefe, trouble, torment, prisonment, and extreme punishment. The Asse hearing his brothers wordes, marked them well, that he trembled euery ioynt of him, and quaked like an Aspin leafe: and a beastly feuer tooke him, with which he went his way home. But before he departed thence, he sayde vnto the Moyle. Brother, if thou wey my life, and wilt keepe me from perill (as thou canst not any waye auoyde it) confesse thy fault is worthy of death: thus shalt thou free thee from the wrath of the Gods and after this corporall punishment of thine, doubtlesse thy spirite shall forthwith be transported to the heauens. Well sayd the Moyle, the last and extreme remidie shall be this. If there be no hope of remedie let it be as it will be: for my bodie well I wote suffereth already to much. Now get thee home, & hide thyselfe, and let it light on me, as the world, Fortune, and the Gods will assigne. The Asse departed from him verye sicke, and sore troubled in his minde, and his payne so helde him, that the same night hee ended his sorrowfull dayes. Whose death a Woolfe that dwelled harde by him greatly lamented, and was a witnesse afterwarde that confirmed all the wicked fact:

fact: who hearde in deede the fame night howe the Affe reprooued the Moyle his brother. The Lyon fent to the Libbard, and commanded his officers they fhoulde vnderftand particularly the Moyles cafe, and to difpatch him roundlye.

Al the beafts got them into the Parliament houfe, and euery one tooke his place according to his degree, and fate them downe: and the houfe being fet, there was brought before them in chaines this folemne traytor the Moyle. And when he was come before the prefence of fuch a fight of Affes and fooles, the Libbard ftandeth vp, and fpeaketh. Right honorable, it is yet frefh in memorie, that the King killed the poore innocent *Chiarino,* fo that from that time hitherto his Maieftie hath not bene quieted in his minde, that hee put him to death by the falfe accufation and enuie of my Lorde the Moyle. His Maieftie therefore hath liked to call vs to Parliament, that euery one of vs fhould witneffe the troth, if we knowe or haue heard anything of his doings, in what maner he did it, what Arte he vfed, with whom he practifed, and by whom he was affifted in this great treafon, to bring his wicked minde to purpofe. Euery one of vs is bound that knoweth ought to vtter it, for the preferuation of the Realme, and his Maiefties moft royall perfon.
And

And then by iuſtice it is meete ſuch traytors ſhoulde be puniſhed, and the good rewarded: by meanes whereof the good may liue vnder his Maieſties reigne and gouvernement with ſafetie, and the yll be rooted out and cut off from the common weale.' Euery one looked other in the face, and helde their peace. The vnhappie Moyle, perceyuing that euerie body was aſhamed to take vppon them to tell ſo yll a tale, cut off Fortune by the waſte euen at that pinche, and ſtepped to the matter himſelfe, riſing vp vpon his feete (being ſet before) and boldly ſayd theſe words.

O noble and vertuous Lordes, what is the cauſe ye are all thus ſilent? O my Lordes, how gladde woulde I be (if I were in fault) of this your ſilence. But bicauſe I knowe mine innocencie, and my ſelfe cleere in that I am accuſed off, it ſhall not grieue me, let euery man ſay hardily that he knoweth. But yet with condicion, that he haue the glaſſe of Veritie before his eies, and that he aunſwere iuſtly to that he is aſked, and ſo ſhall he (what ſoeuer he be) ſatiſfie God, and the worlde, and I ſhall remayne free and contented. It is true that euery bodye ſhoulde bee circumſpect to ſpeake onely that they knowe: and not to ſuffer themſelues to be caried awaye eyther with fauour, enuie, or malice.

malice. For then like ynough that loffe and fhame woulde come to him, that came to a Phifition which had the Pificke, or if I lie not, was well feene in Phificke. In a certaine part of *India Pafturaca*, there was a Phifition in *diebus illis*, the which cured all, all the beafts he vifited: and fure it was a marueilous thing there neuer died any vnder his hands that hee had cure off. This man being deade, was reckened for a Saint. Another Phifition called Maifter Marreal, (in our tongue) beganne to caft waters, fetting euery vrinall by himfelfe, and bought him bookes to reffemble the other as neere as he coulde: and when he had met with any receit, oh he kept it full dearely. Afterwardes he had a toye in his head, that he tooke himfelfe for the fame Phifition that was before him, both for learning and practife, fo that he boafted hee had done great cures, who coulde fcant knowe he was himfelfe aliue, hee was fo poore, and yet he layde on lode as he had bene (yea marrie had he) the cunningeft man in the Realme. It happened fo that the daughter of the King of that Citie (where this Phifition dwelled) fell ficke, and hir difeafe was this. That being with childe, hir nofe gufhed out with bloud very oft. The King that loued his daughter dearely, and gladly would haue
had

had remedie for hir and coulde not, hee was very penſive and heauie, and ſighed ſore for that worthye Phiſition that was nowe deade, the loſſe of whome went to his heart, ſith none died vnder him that he had in cure. This newe come Phiſition knowing the Kinges caſe, went to his Maieſtie, and tolde him that hee ſhoulde not ſorrowe for the loſſe of the other Phiſition, for he offered himſelfe to ſatiſſie him as much in his ſeruice, as that other excellent and famous man his predeceſſor: and that he doubted not but he woulde finde out a preſent and ſouereigne remedie for his Graces daughter. The Kinge reioyced at thoſe wordes, belieuing them as true as he had ſpoken them: ſo he payde him to miniſter to hir, and to applie ſuch preſent remedies as might with ſpeede ceaſe hir diſeaſe, and reſtore hir to hir health. Nowe to ſhowe himſelfe a rare and learned man, he came to his bookes, and toſſed and tumbled them pittifullye, turning their leaues vpſide downe, belieuing they were the bookes of the other famous man, and that thoſe woulde able him in his miniſtration as they did the other. Then he made his man bring him thoſe electuaries, compoundes, and conceytes that the other Phiſition had left behind him, and he beganne to mingle them and worke them togither. But like

like an vnfortunate man in all his doings, there came to his handes a pot of Arfenicke, and bicaufe hee thought hee had kept and preferued it with great care and diligence, hee tooke it for a precious oyntment, fo that he tooke of that the greateft quantity, and mingled it with the others. This Arfenicke (which he fuppofed as good as Ginger) prepared in potion, hee caried it to the Princeffe which fhould haue dronke it: faying that ftreight it would ftoppe the bloud, and reftore hir to health. The King feing he had thus quickly difpatched his medcine, thought him one of the rareft iudgements and fingulareft Phifitions in the worlde. The vnhappie Ladie had fcant dronke off a part of this potion, but fhe felt hir hart labor, and take on vnmercifully: fo leauing the reaft behinde vndronke, making pitifull mone, and fcreking out for payne, fhe wofully in fhort time left hir life. The King feeing his daughter deade, was become the heauieft man aliue, as euery man maye conie&ture: and apprehending this beggarly Phifition, made him drinke vp the reaft, fo that he ftreight fell downe in the place and died. And it happened to him as to the pore olde man, that brake all ye earthen Potles or Pipkins he found with his Cudgell. So that one day he met with a hare brained
yong

yong fellow, of his owne humor and condition, and feeing the Pipkin in his hand, he lift vp his Cudgell and brake it in peeces, fo that all that was in it ranne out.

Therefore my Lordes take no fantafie in your heades that is not honeft, for fo yll woulde come of it: and take not vpon you anything that you are not well informed off, leaft yours bee the fhame and loffe. Let euery man remember his foule, and let him not fay that he knoweth not: but to affirme that he hath feene, I am very well contented with that. Sure it were yll done (my Lordes) for anye man to fpeake that he knoweth not certainely and affuredly, and the wrath of the Gods with fuch lyke yll lucke as mine would be poured vpon them and their lyfe: and this none but I knoweth it better. The maifter cooke of the Kinges kitchin (as fatte as a Hogge) hearing this brauery of his to enforce his credite he tooke hart vpon him, and emboldened himfelfe notwithftanding his nobilitie, and beganne to fpeake in prefence of them all, and thus he fayde.

Right Reuerent and Honorable audience, ye are very well met in this place. Our olde auncient fathers that wrote many bookes of Phifiognomie (of the which I thank the King

I haue greafed a good number, bicaufe I ftudied often times in the kitchen) do tell vs many things, and gaue vs diuers tokens to knowe beaftes and men, whereby we knowing them to be good or bad, they fhould accordingly be rewarded or punifhed. *Id eft* I meane fo, to practife with the good, and to flie the companye of the euill. So it is, yea marrie it is, in faith I am fure of it I. Nowe that I haue ftudied, and according to my fkyll, (I tell ye my Lordes I cannot diffemble) I finde our folemne Moyle here to haue manye yll parts in this matter, which fhowe him in all to be enuious, falfe and a traytor: leauing out that he is verye cruell, and wickedly bent befides. And ye marke him, he euen looketh hier with his lefe eie than his right, and his noftrels he turneth ftill to the right fide, with his eiebrowes very thicke and long of heares, and continually he looketh on the grounde: which are manifeft tokens he is a traytor: and all thefe fignes (looke ye on him that lift) ye fhall fee him haue them rightly I warrant ye. The Moyle feeing the Swyne groyne with fo yll a grace, although he was euen almoft grauelled and out of countenance, yet he turned to him and replied.

My

My Lords, if it were true that this malicious Swyne and greafie verlet here before yee all doth tell yee, that the heauens fhoulde place fignes in vs as a neceffarie caufe of wickedneffe: then ftreight anone as we fawe any beaftes brought forth with thofe peruerfe lines and marks, eyther they were to be forthwith punifhed, or put to death, that they fhould not worke fuch wicked treafons and effectes: and fewe befides that fhould bee borne, that the moft part of them at the leaft were not marked with thefe fignes, that he & his goodely bookes doe imagine. I knowe not if his doctrine fhall be of fuch authoritie receyued amongft you, that it fhall condemne my goodneffe and pure workes. Sure this worfhipfull beaft is deceyued, and doth as they that fee an olde woman prefent a yong woman with anything, or deliuereth hir fome letter with anye pitifull fhowes: ftreight without touch of breft, not knowing no further, they take hir for a Bawde. My worfhipfull Hogge fhoulde knowe thyngs better before hee be thus bolde and faucie to fpeake in this prefence. But none is fo bolde as blinde Bayarde I fee. Thou weeneft to poynt at me, but thy felfe it is that is poynted at, and thou make it well. Thou fuppofeft to detect me, and to open my defectes,

and

and doeſt not looke vpon thy ſelfe what thine owne doe ſhowe thee. But harken to this tale, & then tell me how thou likeſt it.

Our Forefathers and elders ſacked a great Citie, had the ſpoyle of all that was in it, and put all to the ſworde ſaue olde men and women and little children of all ſortes. In tyme theſe little ones grew, and bicauſe they left them nothing, men and women went naked, hyding only their ſecrets and priuities with ſome thing. One daye there came to the towne an olde countrie Cloyne to fell woode, and hee brought with him his two daughters, whereof the one went plainly to worke without any ceremonie, ſhowing ſuch marke as God had ſent hir, and the other comely couered it wyth leaues as well beſeemed hir. The people began to ſay to the unnoſeled Mayde: oh ſhame of the world, fie for ſhame, hyde, hyde, hyde. The olde Cloyne bicauſe he woulde not haue that Maygame be-hinde him, turning him, reuiled every body that ſpake, and was as madde as a March Hare: and leauing him ſelfe bare, gaue hir his furniture to hyde hir ſhame. Then they were all on the iache of him, and reuyled him to badde. His firſt daughter that was couered, ſeeing hir father bare, ſayde vnto him. So ſayth ſhe, ye haue made

made a good hande nowe: had you not bene better haue holden your peace, and to haue kept your owne priuities cloſe as they were at the firſt? This I haue told for thee, maiſter Cooke of the King's kitchen. Thou doeſt not remember the vyle and infinite naughtie ſignes that thou haſt, and the great defectes and deformities placed in thy body. Thou, thou art vyle flowe, rauening. Thou art foule, ſtinking, filthie, lothſome, and a wretched thing: borne of a Sowe, and gotten of a Bore, and not of a Mare and an Aſſe as I am. Thou, a vile deuourer of all thinges, and a ſolemne ſupper of broth and ſwill. Thou, a little neck, a vile viſage, with thy ſnowte forward: a narrow forehead, wide noſtrels, and ſhort noſed, ſo that the office thou haſt is yll beſtowed on thee. For thou haſt no part in thee that is profitable, good, honorable, meete, nor ſightlye for anybody, but when thou art before them in the diſh.

The Hogge ſeeing himſelfe thus well payde home in wordes againe, was glad to holde his peace: and after that neuer a one durſt once ſpeake a word any more. Thus for that time there was nothing elſe determined, but that the Moyle was caried againe to priſon by a Beare, who ſafely kept him, and looked to him. And now

now being the fecond time again clapped into prifon, there came to the Court a great friend of the Affe his brothers, who finding him deade, came to aduertife the Moyle his brother being in prifon, and was verie forie for the death of the Affe, which the Moyle had not hearde of all this while to nowe: and the Moyle tooke it fo inwardly that it pierced his heart, and needes die he would. So turning him to his friende, which was a Foxe well ftricken in yeares, he fayde to him. Brother I am determined to die, and will make thee mine heyre. And making him get Penne, Inke, and Paper, he made his Will and bade him write, and he bequeathed him all he had: which was a rich furniture. A double Coller with three Bafenets. A Nofell netwife for his mouth with a bit to the fame. A coller of leather hungrie to hang ouer his necke with belles, a broade Pattrell with diuers coloured fringes made of Girthweb and Canvas. A Baffe, a great Crouper of wood, a Souzer, a Charger, and mayling cords. A broade long Want, a tying Coller, a paire of Paftornes, and a Cranell: with other ciuill furnitures pertinent to his eftate. And then he confeffed all, and tolde him his wicked practifes and treafon, and that he onely (yea marrie was he) was the caufe of all this fturre.

sturre. The Foxe thanked him hartily, and offered to helpe him with the King, and to trauell for him the best he coulde, bicause he was his chiefe Secretarie in Court and out of Court: and so departed from him. And he was no sooner out of his sight, but bicause he was in deede made heyre of that he had, he went to the Lyonesse and Libbarde, and there confirmed the testament hereditarie of the Moyle. And to further his desire (who desired to die) he reuealed it, and accused the Moyle. So the traytor by another traytor was betrayed.

In the morning betimes all the beasts met in the Parliament house, the Lawyers, Judges, Sergeants, Counsellers, and Attorneys, and all the Kinges officers togithers: and there appeared also the Lyonesse and Lybbarde. The inditement drawne, the witnesses sworne and deposed, they caused the Moyle to be brought *Coram testibus*, and the Judges: and the Clarke of the peace to read his inditement to his face. Now think whether his eares did glow, and his cheeks blush, when he heard the Foxe, the Woolfe, and Libbard sworne as witnesses against him. Hee stamped, hee snuffed, he cried in his Moylishe voice, he flong, he yerked, and tooke on like a furie of Hell. And when he was
wearied

wearied with thefe ftormes and paffions downe he layd him, and rored out amaine. O I am killed, I am killed, I denie it. It is nothing true that is fpoken: and therefore I warrant him it will come to that vilaine the Foxe (who to haue my goodes hath thus falfely accufed mee, accurfed was I when I made him mine heyre) which happened to him that brought vp three Popingeyes or Parats.

In the middeft of *Tatarie* there was a great honeft riche man, that had the moft true, faithfull, honeft, louing, difcretee and gentle wife in all that Realme: So that hir doinges were wonderfull, and fhe alone was inough to giue light to halfe the worlde. This fame Gentleman (hufbande to this wyfe) had a ftraunger to his man, proper of perfon, and comely to beholde. And this handfome feruing man became marueyloullye in loue with his fayre yong Myftreffe, fo that night and daye he could thinke of nothing elfe but which waye to purfue his loue. And when he had manye times (by tarying at home) affayde the ryuer to paffe ouer, there was no pollicie coulde ferue hys turne to obteyne fauor, but to bee enterteyned as a feruant ftill. It fortuned him that one daye being a hunting, he found a Parattes neaft, and

in

in the neaft three yong Parrattes: fo taking them vp he caried them home, and familiarlye brought them vp, and taught them to fpeake fome things in his language, (the Indian tongue) which in that countrie where he dwelled nobody vnderftoode. One of them could piertly faye. Our Myftreffe maketh hir hufbande a Cuccolde. The other. O what a fhame is that. The thirde fayd, it is true, it is true, it is naught. Thefe toyes had the feruant deuifed to be reuenged of hir, for that he could not obteine his purpofe, and bicaufe fhe would not confent to his wickedneffe. Thus all the daye thefe bleffed Parattes tampered on thefe verfes only, and fang them ftil as they were taught. And for that the tongue was ftraunge, there was neuer none of the countrie coulde vnderftande it. There came one daye to the houfe of this honeft man, two Merchants, kinfefolks to his wife, which bicaufe they had trafficked *India* very well, they had the tongue perfitely. And being at the table, they talked of many things, and they fell at length into talke of Parattes. So that the good man of the houfe caufed his men to bring his three Parattes to him, only to fhowe them vnto his kinfemen. The little Parattes being made of, beganne to

fing

fing their verfes, and to repeate it ftill apace. Nowe thinke yee what thoughtes thefe Merchauntes had, hearinge them fpeake fo vile and flaunderous wordes. And thus looking one at another, turninge them to the Gentleman, they demanded of him: Sir know ye what thefe harlotrie Birdes doe fpeake? No not I God knoweth, fayde the Gentleman that ought them: but me thinketh it is a paftime to heare them. Well, let it not miflyke you to vnderftand what they fay; for it behoueth you to knowe it by any meanes. And fo they tolde him all the ftory of the Parattes. The Gentleman was all amazed and troubled in his minde to heare this expofition. And then hee afked them againe: but doe they fing nothing elfe all daye but this, and ftill in one fonge? yea fure fince we came, no other tune nor fonge had they but this. With that, very angry and woode as he coulde bee, he flewe on his wyfe, and woulde haue killed hir. But he was ftayde by the Merchants, and his wife wifely committing hir felfe vnto him, befought hym diligently to inquire out the matter, and not to doe hir the wrong to beleeue thofe foolifhe Birdes: fo he was forced to quiet himfelfe. Firft he fought to knowe and if the Parattes could fay any other thing or no: and
hee

hee coulde not finde they coulde. Then the fault was layde vppon the feruante that had taught them. And calling for his man, hee came ftreight with a Sparrowe hawke on his fift: who was no fooner come before hys Myftreffe but fhee fayd vnto him. O wicked feruante thou, what haft thou taught thefe Birdes to faye? Nothing aunfwered he. They fpeake lyke beaftes of vnderftanding, what they fee and knowe. Why then fayth the hufband, and is it fo as they fpeake? Yea fir, fayde the naughtie feruaunt. With that the Sparrowe hawke on his fift beganne brokenlye to fpeake: Beleeue them not maifter, for they lie in their throtes euery one of them. Thefe wordes were no fooner fpoken, but the Merchantes (kinfefolkes to his wyfe) rofe vp and pulled out both the feruaunts eyes: and then to late he reftored to his miftreffe hir good name agayne, which fell out to his vtter vndoing.

Beholde therefore fayde the Moyle, fee what hate reygneth in mens breftes. O facred Prince, bee not offended with your good fubiectes for fynifter information giuen you. Neither determine any thing that is to the hurt and fhame of your neighbour, through the accufations of the enimies of vertue. The Court doth willingly giue eare one to deftroy another, if the iuftice of of the Prince fteppe not in betweene. And euery man that can preferre and exalt himfelfe (at leaft as long as he hath meanes to doe it) careth not for the loffe, hurt, or fhame, of friend, kinfman or brother. For fuch is the priuilege of auarice and ambition. Euery one that heard the Moyle (knowing his wickedneffe) could not abyde any longe to heare him: and feeing his vnreyned arrogancie, the Lybbard ftepped forth, and gaue euidence before the counfell of that hee had heard and knowen. The Woolfe followed alfo with true and euident tokens, and the Foxe with his owne fubfcribed will confirmed his great treafon. The Kinge gaue fentence his fkinne fhoulde bee turned ouer hys eares, his carkas left for the Rauens, and his bones fhould be burned for facrifice, done in memorie of the Bull and in teftimonie of his innocencie: and to this was a worthie punifhment for fo vile a carkas, that had wrought fuch mifchiefe.

We muft all therefore indeuour, great and fmall, high and lowe, to worke well, and to liue with puritie of minde, and an vpright confcience. For the heauens, after long abftinence and deferring of punifhment, doe by determined iuftice rayne vpon vs a double plague and correction,

rection, to thofe that iuftly deferue it. But the iuft and vertuous fort they recompence alfo, with infinite benefites of lyfe, eftate, commoditie, honor, and eftimation.

Finis.

Here endeth the Treatife of the Royall Philofo-
phie of *Sendebar :* In which is layd open many
infinite examples for the health and life of
reafonable men fhadowed vnder
tales and fimilitudes of brute
beaftes without
reafon.

Imprinted at London by Henrie
Denham, Dwelling in Pater-
nofter Rowe, at the
Signe of the
Starre.
1570.
Cum Priuelegio.

Faultes

FAULTES ESCAPED.

Folio	Page	Line	Faultes.	Correction.
4	1	9	debating with himſelfe	occupying with himſelfe.
12	1	12	of my Genitours etc	of my Progenitours, etc.
42	1	8	if thou wilt not be etc	if thou wilt not be called by, etc.
42	1	8	the goodyere ay-leſt, etc	the goodyere ay-ledſt, etc.
42	1	12	ſo bake.	ſo drinke.
69	1	19	take hart of grace etc	take hart of graffe, etc.
76	1	11	wearied the Bull,	woried the Bull,
94	1	14	Preſeruation their etc	preſeruation of their, etc.

www.ingramcontent.com/pod-product-compliance
Lightning Source LLC
Chambersburg PA
CBHW030315240426
43673CB00040B/1169